FLY FISHING
THE
CANADIAN ROCKIES

JOEY AMBROSI

ROCKY MOUNTAIN BOOKS — CALGARY

Acknowledgements

This book would never have been completed without the valued assistance of a great number of friends who accompanied me on the many miles of backcountry travel, and who had to put up with my inevitable, "Aw c'mon, just one more cast." Very special thanks to Wayne Pierce, Don Shandrowsky, Colleen Boyle, Carlann Fowler, Brad Fuller, Steve Fediow, Raymond Thouret, Dale McIlwrick, Bonnie Bentley, Grant Frater, Connie Goss, Perry Mah, Audrey Gordon, Elizabeth Drury, Rob Lewis, Anne Jackson and Tony Mah. 'Mac' also deserves recognition for his contribution, as does Shep Braun, who straightened 'Mac' out in times of insurrection. I would also like to extend my gratitude to the publishers of this book, Gillean and Tony Daffern, who accepted this project and who have contributed immensely in working it into its final form.

Published by Rocky Mountain Books
106 Wimbledon Crescent, Calgary, Alberta
Text, Diagrams and Maps were produced
on an Apple Macintosh Computer.
Printed and bound in Canada by
Hignell Printing Limited, Winnipeg.

ISBN 0-9690038-7-0

This book is gratefully dedicated to my father
Luigi Ambrosi
and to
Graham Tyler
George Thouret
Henry Lim

"Still the best fishermen I know."

Equipment and Tactics

Table of Contents

The Lakes

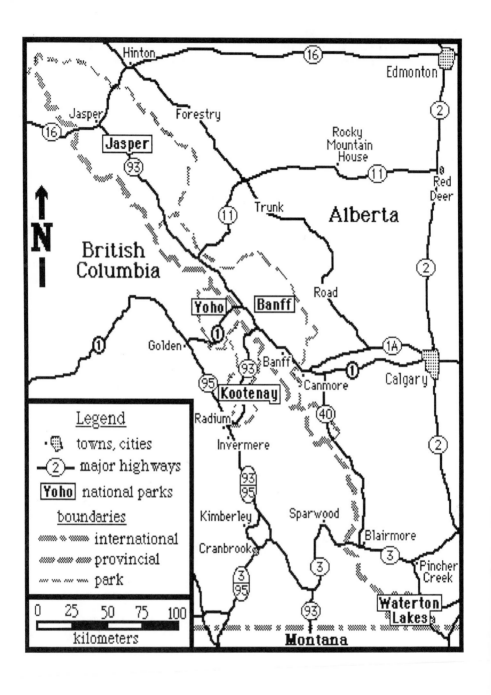

EQUIPMENT AND TACTICS

Fly fishing the Canadian Rockies requires a combination of skill, knowledge and luck. Although most fishermen depend on luck as the most important element in catching fish, its importance can be reduced to a minimum by increasing both skill and knowledge.

Acquiring the proper equipment is the key first step, otherwise casting will prove to be a frustrating proposition. Then there is the basic skill of casting a fly correctly which may appear overwhelmingly difficult to many novices, but with proper instruction and continued practice very quickly becomes second nature. Reading the water, whether stream or lake, and determining where fish are most likely located is essential for all fly fishermen. The ability to choose the right fly for the right conditions, learned through experience, is the final piece in the puzzle. Successful application of all of these elements will produce results time and time again, unless, of course, you are just plain unlucky.

For most fishermen, the determining factor in their choice of fishing equipment is money. However, even within the constraints of a limited budget, a fly fisherman can be outfitted properly. The most important consideration in choosing equipment is balance: that is, fly lines must be matched to fly rods. With improperly balanced equipment, casting is very difficult, and makes the entire fly fishing experience much less enjoyable.

Fly Lines

Fly lines are the unique key to fly fishing. Unlike spin casting where the weight of the lure carries the line out from the reel, fly lines possess the weight which carries the fly. They come in a variety of densities, weights, styles and colours, all of which are important to the fly fisherman. The density of the line determines whether it will float or sink, and before purchasing a line, fishermen must determine whether they will be doing more dry fly fishing (floating line), or wet fly fishing (sinking line). A dry line (floating) is easier to learn with, and it is always exhilirating to see a trout charge and hit a dry fly. However, since trout consume up to 90% of their diet under the surface of the water, a wet line (sinking) is more practical. The choice is yours. To further confuse first-timers, there are float/sink lines (only the last 5 m is sinking line), and several "speeds" of sinking line (ie. slow sink, fast sink, extra-fast sink).

The weight of all fly lines, listed on their packages, corresponds to the weight of the line over a standard length. Every fly rod should have a recommended line weight printed on the shaft (if not, have the salesman determine the proper line weight for the rod). **It is essential that the proper line weight be chosen for the appropriate rod.**

1

Fly lines also come in a variety of styles, each designed for a specific purpose usually related to casting. A level (L) line is a standard fly line with a uniform diameter over its entire length. A double taper (DT) line has a level middle section and is tapered at both ends. (The taper allows for a smoother presentation of the line on the water, while the taper at both ends permits the fisherman to reverse the line on his reel when one end wears out.) The weight forward (WF) line has most of its weight at the front, which makes for longer although much less delicate casts. Color is another attribute of fly lines. Most lines today, especially dry lines, are very brightly colored, so that fishermen can easily see them, and in turn have more effective control. Most sinking lines are dark, and will be less visible to the fish beneath the water.

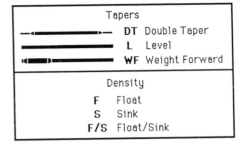

Tapers		
	DT	Double Taper
	L	Level
	WF	Weight Forward
Density		
F	Float	
S	Sink	
F/S	Float/Sink	

Fly Rods

Fly rods can be made of a variety of materials, including bamboo, fibre-glass, graphite or boron, with prices generally varying according to material and workmanship. Lengths also vary, with the most practical ones for the Rockies being in the 2-2.5 m range (7 1/2 ft to 9 ft). All fly rods are very light and very flexible, with the choice of specific weight and flex a personal matter. Also of personal preference is the number of eyes (line guides) and type of ferrules (which join the two sections of rod together). **Of prime importance is matching the fly rod with the proper fly line.** All rods have or should have the recommended line weight printed on the shaft.

Fly Reels

As with lines and rods, fly reels also come in a variety of styles with a wide price range. The basic function of the reel is to hold the fly line, and little more. Variable drags (increase or decrease tension), spool which overlaps rim (allows hand to control tension), and automatic line retrieval are options that are included on more expensive models. Interchangable spools are a definite asset as you can switch lines quickly from wet to dry and vice versa.

Odds 'n' Ends

To complete the outfit, you require backing and leader. Backing is usually made up of 50 m of 10 kg test monofilament which is attached directly to the reel, and then to the fly line. Backing serves two basic purposes. Firstly, it takes up the tightest coils on the reel, allowing the fly line to be wound on in less tight loops which permits better casting. Secondly, it offers "emergency back-up" in case you hook into a very large fish which takes out all of your fly line.

The leader joins the fly to the fly line. It is made of clear mono-filament from 1 to 5 kg test, and is usually set between 2.5-3.5 m in length depending on wind conditions, type of fly being used and personal preference. The main purpose of the leader is to be less visible to the fish than the bulky fly line. Additionally, as it is much finer than the fly line, it makes much less disturbance when landing on the water. You can choose a leader that is either tapered or level, or can create a tapered leader by joining together successively smaller diameter lines. The final half meter of tapered leader before the fly is referred to as the tippet, and its size or strength is usually specified on the package.

Backcountry Fly Fishermen

For those planning to do much backpacking there are a number of alternatives which can save both space and weight in packs. Collapsible fly rods are available, and although they do leave a little to be desired in casting performance, they are much easier to carry than a standard size rod which inevitably snags on every overhead tree branch. A number of under-sized reels are also available on the market, and offer a considerable saving in weight. Their main drawback is that they do not have enough room on the spool for backing. A good suggestion for leader is to buy a 25 or 50 m spool of either 1.5 or 2 kg test monofilament, as it is cheaper than packaged tapered leaders, and a single spool will generally last a good part of the season. There is nothing worse than being 20 kilometres from the nearest road and breaking your last leader. A single small fly box completes the backcountry fisherman's gear.

Our ideal summer resort is one where fish bite and mosquitoes don't.

Connecting the backing, fly line, leader and fly into a usable assemblage requires the knowledge of a few basic knots. Although there are a wide variety of knots that will serve the purpose, the knots shown here are the simplest.

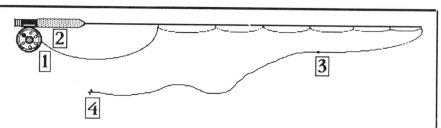

1-Backing to Reel

Basically, any simple slip knot will do, as long as it doesn't release under pressure. Pass the backing around the spindle on the reel and bring it back out the front. Tie a slip knot and pull tight. Wind 50 meters of backing onto reel.

to spool with backing

2-Backing to Fly Line

A number of knots will suffice in this situation, including the "nail" knot and "blood" knot. One of the simplest is the "loop" knot.

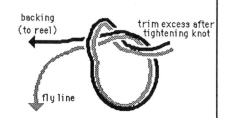

backing (to reel)

trim excess after tightening knot

fly line

3-Fly Line to Leader

Although many knots are effective in this situation, including a "nail" knot, most require cutting off a small piece of the fly line each time the leader is replaced. While it may not allow for the smoothest presentation, this simple "loop" knot is effective, and does save on fly line.

(a)

fly line — fold over
to reel

(b)

trim excess after tightening

keep final loop small

(c)

fly line

attach leader to fly line using clinch knot
(See **4**)

leader

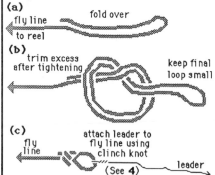

4-Leader to Fly

The final step in the process is connecting the fly to the leader. The clinch knot is the most widely accepted, although other knots, including the "turle" knot and the "improved clinch" knot are also used.

(a)

to fly line

(i) thread leader through eye

(ii) wrap loose end 5-6 times around leader

(iii) push loose end through loop closest to eye

(b)

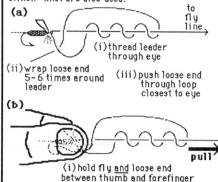

pull

(i) hold fly and loose end between thumb and forefinger
(ii) tighten knot
(iii) trim excess line from loose end

Choosing the Right Fly

The final, and often the most frustrating element to fly fishing, is choosing the right fly for the right fishing situation. An extensive variety of food, most notably in the form of aquatic insects, is available to trout throughout the fishing season. Of equal variety are the shapes, colours and sizes of flies available in most angler's fly boxes. On occasion, any fly cast near the water will catch fish. Conversely, with fish rising all around, a fly fisherman may try every pattern in his box without even so much as a nibble. Both novices and experienced fishermen are strongly advised to consult any one of numerous excellent books available on both entomology and on fly patterns; the better informed a fisherman is before he sets out, the more successful the results are likely to be.

Although an almost unlimited number of fly patterns are available, fly fishermen in the Rockies can generally stick with three basic types, with 20-25 basic patterns.

Dry Flies
Dry flies generally try to imitate either hatching insects, flying insects, or terrestrials (grasshoppers, ants, etc.) that have been caught on the water. The main and most obvious characteristic of dry flies is that they float on the surface of the water, and are generally used in conjunction with a floating fly line. A smooth and delicate presentation of the fly to the fish is very important when working with a dry fly.

Although additional patterns will undoubtedly be added over time, beginners would be well advised to stock up on the following dry flies: Adams, Black Gnat, Black Ant, Cahill (Light and Dark), Elk Hair Caddis, Midge, Grasshopper, Mayfly, Mosquito, Royal Coachman (dry) and Tom Thumb. As they usually imitate small insects, dry flies generally come in smaller sizes (Nos. 10-20), with the Caddis and Grasshopper being the exception.

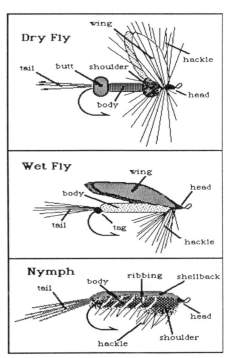

Wet Flies

Many wet flies are classified as "attractor" patterns, as opposed to "imitation" patterns. As the name suggests, these flies attract fish through size, shape or colour, rather than imitate a specific insect. Generally larger in size than dry flies, attractors are often very effective when there is little activity on a lake or stream, and depending on the specific body of water, can be fished either near the surface or very deep. Bucktails and streamers also fall into the wet fly category.

Prominent wet fly patterns include Doc Spratley, Muddler Minnow, Leech, March Brown, Royal Coachman (wet), 52 Buick, Silver Doctor and a Black-Nosed Dace.

Nymphs

Since nymphal forms of aquatic insects provide the greatest portion of a trout's food supply, nymph patterns prove very reliable under most conditions. Fished in a similar manner to other wet flies, nymphs differ only in that they are an imitation instead of an attractor. Fishing a nymph on a wet line in the shallows of many lakes in the early morning or late evening can be extremely effective.

Most nymph patterns are very similar, usually differing only in size or colour. Your basic nymph patterns should include Halfback, Fullback, Stone-Fly Nymph, and Hare's Ear.

There is no use in walking five miles to fish when you can depend on being just as unsuccessful near home.

Mark Twain.

6

"Minutes to learn and a lifetime to master," fittingly describes the action of casting a fly. The first feeble thrashes quickly evolve into an efficient, well-coordinated maneuver. Entire books have been devoted to the intricacies of casting a fly, and the best that can be attempted here is a very brief and general overview of basic fly casting techniques. Newcomers to the sport are very strongly urged to seek personal instruction, either from a friend who fly fishes, or through a fly casting class offered by a fly fishing store or a fly fishing club. My second choice is to refer you to any one of a number of fine books on the subject.

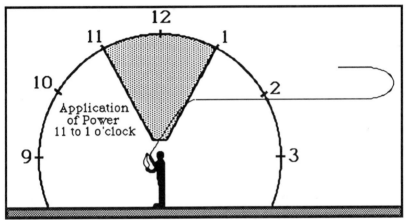

Basic Casting Action

Pull at least 1-2 m of fly line through the top eye of the rod. Holding the rod firmly with the right hand, strip 8-10 m of fly line off the reel (less if just learning), and let it fall to the ground. (All instructions will be made assuming that the fly fisherman is right-handed. The process will be opposite for left-handers). Now imagine a large clock to your immediate right, with 12 o'clock pointing straight up, 9 o'clock straight ahead, and 3 o'clock straight back. All of the power application for casting takes place between 11 and 1 o'clock on the imaginary clock.

Backcast

Holding the fly line tightly with the left hand, the right arm is drawn back in a smooth, powerful motion: the elbow bends, but the wrist remains locked. At the 1 o'clock position, the entire motion is brought to an abrupt stop by tightening the muscles in the right arm. As the arm and rod motion stop, the line uncurls and straightens out behind the fisherman. Once the line has extended fully, the forward cast begins.

Forward Cast

The motion and power application for the forward cast are similar to the backcast. The arm and rod are brought forward in a powerful, smooth motion: the elbow bends, but the wrist is locked. At the 11 o'clock position, the motion is brought to an abrupt stop. As the rod reaches the 11 o'clock position, loosen the grip on the fly line with your left hand, and allow some line to be pulled through the eyes of the rod as the line straightens. How much line you allow to be pulled out on your forward cast will depend largely on skill - novices should keep it to a few metres at a time. After the line has straightened out the front, tighten the grip on the fly line with your left hand, and begin the backcast procedure once again.

Called false casting, the backcast-forward cast combination is repeated several times depending on skill, until the fishermen feels he has enough line out. If necessary, additional line can be pulled off the reel during the backcast, and released during the forward cast. Also, proficient fly casters can let line out during the backcast as well as the forward cast. Once satisfied with the amount of line out, the final forward cast is made. Once the rod reaches the 11 o'clock position on the final forward cast, loosen the grip on the fly line with the left hand, and allow the remaining fly line to be pulled through the guides. Although novices may be a little frustrated in the beginning, patience, perserverance and practice will pay off, and the first feeble thrashes will soon evolve into an efficient, well coordinated maneuver.

Roll Cast

Mastering the roll cast is one of the keys to successful fly fishing in the Rockies. The roll cast has no backcast, an important factor to consider when heavy vegetation behind the fisherman prevents a normal cast from being made.

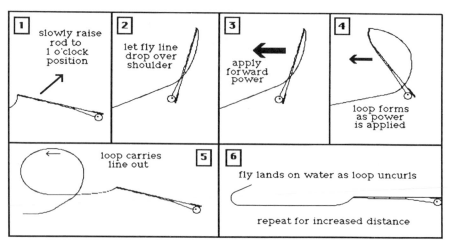

1. slowly raise rod to 1 o'clock position
2. let fly line drop over shoulder
3. apply forward power
4. loop forms as power is applied
5. loop carries line out
6. fly lands on water as loop uncurls

repeat for increased distance

Begin with at least 5 m of fly line pulled out of the end of the rod. If it is the first cast, false cast out a few metres; otherwise, do not retrieve the last 5 m of fly line, and begin the roll cast at this point. Now strip 10-15 m of fly line off the reel and let it fall to the ground at your feet. Slowly raise the rod to the 1 o'clock position, letting the fly line drop over the outside of your right shoulder. Apply power from the 1 o'clock position through the 9 o'clock position while bringing the rod forward. As the rod reaches the 10 o'clock position, loosen the grip on the fly line with the left hand, and allow some line to be pulled out through the eyes as the line straightens. The line should stretch out and land on the water. Slowly draw the rod back to the 1 o'clock position again, while holding the fly line tight with the left hand. Repeat the forward cast procedure until satisfied with the distance.

Retrieving the Line

Loop the fly line over the index finger of the right hand (hand holding the rod), and retrieve by pulling lengths of fly line with the left hand.

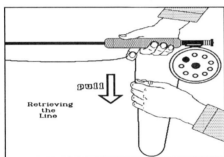

The length and speed of the retrieval is a matter of personal preference and usually depends on the type of fly being used. Long, slow retrievals of up to a metre at a time, or short, quick pulls of 10-15 cms are both commonly used. Nearing the end of the retrieval, be careful not to pull the leader inside the top eye.

Setting the hook and playing a fish

While retrieving the line, it is generally a good idea to keep the rod tip close to the surface of the water. When a fish strikes, the fisherman should raise the rod, and at the same time retrieve a short section of line, these two actions setting the hook, and leaving the rod in a position (tip of the rod as high as possible) where the fisherman can properly play the fish. Although the fisherman must be firm when setting the hook, pulling too hard often tears the fly from the mouth of the fish. Keeping the rod tip high, the fly line is retrieved by hand. After retrieving a length of line, tighten the grip on the fly line with the index finger of the right hand to prevent the fish from taking line out, then with the left hand, take hold of the the fly line and retrieve another length. Once hooked, trout generally make several runs which usually take line out, the tension during runs being controlled by the index finger of the right hand. Large fish can pull out all of the fly line, forcing the fisherman to use the monofilament backing. Backing must be wound back onto the reel, as it extremely difficult to retrieve monofilament by hand and cut fingers will very likely be the result.

Licenses and Regulations

Fishermen in the Canadian Rockies are covered by three different sets of fishing regulations, Alberta, British Columbia or National Park, depending on the specific body of water involved. Fishermen must be aware of which regulations are in effect, and ensure that they have the proper license. A synopsis of fishing regulations is issued with each license, and fishermen should familiarize themselves with the regulations each year as there are always changes. This guide covers some of the major closures that have been in effect for a number of years, **but it is not a replacement for the official regulations.** Be sure to check the regulations each season.

Catch and Release

The practice of "catch and release", which is becoming more and more popular among fishermen, is very important to the maintenance of fish populations, particularly in lakes where there are no re-stocking programs in effect. Although very few bodies of waters in the Rockies have enforced catch and release regulations, it is very strongly suggested that fishermen limit their kills to a minimum, particularly in many backcountry lakes where dwindling fish populations will very soon be eliminated if conservation measures are not undertaken by fishermen. There is no more sportsmanlike gesture than returning a fish, unharmed, back to the water after an exhilerating fight.

If releasing fish, there are a number of very important points to remember. Do not play the fish for an excessively long time, or it will become too exhausted to recover. Take great care to handle the fish gently, keeping it in the water if possible. **Be sure to keep fingers out of the gills.** Flies are usually only hooked in a lip, and can be easily removed. If the hook is deep in the throat, cut the leader and leave the hook in the fish. If the fish does not recover immediately after being released, and floats belly up, turn it over and face it upstream if in a creek, or move it back and forth if in a lake, in order to pump water through the gills. Once it begins to struggle and swim normally, release the fish.

Spawning Fish

Although opening and closing dates of most waters listed in the fishing regulations are designed to allow fish to spawn unmolested, there will undoubtedly be occasions when fishermen will be fishing while some fish are spawning. As well as being extremely unsportsmanlike, keeping spawning fish severely inhibits a lake or stream's ability to maintain its population naturally. Be aware of the spawning season for each species. When caught inadvertently, spawners should be released immediately.

Reading the Water

To be a successful fisherman, fly or otherwise, you must be able to accurately "read" the water, and determine where fish will most likely be located. Casting with perfect technique, and using the perfect fly mean little if you are fishing in an area that holds no fish. Two main factors determine where fish will be located: (1) safety: whether or not there is protection for the fish, and (2) food: whether or not there is an adequate food supply. Under most circumstances, safety is the most important factor to the fish, although food supply cannot be overlooked.

For both lakes and streams, a combination of a number of types of likely-looking waters will greatly increase the potential for holding fish. For example, a zone between deep and shallow water, strewn with deadfall, and located near an inlet creek would be ideal. In addition to being able to read the water, the fisherman should be aware of a number of other factors. If undisturbed, fish can be found very close to shore, particularly in mountain lakes, so when approaching a lake for the first time, one should adopt "the bomb squad" approach; that is, pretend the lake is a bomb, and you have been sent to defuse it. Approach very slowly and cautiously, keeping a sharp eye out for any fish near the shoreline, and if necessary, begin your cast well back from the lake. You might also try "patrolling the shore" in very clear lakes, a preferable alternative to casting into waters that hold no fish.

Trolling either a wet or dry fly behind a slow moving boat or canoe is an effective alternative to casting. Trolling allows the fisherman to cover large areas of a lake, and is the great equalizer for those with limited casting skills. Simply cast out behind the boat, and row, paddle, or motor through likely-looking waters.

Although fly fishing is the most practical and effective way to present a fly to a waiting fish, it is not the only option. At times, spin casters can be productive with a bubble and a dry fly, or a weight and a wet fly arrangement.

Lakes

Inlet Creek: As well as providing a constant food supply, inlet creeks are generally a source of cooler water, a feature which often attracts trout.

Zone between Shallow and Deep Water: Perhaps the most productive area in lakes, this zone offers the protection and safety of deeper water, and the food supply of the shallow water. Finding this zone is the key to success in many mountain lakes.

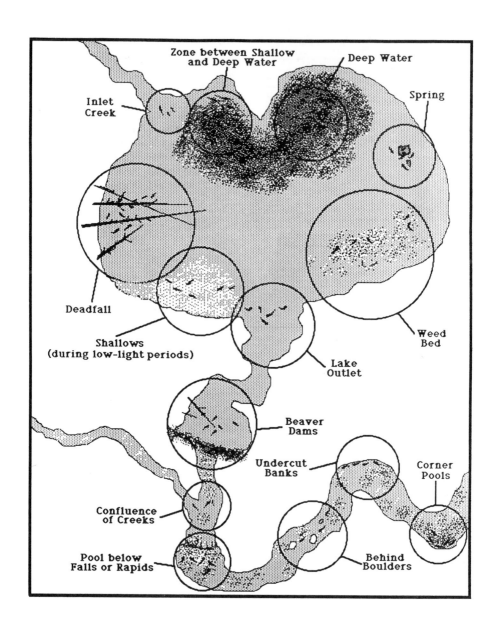

Deep Water: Although the food supply is limited in deep water, it offers protection, and is generally much cooler than other areas of a lake. However, determining precisely where fish are in deep water is a difficult proposition. Also, in many lakes, the deep water is well beyond normal casting distance if the fisherman is relegated to shore.

Spring: Some mountain lakes have small, cold springs as their main source of water inflow to which fish are usually attracted.

Weed Bed: Weed beds provide both cover and a food supply for trout. However, tactics are generally limited to dry fly only.

Lake Outlet: The outlet of most lakes hold a few trout, either in small pools immediately below the outlet, or in the first few hundred metres of the outlet stream.

Shallows: Although a prime feeding area for trout, the shallows of most lakes offer very little in the way of protective cover, and as a result, fish generally avoid shallows except during the low light periods of early morning and late evening.

Deadfall: Fallen and sunken deadfall, along with logjams, provide ideal protective cover for trout. Unfortunately, they can be major problems for fly fishermen as flies inevitably become snagged on the underwater woodwork.

Streams

Beaver Dams: Beaver pond complexes are prevalent throughout the Rockies, and the majority contain trout. Posing difficulties for fly fishermen, beaver ponds are usually surrounded by brush and contain plenty of submerged deadfall. Fish are generally spooky due to the shallow nature of most ponds.

Confluence of Creeks: Pools at the confluence of creeks usually hold fish, particularly when a tributary is much clearer than the main stream or river.

Pools below Falls or Rapids: Large pools below falls or rapids provide the best fishing potential on many streams in the Rockies, cover and food supply being at a maximum. These type of pools often hold the stream's larger fish.

Behind Boulders: Large boulders or other obstructions in midstream offer cover for trout, and fly fishermen should concentrate their efforts in and around, and particularly downstream from boulders.

Undercut Banks: On many streams, especially those with vegetation along the banks, undercuts occur along many corner pools. With a ready food supply and reasonable cover, undercut banks invariably hold trout.

Corner Pools: Deep pools which are often formed when streams or rivers make wide bends are usually excellent fish-holding waters.

Cutthroat trout

Native to many watersheds on both the east and west slopes of the Rocky Mountains and prominent in alpine lakes and many of the smaller creeks, the cutthroat trout has long been a favourite of fly fishermen. Although cutthroat seldom jump when hooked, they are strong fighters, and battle pound-for-pound as well as any trout. Cutthroat spawn in the spring or early summer soon after ice-out.

Rainbow trout [Kamloops trout]

Stocked in many lower elevation lakes, rainbow trout are the most popular game fish of the Rockies. Excellent fighting fish, rainbows are renowned for their spectacular jumps when hooked. Spring spawners, rainbow and cutthroat often hybridize if found in the same waters.

Brook trout [Speckled trout]

Adaptable to a wide range of growing conditions, brook trout have been planted successfully in waters throughout the Rockies, ranging from valley bottom to high alpine. Being a char, brook trout are closely related to the lake and bull trout, and spawn in the fall.

Lake trout

Growing to enormous sizes in some of the Rockies' larger lakes, lake trout are sought after by many anglers. Unfortunately for fly fishermen, bait and spin fishermen have a distinct advantage, due to the dietary nature of the lake trout. Late spring, immediately after ice-out offers the best opportunities for taking lake trout on flies. Lake trout spawn in the late fall.

Splake

A hybrid of speckled (brook) and lake trout, splake were stocked in a number of lakes in the National Parks with very limited success. Very few lakes are thought to still contain splake.

Bull trout [Dolly Varden, char]

Found in most major river systems of the Rockies, bull trout have recently been recognized as a separate species from the Dolly Varden which is found in rivers along the west coast. Generally easy to catch, bull trout have been badly overfished in years past, and their numbers have fallen off dramatically. Only strict regulation by government along with ardent conservation by anglers will ensure that bull trout remain in the Rockies. Bull trout spawn in the early fall.

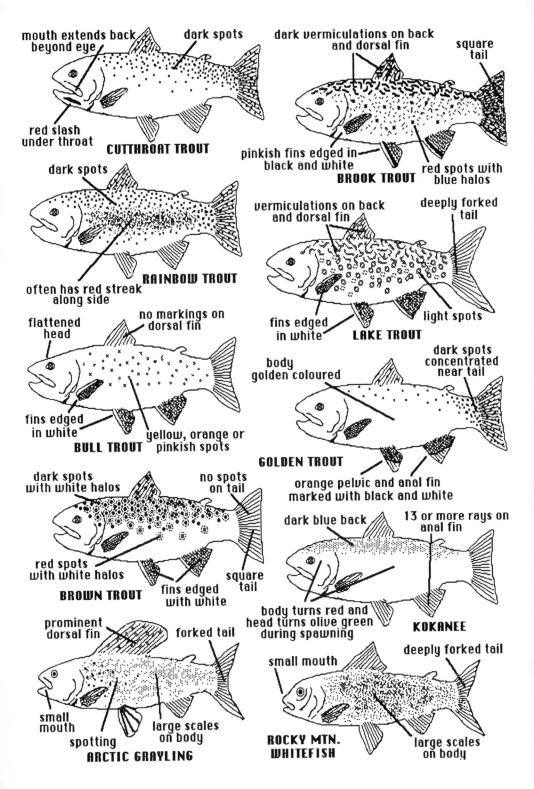

CUTTHROAT TROUT
mouth extends back beyond eye
dark spots
red slash under throat

BROOK TROUT
dark vermiculations on back and dorsal fin
square tail
pinkish fins edged in black and white
red spots with blue halos

RAINBOW TROUT
dark spots
often has red streak along side

LAKE TROUT
vermiculations on back and dorsal fin
deeply forked tail
fins edged in white
light spots

BULL TROUT
flattened head
no markings on dorsal fin
fins edged in white
yellow, orange or pinkish spots

GOLDEN TROUT
body golden coloured
dark spots concentrated near tail
orange pelvic and anal fin marked with black and white

BROWN TROUT
dark spots with white halos
no spots on tail
red spots with white halos
fins edged with white
square tail

KOKANEE
dark blue back
13 or more rays on anal fin
body turns red and head turns olive green during spawning

ARCTIC GRAYLING
prominent dorsal fin
forked tail
small mouth
spotting
large scales on body

ROCKY MTN. WHITEFISH
small mouth
deeply forked tail
large scales on body

15

Golden Trout

Stocked in only a few prisitine alpine lakes in the Rockies, golden trout are the rarest of the Rockies' game fish. Very susceptible to overfishing, catch-and-release is the only viable option if golden trout are to survive. Spawning occurs after ice-out, which is usually early July in the high country.

Brown Trout

A particular favourite of fly fishermen due to their wariness and selectivity, brown trout are found in a very limited number of lakes and rivers, mostly in the foothills of Alberta. Unlike their close relatives the cutthroat and rainbow trout, browns spawn in the fall.

Kokanee

Kokanee are land-locked sockeye salmon, but do not grow as large as the saltwater variety. Inhabiting a small number of lakes and rivers on the western side of the divide, kokanee exhibit characteristic salmon spawning habits. In the fall, after four years of life, bright red and green mature kokanee make their way to the stream of their birth where they mate and then die.

Arctic Grayling

Common to much of northern Canada, arctic grayling are found in the Rockies only in the northern portion of Jasper National Park and in the Willmore Wilderness Park. Grayling are superb fighting fish, and are particularly favourable to flies. Spawning occurs in the spring after ice-out.

Rocky Mountain Whitefish

Whitefish are distributed throughout the Rockies in all major river systems. Fly fishing can be very effective for the hard-fighting whitefish, although care must be taken when playing them due to their tiny and fragile mouths. Whitefish spawn in the late fall.

Lake Whitefish

Somewhat larger that the Rocky Mountain whitefish, lake whitefish have a much more limited range in the Rockies, and are only found in a few of the region's larger lakes. As with Rocky Mountain whitefish, lake whitefish also spawn in the late fall.

Hypothermia

Inevitable wet hands and wet feet make fishermen very susceptible to hypothermia which occurs when the body temperature falls below normal. If left unchecked, it can lead to death within hours. As it can strike in temperatures well above freezing, fishermen must be aware of the symptoms, and of the safeguards. Dress properly, protecting your body from the wind, wet and cold, taking particular care during cool spring or fall days, especially if there is any precipitation. One sure sign of the early stages of hypothermia for fishermen to be conscious of is the loss of dexterity in the fingers. If you're having trouble tying a fly to the leader, it's time to take a break and warm up.

Bears

Bears constitute a special problem for fishermen. Bears love fish as much or more than fishermen do and since it is virtually impossible to prevent bear encounters, especially in the backcountry, fishermen must take a number of precautions. Be alert at all times. Be particularly cautious around streams where sounds are drowned out, and around prime feeding areas for bears such as berry patches. At all times, avoid a direct confrontation with a bear. Give a wide berth to a black bear, and totally avoid a grizzly, even if it means turning back. Be particularly aware of cubs, as overprotective sows will often attack.

If confronted, do not antagonize the bear. Keep calm and try to assess the situation. You cannot outrun a bear, but other options include climbing a tree, backing off slowly or if all else fails, playing dead. If you have the smell of fish on your clothes or your body, the problem is compounded. Dropping some fish on the ground while slowly retreating may provide you with a few precious seconds if the bear chooses to examine the fish instead of you.

Although backcountry bears are generally predictable, and usually flee from humans, garbage bears that hang around campgrounds are very unpredictable, and much more dangerous. This is particularly true if they have become accustomed to humans and directly associate people with their food supply.

Properly disposing of the entrails after cleaning fish can often be a problem, especially in the backcountry, and if possible, they should be packed out along with other garbage and disposed of in a proper facility. If it is not possible to pack out the entrails, one option is to burn them in a fire. **Do not dispose of them in a lake or stream,** as water sources are very fragile, and are easily polluted. **Do not throw them away**, as bears and other animals will invariably be attracted.

Backcountry Travel

For those fishermen entering the backcountry, or visiting an un-familiar area, it is essential to carry a map and compass. These simple items can save your life. Other important items are warm clothes, rain gear, first aid/survival kit, and a flashlight. Fishermen would also be strongly advised to take along sun-glasses, insect repellent, sunscreen, knife and fishing licenses.

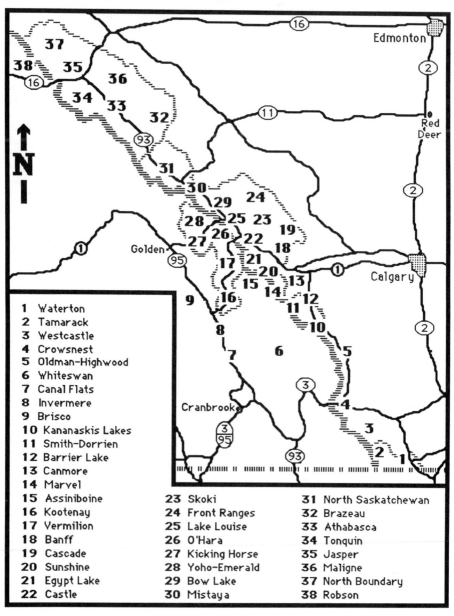

1 Waterton	23 Skoki	31 North Saskatchewan
2 Tamarack	24 Front Ranges	32 Brazeau
3 Westcastle	25 Lake Louise	33 Athabasca
4 Crowsnest	26 O'Hara	34 Tonquin
5 Oldman-Highwood	27 Kicking Horse	35 Jasper
6 Whiteswan	28 Yoho-Emerald	36 Maligne
7 Canal Flats	29 Bow Lake	37 North Boundary
8 Invermere	30 Mistaya	38 Robson
9 Brisco		
10 Kananaskis Lakes		
11 Smith-Dorrien		
12 Barrier Lake		
13 Canmore		
14 Marvel		
15 Assiniboine		
16 Kootenay		
17 Vermilion		
18 Banff		
19 Cascade		
20 Sunshine		
21 Egypt Lake		
22 Castle		

THE LAKES

The second part of this guide is a comprehensive listing of fishable waters in the Canadian Rockies, and is divided into 38 chapters, each reprepsenting a unique geographical area. The boundaries of the guide extend from Waterton Lakes National Park in the south to Jasper National Park in the north and spans both sides of the continental divide. Each chapter begins with a brief outline of the area in general, including location and access, plus an area map, while within each chapter you'll find more specific information on the area's lakes and streams, including type and size of fish present, location, setting, and applicable tactics. Every lake or stream listed can be located on its appropriate area map. Finally, the Index gives a complete listing of all lakes and streams included in the guide.

Information on all fishable waters include a note on which regulations are in effect, and the type of license required (**PC** = Parks Canada; **BC** = British Columbia; **AB** = Alberta). Special regulations that have been in place for a number of years, including closures, are listed in the text, although all fishermen must closely examine fishing regulations each year for changes; this guide **is not** a replacement for provincial or Parks Canada fishing regulations. The type of game fish in each lake or stream is listed, as well as a rough guideline to the size of fish present. Lengths and weights indicate the maximum limits of fish in each body of water and are **approximations only**, since fishermen will undoubtedly catch a few fish exceeding the maximum size limits listed in this guide. General location and access is given for each water, as is a brief outline of the immediate surroundings (whether marsh or meadow, forest or rock), and its overall conduciveness to fly fishing. Where applicable, specific information on fishing tactics for a particular lake or stream is also included. The following legend applies to all of the maps included in this guide.

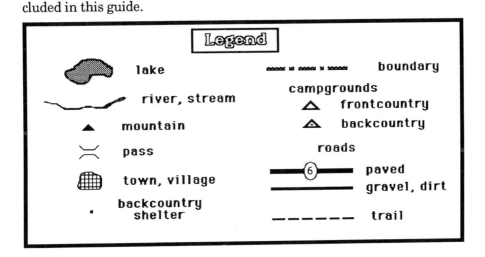

Legend

lake	boundary
river, stream	campgrounds
mountain	△ frontcountry
pass	⬟ backcountry
town, village	roads
backcountry shelter	paved
	gravel, dirt
	trail

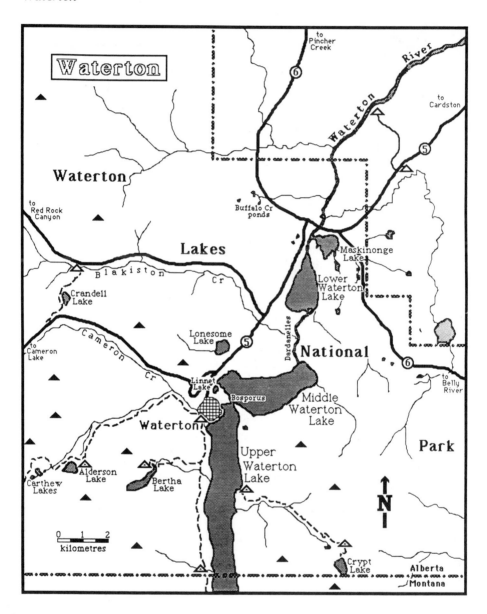

WATERTON

Each year hundreds of thousands of tourists flock to Waterton Lakes National Park to take in the magnificent scenery. In addition to its scenery, the park offers excellent fishing opportunities with the Waterton Lakes and Waterton Townsite serving as the focal point of the region. The park itself can be reached from Pincher Creek via Highway 6, from Cardston via Highway 5, and from the United States via the Chief Mountain Highway (Highway 6). The townsite has a major campground, as well as motels, restaurants, gas stations and a variety of tourist-related stores including stores selling fishing tackle and offering current fishing information. The Parks Canada Information Centre (opposite the Prince of Wales Hotel turnoff) and the warden office (in the park compound), are located just east of the townsite on Highway 5.

All three Waterton Lakes are readily accessible, and are very popular with anglers. Daily boat tours take sightseers down the entire length of Upper Waterton Lake and arrangements can be made with the operators for drop-offs and pick-ups at the Crypt Lake trailhead. From the townsite, trails branch to Bertha Lake and to Alderson and Carthew Lakes via the Carthew Trail. Crandell Lake is located at the midway point, by trail, between the Akamina Highway and the Red Rock Canyon Road. Noted for its fine stream fishing, the Belly River is located in the extreme southeast corner of the park alongside Highway 6.

Waterton Lakes [Upper and Middle] (PC)

lake trout to 90 cm (10.0 kg)
rainbow trout to 65 cm (3.0 kg)
cutthroat trout to 60 cm (2.5 kg)
brook trout to 60 cm (2.5 kg)
bull trout to 75 cm (5.0 kg)
whitefish to 50 cm (1.5 kg)

World-renowned for their spectacular beauty, Waterton Lakes offer some superb angling for a wide variety of fish. Although the sheer size of the lakes dictate that fishing from a boat will be the most effective method, fishing from shore can be productive from many locations. Areas around the numerous inlet creeks are generally the best waters, with Bertha Bay and Boundary Bay particularly noted for their good fishing. In late-summer, early-fall, whitefish can be taken in good numbers from the Bosporus, the narrow channel that separates the Upper and Middle Waterton Lakes. Lake trout are usually taken by bait or lure fishermen in the deep waters, even though the odd laker will be taken by a fisherman trolling a fly. Whether trolling or casting from shore, rainbow, cutthroat, and brook trout can all be taken on flies. Bull trout, suckers, chub, ling and the odd northern pike are also taken from the Waterton Lakes. Boat rentals are available in Waterton Townsite. Be aware that Waterton Lakes are well-known for their strong winds which will keep most small craft off the lakes and foil most attempts at fly fishing. Boaters and canoeists should pay particular attention to changing weather conditions as storms can arrive very quickly.

Lower Waterton (Knight's) Lake (PC)

rainbow trout to 45 cm
cutthroat trout to 45 cm
brook trout to 45 cm
whitefish to 50 cm (1.5 kg)
bull trout to 60 cm (4.0 kg)
northern pike to 70 cm (5.0 kg)

Two kilometres downstream from the outlet of Middle Waterton Lake, Lower Waterton Lake holds virtually the same variety of fish as the upper two lakes. However, since Lower Lake is much shallower than either Middle or Upper Waterton, very few lake trout are present, while northern pike are more abundant. The inlet and outlet areas have the best potential for anyone fishing from shore.

Maskinonge Lake (PC)

northern pike to 80 cm (6.0 kg)

Little more than a large slough, the shallow (seldom more than 1 m deep) waters of Maskinonge Lake hold only northern pike, and are of little interest to most fly fishermen. For those fishing for pike, the best area is near the lake's outlet.

Waterton River (PC-AB)

cutthroat trout to 45 cm
rainbow trout to 45 cm
bull trout to 75 cm (5.0 kg)
whitefish to 35 cm

Flowing between Middle and Lower Waterton Lakes, and then out of Lower Waterton Lake, Waterton River offers some fine stretches of fishable water. Particularly good for cutthroat and rainbow trout is the two kilometre section between the two lakes called the Dardanelles. The odd pike is taken in the river near Maskinonge Lake, while in the fall, whitefish are taken regularly from all stretches of the river. Downstream from the park boundary, approximately 3 km below Lower Waterton Lake, an Alberta fishing license is required.

Crypt Lake (PC)

cutthroat trout to 55 cm (2.0 kg)

A unique access trail which includes a boat crossing of Waterton Lake and a crawl through a 20 m tunnel leads to a rocky amphitheatre containing Crypt Lake. The lake's emerald green waters hold wary cutthroat trout averaging 30-40 cm in length which can be seen from most locations around the lake cruising the shoreline in schools. Backcasting room is available along most of the shoreline. Due to its sheltered position, Crypt is usually frozen into early July, and ice floes remain on the lake for the entire summer.

Bertha Lake (PC)

rainbow trout to 50 cm (1.5 kg)

Nestled in a hanging valley 6 km from Waterton Townsite by trail, Bertha Lake is very popular with local fisherman. Its waters hold a fair number of rainbow trout, most averaging 25-30 cm in length. Although fly fishing is usually productive, most of Bertha's shoreline has heavy brush, and roll casting ability is essential.

Alderson Lake (PC)

cutthroat trout to 55 cm (2.0 kg)

Alderson Lake sits in a spectacular basin 8 km from Waterton Townsite along the Carthew Trail. Cutthroat trout averaging 25-35 cm inhabit Alderson's beautiful blue waters. Roll casting will be necessary from much of the shore, particularly when fishing the deep waters along the scree slopes which guard the northwest corner of the lake.

Carthew Lakes (PC)

cutthroat to 50 cm (1.5 kg)

Two kilometres beyond and almost 400 m above Alderson Lake on the Carthew Trail, a windswept alpine basin holds the Carthew Lakes which are comprised of the Upper and Lower Carthew Lakes plus the diminutive Carthew Pond. Although all three lakes hold cutthroat trout ranging from 20-35 cm., the upper lake at one time contained a few rainbow trout most of which have now been absorbed into the cutthroat population. The alpine surroundings ensure ample backcasting room from most locations. Due to their lofty elevation, the lakes are usually frozen and access trails snowbound into early July.

Crandell Lake (PC)
rainbow trout to 35 cm
brook trout to 35 cm

Accessible by short hiking trails from both the Akamina Highway and the Red Rock Canyon Road, Crandell Lake's crystal clear waters are a favourite of local anglers. Both rainbow, which predominate, and brook trout are caught in Crandell, most averaging 20-25 cm in length. Crandell's open shoreline offers ample backcast room around the entire lake.

Lonesome Lake (PC)
status: devoid of fish

Located near the Waterton Golf Course, Lonesome Lake at one time contained both rainbow and brook trout, but both species failed to re-produce.

Linnet Lake (PC)
status: devoid of fish

Situated just north of Waterton Townsite, Linnet Lake was stocked in the past with rainbow, cutthroat and brook trout, all of which failed to take hold.

Buffalo Creek ponds (PC)
rainbow trout to 25 cm
brook trout to 25 cm

A series of beaver dams west of the park gates along Highway 6 contain small rainbow and brook trout. As with most beaver ponds, heavy brush is a certainty as are wet feet.

Belly River (PC)
cutthroat trout to 40 cm
rainbow trout to 40 cm
brook trout to 40 cm
bull trout to 75 cm (5.0 kg)

Located in the extreme southeast corner of Waterton Park, the Belly River offers some fine stream fishing in deep pools holding a variety of trout. The Belly River is accessible at the point where it parallels Highway 6 for 3 km, and can also be reached by following the Belly River Wagon Road, a 3 km-long trail that eventually crosses the International Boundary.

Giant's Mirror (PC)

rainbow trout to 30 cm
brook trout to 30 cm

Heading southeast on Highway 6, you come to Giant's Mirror, a small lake located just east of the highway as it reenters Waterton Lakes National Park from the Blood Indian Reserve. Not far from the rushing waters of the Belly River, the placid waters of Giant's Mirror hold small rainbow and brook trout.

The only thing guaranteed about fishing in the Canadian Rockies is that nothing is guaranteed. At the same lake, under the same conditions, you may catch a fish on every cast one day, and not even get a bite the next. A lake that everyone swears has been dead for years may provide you with the best fishing of your lifetime. Be prepared for anything.

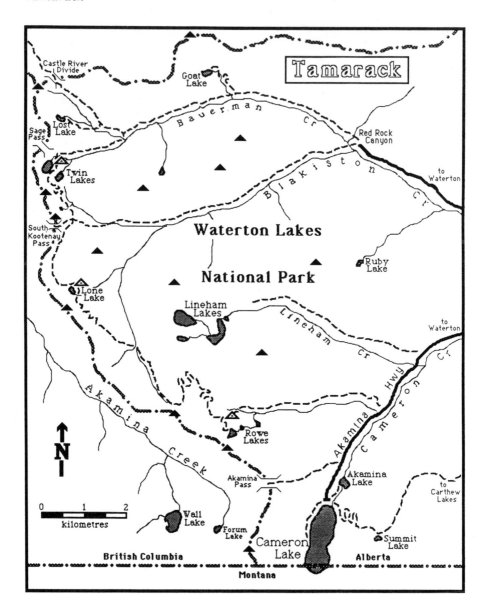

TAMARACK

Encompassing the western section of Waterton Lakes National Park, this region is centered on the 36-km long Tamarack Trail which leads hikers through some spectacular country from the Akamina Highway to Red Rock Canyon. In addition to the promise of out-standing scenery, the trail passes close to several fine lakes, in-cluding Rowe, Lineham, Lone, Twin, Lost and Goat. The Lineham Lakes basin can also be reached via a difficult route from the Akamina Highway that includes a 100 m-high cliff. Red Rock Canyon is the northern terminus of the Tamarack Trail, as well as the Blakiston Creek access to Twin Lakes. Cameron Lake, at the western end of the Akamina Highway, is popular with anglers throughout the summer and serves as a starting point for short hikes to Akamina and Summit Lakes. After crossing Akamina Pass into British Columbia, prospective anglers can hike to Wall or Forum Lake.

Cameron Lake (PC)
rainbow trout to 50 cm (1.5 kg)
brook trout to 50 cm (1.5 kg)

Set in a large subalpine basin 15 km from Waterton Townsite along the Akamina Highway, Cameron Lake is one of the more popular fishing spots in Waterton Park. Both rainbow and brook trout are caught regularly during the summer, with most fish averaging 25-35 cm in length. Fishing from shore is usually not overly productive due to the size of the lake, although areas around the inlet and outlet creeks hold fish. Fortunately, boat rentals are available. Trolling a fly generally works well and requires little skill on the part of the fisherman.

Akamina Lake [Little Cameron Lake] (PC)
rainbow trout to 30 cm
brook trout to 30 cm

Akamina Lake sits in a marshy opening in the midst of heavy forest half a kilometre by trail from Cameron Lake. Fly fishing is difficult as the surrounding vegetation hampers backcasts, and the lake is very shallow for a fair distance from shore.

Cameron Creek (PC)
rainbow trout to 25 cm
brook trout to 25 cm

Cameron Creek, which parallels the Akamina Highway, flows for approximately 16 km from the outlet of Cameron Lake to Waterton Lake. Very accessible from the highway, the many pools along Cameron Creek's tumbling route hold small rainbow and brook trout.

Summit Lake (PC)
status: devoid of fish

Tiny Summit Lake, situated 4 km by trail from Cameron Lake on the Carthew Trail, was at one time stocked with cutthroat trout. However, likely due to winter kill the trout failed to take hold.

Forum Lake (BC)
cutthroat trout to 30 cm

Set in a rocky amphitheatre at the head of Akamina Creek, Forum Lake is a seldom visited lake holding cutthroat trout. Access is difficult, requiring some route finding after you've crossed Akamina Pass and descended its western side; a topographic map is strongly recommended. Total distance from the Akamina Parkway is approximately 4 km.

Wall Lake (BC)
cutthroat trout to 40 cm

Situated on the south side of Akamina Valley beneath a spectacular headwall, Wall Lake offers some fine cutthroat fishing, and despite its remote location, is a popular destination with anglers. A rough 4 km trail leads from Akamina Pass to Wall Lake through heavy forest.

Rowe Lakes (PC)
brook trout to 30 cm (Lower Lake only)

These three small lakes nestled on the flank of Mt. Rowe all contained populations of brook trout at one time. However, recent surveys indicate that the two Upper Lakes are likely devoid of fish, and the Lower Lake has a limited population of small brook trout recently reduced by winter-kill. Lower Rowe Lake, 4 km by trail from the Akamina Highway, has sparse vegetation around its shoreline while the Upper Lakes are set in an alpine basin reached via a steep 1 km spur trail from the Rowe Meadow, a total distance of 6.5 km from the trailhead.

Lone Lake (PC)
cutthroat trout to 35 cm

Situated close to the midway point on the Tamarack Trail, diminutive Lone Lake holds plenty of small cutthroat in its emerald green waters. Most of the fish average 25-30 cm in length, and are generally very eager to take a fly. Except for a break around the area of the outlet stream, the lake is encircled by forest, and requires reasonable roll-casting abilities.

Lineham Lakes (PC)

cutthroat trout to 50 cm (1.5 kg)
rainbow trout to 40 cm (Lineham-South only)

Access to the magnificent Lineham Basin which holds the three Lineham Lakes is extremely hazardous, at one point requiring the hiker to negotiate a 100 m-high cliff. Fishermen using this route must register out with the warden service. For those unwilling to risk the climb on the cliff, an alternate route exists which leads from Lineham Ridge on the Tamarack Trail down a steep, ill-defined trail into Lineham Basin. This route is very arduous, and also requires registering with the warden service. Those who do make it to Lineham Lakes are rewarded with some of the best backcountry fishing in Waterton Park. All three lakes hold plenty of cutthroat trout, with Lineham-South (smallest of the three, set in the southwest corner of the basin) also containing rainbow trout. Adequate backcasting room is available around all of the lakes. Due to their high elevation and sheltered location, the Lineham Lakes are seldom open until mid-July. Accordingly, spawning often occurs into late-July.

Twin Lakes (PC)

brook trout to 35 cm
rainbow trout to 35 cm (Upper Lake only)

These two small lakes, situated 11 km from the Red Rock Canyon trailhead, are a very popular destination for backpackers. Both lakes contain brook trout, with the Upper Lake also holding a few rainbow. Lower Twin Lake serves as an ideal training ground for the novice fly fisherman as it has plenty of small (15-25 cm) brook trout eager to bite, backcasting room is available around much of the shore and casts of 5-10 m are usually all that are required to reach the fish. The upper lake offers little room for backcasting because of heavy vegetation growth around much of the shore while remaining areas are also limited to roll casting because of steep terrain.

Lost Lake (PC)

status: doubtful

A tiny lake 2 km by trail from the Snowshoe Fire Road, Lost Lake has been stocked in the past with cutthroat, brook and rainbow trout, all of which, according to Park records, failed to reproduce. For those eternal optimists wishing to test the waters of Lost Lake, be forewarned that fly fishing will be a difficult proposition as the lake is completely surrounded by heavy underbrush.

Goat Lake (PC)

cutthroat trout to 35 cm
cutthroat-rainbow hybrid to 35 cm

Set in a splendid hanging valley 7 km by trail from Red Rock Canyon, the beautiful green waters of Goat Lake hold cutthroat trout as well as a few rainbow-cutthroat hybrid, the result of stocking the lake with rainbows a number of years ago. The small pond at Goat's outlet usually holds a few fish, although they will be spooky. The relatively sparse sub-alpine vegetation around the lake offers numerous locations for adequate casting.

Ruby Lake (PC)

rainbow trout to 30 cm

Ruby Lake, seldom visited and seldom fished, is nestled high in a basin beneath the east face of Mt. Blakiston. A topographic map is recommended, as no well-defined trail leads up Ruby Creek to Ruby Lake, although the general route is straightforward. Those fishermen completing the 5 km trek are rewarded with rainbow trout averaging 25-30 cm.

Blakiston Creek (PC)

cutthroat trout to 25 cm
rainbow trout to 25 cm
brook trout to 25 cm
bull trout to 40 cm
whitefish to 25 cm

Despite its variety of fish, Blakiston Creek holds few in number, and is generally regarded as poor fishing. Accessible from the Red Rock Canyon Road, its best potential lies in the lower half of the creek between Crandell Mountain Campsite and the Waterton River.

WESTCASTLE

Excellent stream fishing and secluded lakes typify the Westcastle region. The Castle and West Castle Rivers, both noted for their fine angling, flow from south to north through the heart of the area and are accessed from Pincher Creek via Highway 774 to the Westcastle Ski Hill and by logging roads extending further up both main valleys. Beaver Mines Lake, accessible by road, has a provincial campground, and receives heavy fishing pressure throughout the summer. Both Southfork Lakes and Rainy Ridge Lake contain populations of golden trout, the only lakes in the Canadian Rockies where this rare species has survived. Grizzly, Bovin and East Scarpe Lakes, all long day hikes, are popular backcountry fishing destinations.

Beaver Mines Lake (AB)

rainbow trout to 50 cm (1.5 kg)

Situated beneath the impressive form of Table Mountain 1 km west of the Castle River road, Beaver Mines Lake is busy with fishermen all summer long; its accompanying provincial campground invariably crowded with tents and trailers. The lake's popularity arises from its abundance of feisty rainbow trout which average 25-35 cm in length. Fishing from a boat generally increases the potential for catching trout, although shore-bound fishermen take their share. Working east from the campground, Beaver Mines Lake's southern shore affords numerous locations to cast from. Much of the remaining shoreline is closed in with heavy brush and deadfall, and walking, let alone casting, is difficult. The area is well-known for its ravenous insect population, and extra repellent is strongly advised.

West Castle River (AB)

cutthroat trout to 40 cm
rainbow trout to 40 cm
bull trout to 60 cm (2.5 kg)
whitefish to 35 cm

Very similar in character to the Castle River, the West Castle River provides many kilometres of superb stream fishing. The only route into the West Castle drainage is via Highway 774 from Pincher Creek which ends at Westcastle Ski Hill, beyond which a rough logging road continues south along the river. As with the Castle River, cutthroat, rainbow and bull trout can all be caught in the West Castle, with whitefish taken on occasion as well. Major tributaries of the West Castle include Syncline Creek and Gravenstafel Brook. Check fishing regulations for stream closures.

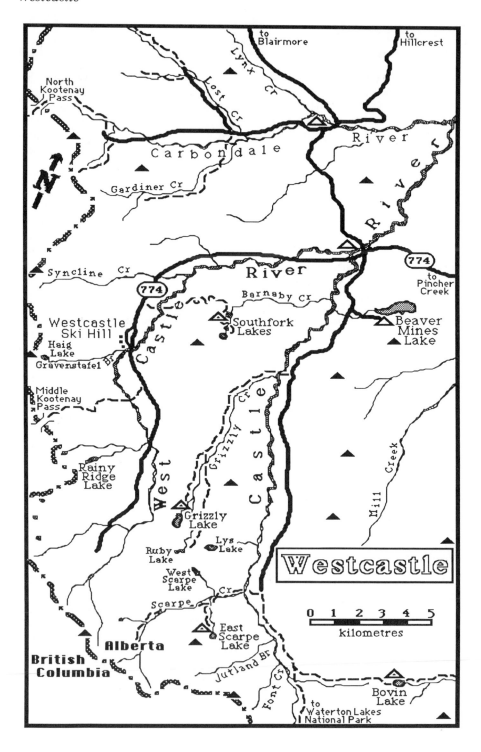

Castle River [South Castle River] (AB)

cutthroat trout to 40 cm
rainbow trout to 40 cm
bull trout to 60 cm (2.5 kg)
whitefish to 35 cm

Long noted for its fine fishing, the Castle River receives the attention of many anglers each season. Generally slow-moving as it winds its way along the valley floor, the Castle creates innumerable pools offering many kilometres of fishable water. The main access along the Castle is provided by a gravel logging road which branches south off Highway 774 just east of the Castle River bridge. Known as the Castle River road, it is impassable for vehicles beyond Scarpe Creek approximately 20 km south of the Castle River bridge. Cutthroat trout in the 20-30 cm range predominate in the Castle, with rainbow and bull trout as well as whitefish taken regularly. Spring run-off is usually complete by early July and as water levels on the Castle subside, fishing picks up tremendously. Major tributaries of the Castle include the West Castle and Carbondale Rivers, Barnaby, Grizzly, Scarpe, Jutland and Font Creeks. Be sure to check fishing regulations as the Castle River and its tributaries are only open to angling in alternate years.

Rainy Ridge Lake (AB)

golden trout to 55 cm (2.0 kg)

Set against the backdrop of the continental divide, delightful Rainy Ridge Lake offers much for the prospective angler. The lake contains beautifully-coloured golden trout originally stocked in the late 1950's and now able to maintain their population through natural reproduction. Most goldens taken from Rainy Ridge are in the 25-35 cm range, although much larger ones are taken on occasion. Casting room is available around most of the lake with the area along the scree slopes on the south shore generally the most productive. Trails into Rainy Ridge Lake are ill-defined at best, and many anglers simply work their way through heavy timber up the outlet creek from the West Castle River. A map and compass are essential. Check regulations for possession limits and season.

Haig Lake (AB)

status: doubtful

Four kilometres above Westcastle Ski Hill, Haig Lake lies nestled in a cirque immediately below the east face of Mt. Haig. Never stocked, it is highly doubtful that trout could have made their way up torrential Gravenstafel Brook into Haig Lake.

Bovin Lake (AB)

brook trout to 40 cm

Fished infrequently due to lengthy access routes, Bovin Lake promises a high quality of angling for those reaching its shore. One trail to Bovin begins at the southern terminus of the the West Castle River road at Scarpe Creek, and the other begins on South Drywood Creek which flows east from the lake. Both routes are approximately 10 km in length, making Bovin Lake either an overnight or very long day trip. The lake contains plenty of brook trout, most in the 20-30 cm range. Casting room is adequate around most of the shoreline, and fishing a wet fly along the drop-off zone is generally very productive.

East Scarpe Lake (AB)

rainbow trout to 55 cm (2.0 kg)

Set in a large cirque on the flank of Jutland Mountain, East Scarpe Lake attracts many fishermen each summer despite its secluded location. From the 2 km point along the Scarpe Creek trail which begins at the end of the West Castle River road, a steep less-defined trail heads up the west side of East Scarpe Lake's outlet creek and leads in just over a kilometre to the shore of the lake. Rainbow trout in the lake are numerous, most averaging 30-45 cm in length. Unfortunately, backcasting room is virtually non existent around much of the shore, so roll casting ability is a necessity. The lake drops off very quickly, and a wet fly fished deep is generally productive. It's designated as a High Mountain Lake in the fishing regulations.

West Scarpe Lake (AB)

rainbow trout to 50 cm (1.5 kg)

West Scarpe Lake is situated on the southern end of Lys Ridge 2 km above Scarpe Creek. Stocked a number of years ago with golden trout which apparently failed to reproduce, West Scarpe was long thought to be incapable of sustaining fish. However, recent plantings of rainbow trout have apparently been successful, and rainbows are now present in fair numbers. As access from Scarpe Creek is difficult because of a lack of trails over the final 2 km, this lake can only be recommended to the most adventuresome.

Lys Lake (AB)

rainbow trout to 55 cm (2.0 kg)

Set in a narrow basin off the southeastern end of Lys Ridge 2 km north of West Scarpe Lake, Lys Lake receives relatively little fishing pressure due to its isolated location. Lys holds rainbow trout in the 30-45 cm range in good numbers which can be taken from most locations around the lake. Main access is on ill-defined trails up the outlet creek from the Castle River. You'll find it listed in the fishing regulations as a High Mountain Lake.

Grizzly Lake (AB)
brook trout to 40 cm

A 10 km hike from the Castle River leads to Grizzly Lake situated at the south end of Barnaby Ridge. Popular with fishermen despite its lengthy access, Grizzly's pretty green waters hold an abundance of brook trout, most in the 20-30 cm range. Although backcasting room is generally restricted around much of the lake, trout can be taken within a few metres of shore, so long casts are not essential. The area around the scree slopes in the southwest corner is generally the most productive, although fish can be taken from almost any spot along the lakeshore.

Ruby Lake (AB)
status: devoid of fish

Set in a basin near treeline 1 km above Grizzly Lake, tiny Ruby Lake has never been stocked and contains no fish.

Grizzly Creek (AB)
brook trout to 30 cm
cutthroat trout to 25 cm

Flowing north from Grizzly Lake to the Castle River, Grizzly Creek contains small brook trout in its upper reaches and small cutthroat trout near its confluence with the Castle. The creek is paralleled for its entire length by the Grizzly Lake trail.

Southfork Lakes [Barnaby Ridge Lakes] (AB)
golden trout to 55 cm (2.0 kg)

Set in an exquisite alpine basin beneath Southfork Mountain, the three Southfork Lakes stand out collectively as the gem of the entire region. Along with Rainy Ridge Lake, these lakes are the only lakes in the Canadian Rockies where golden trout have been successfully planted. Access is by a steep 5 km trail which leads into the Southfork Lakes basin from the West Castle River. Goldens in the lakes average 25-35 cm in length with larger ones present in good numbers. The first lake, set at a lower elevation than the other two, has adequate backcasting room around its shoreline. The upper two lakes both have plenty of room for casting, the larger one holding a far more substantial population of trout. As goldens are generally spooky by nature and the water is extremely clear in all three lakes, fishermen must be very cautious even when approaching the lake as fish are often sighted within a few metres of the shore. When casting, a delicate presentation is very important which will pose a problem for many fly fishermen. Special limits and season apply to Southfork Lakes, so check regulations.

Carbondale River (AB)

cutthroat trout to 35 cm
bull trout to 40 cm
rainbow trout to 35 cm

A major tributary of the Castle River, the Carbondale River begins in meadows below North Kootenay Pass. Turbulent in its upper reaches, the river offers excellent stream fishing below its confluence with Gardiner and Lost Creeks to its junction with the Castle. Cutthroat trout are the dominant species, most averaging 15-25 cm in length. The occasional bull or rainbow trout are also taken. The Carbondale River road, accessible from Hillcrest, is the major route into the Carbondale drainage and has branches extending north up Lynx and Lost Creeks and south to join Highway 774 at the Castle River bridge. The Carbondale River and its tributaries are open to angling in alternate years only, so check regulations.

Lynx Creek, Gardiner Creek, Lost Creek (AB)

cutthroat trout to 30 cm

Tributaries of the Carbondale River, Lynx, Gardiner and Lost Creeks all contain small cutthroat trout in good numbers, and provide fine stream angling.

The fishing was so bad on our vacation that even the liars didn't catch any.

CROWSNEST

The Crowsnest River and Crowsnest Mountain lend their name to this area which is centered on the coal mining communities of Blairmore, Coleman and Bellevue. Highway 3 (Crowsnest Highway) cuts through the middle of the region, leading east to Fort Macleod and west to Sparwood and Cranbrook in British Columbia. The Crowsnest River, which begins at the Alberta-B.C. boundary and parallels Highway 3 as it flows east, is regarded as one of the most outstanding fly fishing streams in the Rockies. The numerous minor tributaries of the Crowsnest all hold trout, and are very popular among creek fishing enthusiasts. Crowsnest Lake, Island Lake and Emerald Lake at the head of the Crowsnest River are most popular with local anglers as is Chinook Lake just off the Allison Creek Road. Window Mountain Lake, a short hike off the upper Allison Creek Road provides one of the area's few backcountry fishing opportunities.

Crowsnest River (AB)
rainbow trout to 60 cm (2.5 kg)
brown trout to 70 cm (4.0 kg)
bull trout to 70 cm (4.0 kg)
whitefish to 40 cm

Renowned as one of the finest fly fishing streams anywhere in the Rockies, the Crowsnest River flows passively eastward from headwaters in the Crowsnest Pass. Easily accessible from nearby Highway 3 (Crowsnest Highway) which accompanies the river for its entire length, the Crowsnest receives very heavy angling pressure throughout the summer. Rainbow trout averaging 20-30 cm in length predominate in all sections of the river and are generally very susceptible to the fly. The occasional large brown or bull trout is taken, and whitefish are present in fair numbers. A very slow, meandering river, the Crowsnest is blessed with an abundance of fishable water typified by deep, dark pools and long stretches of quiet water bounded by grassy banks. In sections of the river cut off by private property, permission must be received by the landowner for access. Although fish can be taken at almost any spot along the river, the stretch below Lundbreck Falls is by far and away the most popular and is always crowded with fishermen. Specific opening and closing dates for angling are in effect on the Crowsnest, so check regulations.

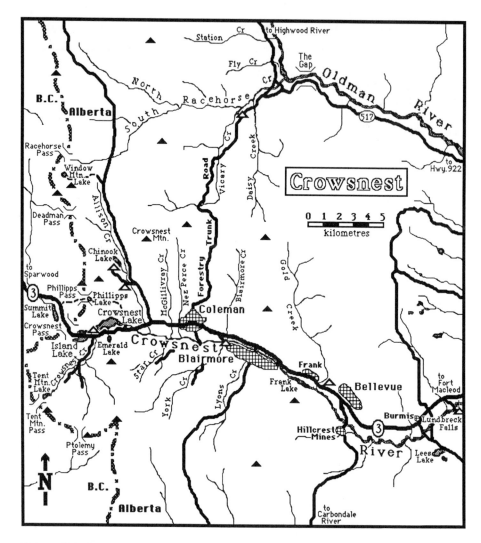

Island Lake (AB)

rainbow trout to 55 cm (2.0 kg)
whitefish to 40 cm

Constituting the headwaters of the Crowsnest River, Island Lake is located just east of Crownest Pass, and is divided in half by Highway 3. Stocked regularly, it contains a good population of rainbow trout, most averaging 25-35 cm in length, as well as a few whitefish. Due to the lake's size, a boat is advisable, although fish can be taken from shore near the inlet or outlet streams. Strong winds frequently sweeping through Crowsnest Pass cause problems for most fishermen.

Allison Creek, McGillivray Creek, Nez Perce Creek, Blairmore Creek, Gold Creek, Crowsnest Creek, Star Creek, York Creek, Lyons Creek (AB)

rainbow trout to 30 cm
cutthroat trout to 30 cm

All minor tributaries of the Crowsnest River, these creeks hold small trout in good numbers. Rainbow generally predominate in the lower portions of the creeks and cutthroat in the upper. Catching a cutthroat or rainbow longer than 25 cm would be very much a surprise, but despite the small size of the trout, these tributaries of the Crowsnest remain very popular, especially among local youngsters. Abandoned logging or mining roads found in the drainages of most of these creeks provide access for fishermen. These creeks are open in alternate years only, so check regulations before you go.

Frank Lake (AB)

rainbow trout to 60 cm (2.5 kg)
bull trout to 70 cm (4.0 kg)
whitefish to 40 cm

Little more than a widening of the Crowsnest River, Frank Lake possesses the same characteristics as the river. Situated in the midst of the Frank Slide, Frank Lake is strewn with enormous bounders which form potential hiding spots for fish. Rainbow trout are in the majority and average 20-30 cm in length with larger ones taken regularly. Bull trout and whitefish are also taken frequently. Casting is no problem as there is limited vegetation along the shoreline and the lake is seldom more than twice the width of the Crowsnest River.

Crowsnest Lake (AB)

rainbow trout to 60 cm (2.5 kg)
whitefish to 45 cm
lake trout to 90 cm (10.0 kg)

With the Crowsnest River acting as both the inlet and outlet creek, Crowsnest Lake, 1 km east of Island Lake, is the largest lake in the region. Its dark waters hold rainbow trout ranging from 25-40 cm in length with larger ones taken regularly. The lake also holds a fair number of whitefish and the odd "monster" lake trout. Trolling a wet fly behind a slow moving boat generally produces well for rainbows. As with other lakes in the immediate pass vicinity, strong winds are accepted as a fact of life, and fly casting is often a virtual impossibility.

Emerald Lake [Hart Lake] (AB)
brook trout to 40 cm

The pretty green waters of Emerald Lake are situated on the south side of Highway 3, 5 km west of Coleman opposite Crowsnest Lake. Holding brook trout averaging 25-35 cm in length, Emerald offers plenty of opportunities for shore-bound fishermen. Backcasting room is generally available, although wind will nearly always be a major concern.

Tent Mountain Lake (AB)
cutthroat trout to 35 cm

Tent Mountain Lake is a small brush-fringed lake set at the head of Crowsnest Creek immediately below Tent Mountain Pass. The lake is accessible from the Tent Mountain Collieries Road which branches south from Highway 3 between Island and Crowsnest Lakes. Although casting is generally difficult due to the heavy vegetation growth, cutthroat trout in the 20-25 cm range can be taken within a few metres of shore.

Phillipps Lake (AB)
cutthroat trout to 40 cm
rainbow trout to 40 cm

A small, circular sinkhole lake, Phillipps Lake is located at the summit of Phillipps Pass, 2 km due north of Crowsnest Pass. Whichever route you take, a steep 3 km hike is required to reach the lake either from Highway 3 on the B.C. side of Crowsnest Pass or from the east end of Crowsnest Lake. Phillipps holds both cutthroat and rainbow trout averaging 25-35 cm in length, with the cutthroat now predominating. Kokanee were at one time stocked in the lake, but failed to reproduce. Backcasting room is available around most of the shoreline and the lake's round shape means that all locations offer equal opportunity for catching fish. It is listed in the regulations as a High Mountain Lake.

Chinook Lake [Allison Reservoir] (AB)
cutthroat trout to 40 cm
rainbow trout to 35 cm

A popular fishing spot situated west of Coleman and north of Highway 3, Chinook Lake and its nearby campground are busy all summer long. Extensive flooding caused by the dam at the south end of the lake has left an abundance of sunken deadfall around the entire shoreline. Cutthroat trout are the dominant species, although rainbow trout are also present as well as a fair number of suckers. A boat is recommended, although those anglers with reasonable roll casting skills will be able to take trout from most locations along shore.

Window Mountain Lake (AB)
cutthroat trout to 50 cm (1.5 kg)

An exquisite body of water tucked into the side of Mt. Ward, Window Mountain Lake is one of the region's hidden treasures. After a 15 km drive on the Allison Creek Road, a 2 km hike leads in short order to the lake. The deep waters of Window Mountain Lake contain plenty of cutthroat trout most averaging 30-40 cm in length, and there may also be the odd rainbow present as well, although most have been absorbed into the cutthroat population. Casting is difficult from most locations around the lake so roll casting ability is important. Fishing a wet fly deep generally produces well in Window Mountain. It's designated as a High Mountain Lake, so check regulations.

Lees Lake (AB)
rainbow trout to 60 cm (3.0 kg)

Located 3 km southeast of Burmis by road, Lees Lake is popular with local anglers. At last report a small fee was being charged to gain access to the lake as it is completely enclosed by private property. The lake itself holds plenty of rainbow trout averaging 30-40 cm in length, with much larger ones taken on occasion. Casting or trolling a fly seems to work with equal effectiveness.

Racehorse Creek (AB)
cutthroat trout to 30 cm

Racehorse Creek, including both North and South Racehorse, is a major tributary of the Oldman River which it joins just west of The Gap. It contains cutthroat trout in good numbers averaging 20-25 cm in length. Lower Racehorse Creek is accessible from the Forestry Trunk Road and from trails that lead west from the Racehorse Creek campground, while the upper reaches of North and South Racehorse Creeks can be reached from the Allison Creek Road which joins Highway 3 west of Coleman. Racehorse Creek is open to angling in alternate years only, so check regulations.

Vicary Creek, Daisy Creek (AB)
cutthroat trout to 30 cm

Tributaries to Racehorse Creek, Vicary and Daisy Creeks have long been favourites of local anglers as both contain good populations of small cutthroat trout averaging 15-25 cm in length. Abandoned logging roads up both creeks offer easy access to fishermen. Fishing is allowed in alternate years only, so consult regulations.

Fly Creek, Station Creek (AB)
cutthroat trout to 25 cm

Two minor tributaries which join the Oldman River just north of The Gap, Station and Fly Creek contain cutthroat trout in small sizes seldom exceeding 20 cm. Both creeks have trails that lead upstream from the Forestry Trunk Road. Before you go, check regulations as these creeks are open to angling in alternate years only.

God grant that I may love to fish
Until my dying day,
And when it comes to my last cast,
I'll then most humbly pray,
When in The Lord's safe landing net
I'm peacefully asleep,
That, in His mercy, I'll be judged
As good enough to keep.

OLDMAN-HIGHWOOD

The Oldman, Livingstone and Highwood River drainages serve as the mainframe of this area which is abundant with fishable creeks. The majority of the region's lakes, including Carnarvon, Loomis, Storm and Lake of the Horns, are located high among the peaks that form the continental divide between B.C. and Alberta. Running north to south, the area's main thoroughfare is Highway 40 (Kananaskis Trail) between Peter Lougheed Provinicial Park and Highwood Junction, and Forestry Road 940 between Highwood Junction and Coleman in the Crowsnest Pass. Highway 541 (Highwood Trail) and Highway 532 (Johnson Creek Trail) provide access from the towns of Longview and Nanton to the east. A gas station, open only during the summer, is located at the junction of the Forestry Trunk Road, Highway 40 and Highway 541 at Highwood Junction.

Highwood River (AB)
rainbow trout to 50 cm (1.5 kg)
brook trout to 40 cm
cutthroat trout to 40 cm
bull trout to 70 cm (3.5 kg)
whitefish to 40 cm

The Highwood River, beginning as a tiny stream in the Highwood Pass vicinity, flows south and east, eventually joining the Bow River as a major tributary east of Calgary. The upper Highwood, bracketed by the Elk Range to the west and the Highwood Range to the east, is readily accessible and offers many kilometres of fine river fishing. Rainbow trout predominate, with most averaging 25-35 cm in length. Bull trout and whitefish are also taken in good numbers together with the occasional brook and cutthroat trout. Access is easy. Highway 40 (Kananaskis Trail) parallels the Highwood River from Highwood Pass to Highwood Junction, after which Highway 541 parallels the river on its journey eastward out of the mountains. Areas around the Highwood's confluence with its many tributary creeks generally hold trout as do the numerous beaver pond complexes along the river. Be sure to check regulations as the Highwood drainage is open to angling in alternate years only.

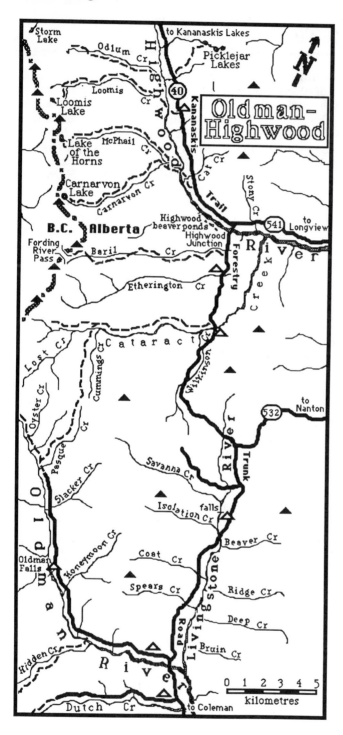

Highwood River ponds (AB)
rainbow trout to 40 cm
brook trout to 35 cm

The wide, forested Highwood River valley provides excellent habitat for the local beaver population, a fact attested to by the area's seemingly endless number of beaver ponds. Many of the ponds contain rainbow or brook trout or both in the 15-30 cm range. Some of the ponds are subject to winter kill and only personal inspection will determine which ponds hold trout and which don't. You'll find some of the best complexes are those immediately west of Highwood Junction and those at the Trout Ponds Day Use Site just south of the confluence of Picklejar Creek and the Highwood River.

Odlum Creek, Loomis Creek, McPhail Creek, Carnarvon Creek, Stony Creek, Cat Creek, Baril Creek, Etherington Creek (AB)
rainbow trout to 30 cm
cutthroat trout to 30 cm
brook trout to 30 cm
bull trout to 35 cm

All tributaries to the upper Highwood River, these creeks contain a variety of small trout seldom exceeding 25 cm in length. Generally, the lower portions of the creeks near their junction with the High-wood contain rainbow and brook trout while the upper reaches hold cutthroat and bull trout.

Picklejar Lakes
cutthroat trout to 50 cm (1.5 kg)

The four Picklejar Lakes are set just below treeline in a pretty cirque located 4 km by trail east of Highway 40 (Kananaskis Trail). Since cutthroat trout from the lakes have been used in the past for breeding stock by the Fish and Wildlife Division, the lakes were closed to angling for a number of years. However the lakes have recently been reopened to angling, and most reports have been favourable with the first (lower) lake offering the best opportunities for fly fishermen.

Storm Lake (AB)
cutthroat trout to 35 cm

Tiny Storm Lake, nestled in a small basin immediately beneath the continental divide, is seldom visited by fishermen. Although no trail leads to the lake, those armed with map and compass will have no trouble negotiating the 3 km-long side valley southwest of Highway 40 (Kananaskis Trail). Cutthroat trout in Storm average 20-30 cm in length. It's listed in the regulations as a High Mountain Lake.

Loomis Lake (AB)
cutthroat trout to 50 cm (1.5 kg)

A 12 km hike which includes a ford of the Highwood River and poor trails over the final 2 km leads from Highway 40 (Kananaskis Trail) to the pretty blue waters of secluded Loomis Lake. Despite its lengthy access, Loomis is popular with backcountry fishermen due to the number and size of its cutthroat trout which average 30-40 cm with large ones taken regularly. Backcasting room is available around most of the shoreline. It's designated a High Mountain Lake in the fishing regulations.

Lake of the Horns [McPhail Lake] (AB)
cutthroat trout to 60 cm (2.5 kg)

Nestled in a rocky amphitheatre high on the flank of Mt. McPhail, Lake of the Horns offers the reward of excellent fishing for those making the effort to reach its shores. A ford of the Highwood River at the beginning and a tricky ascent of a cliff band requiring good scrambling ability just below the lake loom as major hazards on this hike. The lake itself is above treeline, and there is plenty of casting room. Cutthroat trout in Lake of the Horns average 30-40 cm in length with fish exceeding 50 cm taken frequently. As it is a very deep lake and the bottom drops off quickly, a wet line fished deep is generally a successful technique. It's designated a High Mountain Lake, so check regulations.

Carnarvon Lake (AB)
cutthroat trout to 50 cm (1.5 kg)

Similar in character to other lakes in the region, Carnarvon Lake is located in an enclosed basin high on Mt. Strachan immediately east of the continental divide. A ford of the Highwood River and a short climb up exposed rock (difficult in foul weather) protect Carnarvon Lake from the majority of hikers and fishermen. Set amid stark, rocky surroundings, Carnarvon's exquisite blue waters hold plenty of cutthroat trout mostly in the 30-40 cm range. Although the lake drops off quickly around most of the shore, a shelf exists on the west end of the lake near the primitive campsite where hungry trout continually cruise the shallows. Except for the shallows where a dry fly is sure to attract attention, a wet line fished deep is the best option. It's listed as a High Mountain Lake in the fishing regulations.

Cataract Creek (AB)

brook trout to 40 cm
rainbow trout to 40 cm

Cataract Creek, as its name suggests, contains many splendid water-falls along its length. Joining the Highwood just east of the junction of the Forestry Trunk Road, Highway 40 and Highway 541, it possesses several stretches of fine fishing with numerous falls and deep pools characterizing the lower sections, while slower waters and abundant accompanying beaver ponds are typical of the upper section which is much more easily accessed by a major logging road branching west from the Forestry Trunk Road north of Cataract Creek campground. Brook trout predominate, most averaging 15-30 cm in length. Rainbow in the 20-30 cm range are also caught in the section between the Forestry Trunk Road and Cataract's junction with the Highwood. Special regulations and possession limits apply to the lower portion of the creek, so check regulations.

Lost Creek, Cummings Creek, Wilkinson Creek (AB)

brook trout to 30 cm

Tributaries of upper Cataract Creek, Lost, Cummings and Wilkinson Creek all contain small brook trout mostly in the 15-25 cm range. Wilkinson Creek parallels the Forestry Trunk Road which provides easy access while Cummings and Lost Creek are reached by logging roads along Cataract Creek.

Livingstone River (AB)

cutthroat trout to 40 cm
bull trout to 50 cm (1.5 kg)
whitefish to 35 cm

A major tributary of the Oldman River, the Livingstone River flows south from its headwaters on Plateau Mountain and is paralleled for its entire length by the Forestry Trunk Road which offers easy access for anglers. Cutthroat trout are in the majority in the Livingstone and average 15-30 cm in length. Bull trout and whitefish are also present in limited numbers. Trout can be taken almost anywhere along the river though the stretch around Livingstone Falls is particularly promising despite being overfished. The Livingstone drainage is open for fishing in alternate years only, so check regulations.

Savanna Creek, Islolation Creek, Coat Creek, Spears Creek, Beaver Creek, Ridge Creek, Deep Creek, Bruin Creek (AB)

cutthroat trout to 30 cm

All of the tributaries of the Livingstone River contain populations of small cutthroat trout few larger than 20 cm in length. Although the trout are small, they are plentiful, and even the most inexperienced angler will catch fish.

Oldman River (AB)

cutthroat trout to 40 cm
bull trout to 70 cm (3.5 kg)
whitefish to 35 cm

An excellent trout stream in its upper reaches, the Oldman River is accessed by the Forestry Trunk Road, and by a logging road that branches west at the Oldman River campground along the Trunk Road. Be aware that the Oldman is usually very turbulent and dirty until early July when run-off is complete. Upstream from the Forestry Trunk Road, the Oldman provides fine fishing during the summer over its many kilometres of pools and riffles with cutthroat trout averaging 20-30 cm in length predominating. Downstream from Oldman Falls, bull trout and whitefish are also taken in fair numbers. The entire upper Oldman drainage is open to angling in alternate years only, so check regulations before you set out.

Oyster Creek, Pasque Creek, Slacker Creek, Honeymoon Creek, Hidden Creek (AB)

cutthroat trout to 30 cm

Tributaries of the upper Oldman River, these creeks contain small cutthroat trout in good numbers. All can be accessed from logging roads radiating out from the the upper Oldman road. Trout in the creeks are numerous but small, mostly in the 15-20 cm range.

Dutch Creek (AB)

cutthroat trout to 35 cm
bull trout to 45 cm
whitefish to 35 cm

A major tributary of the Oldman River, Dutch Creek offers good stream fishing over its entire length. Lower Dutch Creek can be reached from logging roads branching west from the Forestry Trunk Road while upper Dutch Creek can be accessed from logging roads on Racehorse Creek. Although bull trout and whitefish are caught in Dutch Creek, it is the cutthroat trout averaging 15-30 cm in length which is the dominant species.

48

WHITESWAN

Its deep dark waters hemmed in by a narrow valley, Whiteswan Lake lies at the central core of this mountainous region and is very popular with anglers in search of plentiful rainbow trout. Open to fly fishing only, Alces Lake receives much less fishing pressure than nearby Whiteswan and usually produces well. Beyond Whiteswan Lake, logging roads lead up all branches of the White River where some excellent stream fishing opportunities exist. Connor Lakes, set in a remote corner of the region between the Elk and White River drainages also offers excellent backcountry cutthroat fishing. Top of the World Provincial Park south of Whiteswan Lake is noted for its exquisite alpine meadows, and is located 55 km by logging road from Highway 93/95. The park's main attraction for anglers is Fish Lake which offers superb fishing for cutthroat trout.

Whiteswan Lake (BC)
rainbow trout to 80 cm (6.0 kg)

Located 24 km by gravel road from Highway 93/95, Whiteswan Lake and its provincial park are enormously popular during summer weekends when campgrounds are invariably filled to overflowing. A long, narrow lake sandwiched between the rugged peaks of the Hughes and Van Nostrand Ranges, Whiteswan's dark waters hold rainbow trout averaging 30-45 cm in length with larger individuals present in good numbers as well. Gang trolls and flatfish predominate among fishing equipment on Whiteswan Lake, and fly fishermen are in a definite minority. However, some excellent fly fishing opportunities do exist: simply trolling a wet fly behind a boat at slow speeds is usually productive, or in the late evening, if wind conditions are favourable, there is superb dry fly fishing in the shallower waters at the east end of the lake. Wind can be a problem at Whiteswan as it generally picks up in intensity by mid-day and remains strong throughout much of the afternoon. All of Whiteswan's inlet and outlet creeks are closed to angling. Check regulations, as there are special limits on trout taken. Be aware of logging and mining trucks on the main access road.

Alces Lake [Moose Lake] (BC)
rainbow trout to 80 cm (6.0 kg)

Alces Lake, situated alongside the main road 2 km west of Whiteswan Lake, is restricted to fly fishing only, a factor which keeps Alces Lake much less busy than nearby Whiteswan. Alces' pleasing blue-green waters hold good numbers of rainbow trout averaging 30-40 cm in length. Trolling a fly along the margin that separates the shallows from the deeper water is generally an effective technique. Working the shallows in the evening with a dry fly also produces well.

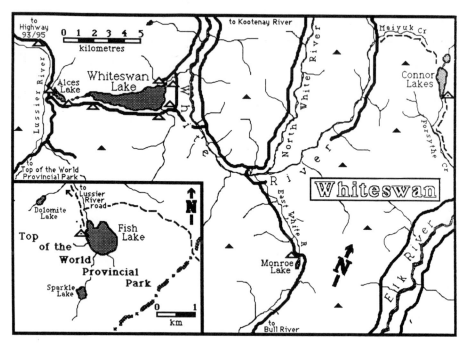

Lussier River (BC)

cutthroat trout to 40 cm
rainbow trout to 40 cm
bull trout to 60 cm (2.5 kg)
whitefish to 35 cm

Flowing from headwaters in Top of the World Provincial Park to its confluence with the Kootenay River, the Lussier River offers fine streamside angling over much of its course. Although lower sections are difficult to reach because of the deep canyon alongside most of the Whiteswan Lake road, the upper Lussier drainage beyond the Alces Lake turnoff is crisscrossed with logging roads and is readily accessible. Cutthroat predominate in the Lussier with bull trout and whitefish present in fair numbers as well. Occasionally, rainbow trout are also taken from the river.

White River (BC)

cutthroat trout to 50 cm (1.5 kg)
rainbow trout to 60 cm (2.5 kg)
bull trout to 70 cm (4.0 kg)
whitefish to 40 cm

The major river of the region, the White River, flows south and west and whitefish along with cutthroat are found along the river's entire length, with rainbow trout populating the area below the White River's confluence with Whiteswan Lake's outlet creek.

North White River (BC)
cutthroat trout to 50 cm (1.5 kg)
bull trout to 70 cm (4.0 kg)
whitefish to 40 cm

Possessing most of the characteristics of the upper White River, the North White River is accessed from logging roads branching off the White. Cutthroat trout averaging 30-40 cm are plentiful with bull trout and whitefish also present in fair numbers.

East White River (BC)
cutthroat trout to 40 cm
bull trout to 60 cm (2.5 kg)
whitefish to 35 cm

A major tributary of the White River, the East White River flows northwest from its source at Monroe Lake. Whitefish, cutthroat and bull trout can be caught along its entire length which is paralleled by logging roads leading from the White River and Bull River.

Monroe Lake (BC)
cutthroat trout to 40 cm

A small lake at the head of the East White River drainage, Monroe's green waters receive little fishing pressure each season. Cutthroat trout in the 25-35 cm range are best fished from a boat as shallows extend out from shore around much of the lake, and forest cover inhibits backcasting. There are special limits on cutthroat trout taken from Monroe Lake, so check regulations.

Connor Lakes (BC)
cutthroat trout to 70 cm (4.0 kg)

In years past Connor Lakes played host to only a few float plane and horse parties each season and gained a reputation of harbouring some immense cutthroat trout. In recent years, more and more hikers and horse parties have made their way into the lakes, either from the Elk River Valley via Forsythe Creek or from the upper White River via Maiyuk Creek. While the quality of fishing has declined somewhat, large cutthroat are still present in fair numbers, and most fishermen making their way into Connor are not disappointed. Be sure to consult regulations, as special limits on catches apply to Connor Lakes.

Fish Lake (BC)

cutthroat trout to 50 cm (1.5 kg)
bull trout to 75 cm (6.0 kg)

Fish Lake, a very popular backcountry destination, is located in the heart of Top of the World Provincial Park and is reached via a 6 km trail from logging roads on the upper Lussier River. Cutthroat trout in the 20-35 cm range abound in the lake's sparkling green waters with large bull trout also present in small numbers. Fishing from shore is limited from most locations due to heavy forest cover which rings the lake; however, a few rafts are usually available which improve the quality of fishing greatly. A large cabin at the lake maintained by the provincial park is open to the public for a small fee on a first-come, first serve basis. There are special limits on the number of trout taken from Fish Lake, so check regulations.

Dolomite Lake (BC)

status: devoid of fish

A small lake hidden in a densely forest valley just over a kilometre northwest of Fish Lake, Dolomite Lake has never been stocked and contains no fish.

Sparkle Lake (BC)

status: devoid of fish

Set in a windy basin above the inlet to Fish Lake, diminutive Sparkle Lake has never been stocked and contains no fish.

Springtime: *when fishermen begin to get that faraway lake in their eyes.*

CANAL FLATS

Columbia Lake, headwaters of the Columbia River is the centerpiece of the area which is serviced by the village of Canal Flats situated at the south end of the lake. Bisecting the region is Highway 93/95, which leads north to Invermere and south to Cranbrook. Columbia Lake has never been renowned for great fishing, although large bull trout are taken on occasion. On the other hand, Dutch Creek, which empties into the north end of Columbia Lake, has some fine stretches of fishable water. The Kootenay River, murky much of the summer, and Findlay Creek, a major tributary of the Kootenay, both offer good river fishing, while Whitetail Lake, 28 km by road up Findlay Creek, holds plenty of large rainbow trout and is very popular with local fishermen.

Columbia Lake (BC)
bull trout to 90 cm (10.0 kg)
cutthroat trout to 50 cm (1.5 kg)
rainbow trout to 50 cm (1.5 kg)
whitefish to 40 cm

The pretty, aquamarine waters of Columbia Lake serve as the source of the mighty Columbia River which eventually flows into the Pacific Ocean at Astoria, Oregon. Although Columbia's fishing is generally regarded as poor due mainly to the large sucker and squawfish population, anglers are occasionally rewarded with huge bull trout often weighing 7 kg or more. The waters around Dutch Creek tend to be the most productive, although cutthroat and rainbow trout as well as whitefish can be taken from many locations on the lake.

Kootenay River (BC)
cutthroat trout to 50 cm (1.5 kg)
bull trout to 75 cm (5.0 kg)
whitefish to 40 cm

Flowing out of the Kootenay Valley into the Columbia Valley, the Kootenay River misses Columbia Lake by only a matter of 2 km. A relatively large river as it flows south from Canal Flats, the Kootenay receives heavy run-off in the spring, and is often muddy until mid to late summer, after which cutthroat and bull trout can be taken in increasing numbers as the river clears. Fall is the best time for whitefish.

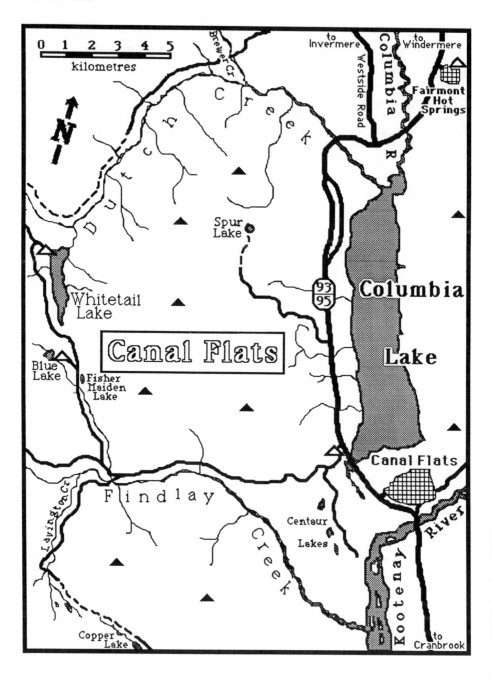

Dutch Creek (BC)

cutthroat to 50 cm (1.5 kg)
bull trout to 75 cm (5.0 kg)
whitefish to 40 cm

Regarded by many as the "true source" of the Columbia River, Dutch Creek has gained a reputation over time as an excellent trout stream. Cutthroat in the 30-40 cm range can be taken from the many pools along the entire length of the creek while bull trout exceeding 60 cm in length are found in some of the larger holes. Whitefish runs in the fall attract many anglers. While the lower reaches of Dutch Creek in the vicinity of Highway 93/95 are overfished, much of the upper river, which is easily accessed by logging roads branching west from the Westside Road, sees few fishermen each year and holds the promise of great fishing.

Brewer Creek (BC)

cutthroat trout to 40 cm
bull trout to 60 cm (2.5 kg)
whitefish to 35 cm

A major tributary of Dutch Creek, Brewer Creek can be reached from logging roads connecting with the Westside Road. Cutthroat averaging 20-30 cm in length are the dominant species with a few bull trout and whitefish present as well.

Spur Lake (BC)

rainbow trout to 55 cm (2.0 kg)

This small forest-encircled lake located 6 km by rough road and trail from Highway 93/95 is overlooked by most fishermen because of its confusing access, yet Spur contains an abundance of rainbow trout mostly in the 25-35 cm range. Although fish can generally be taken fairly close to shore, backcasting is difficult around most of the lake because of the proximity of forest cover.

Whitetail Lake [Deer Lake] (BC)

rainbow trout to 70 cm (4.0 kg)
brook trout to 40 cm

Set between Dutch and Findlay Creek drainages, Whitetail Lake has been designated as a trophy lake, and consequently special limits on number and size of trout kept are in effect as well as restrictions on bait and type of hook. The quality of fishing in Whitetail has been increasing every year, and it presently ranks favourably with the best lakes in the Rockies; rainbow trout upwards of 40 cm. are taken with amazing regularity while large fish of 60 cm. or more are not uncommon. While trolling a fly is generally a successful technique on Whitetail Lake, dry fly fishing in the evening often produces spectacular results.

Blue Lake (BC)
rainbow trout to 45 cm

Blue Lake, a small but colourful lake located 2 km south of Whitetail Lake, contains rainbow trout averaging 25-35 cm in length.

Fisher Maiden Lake (BC)
rainbow trout to 35 cm

Located alongside the Whitetail Lake road, tiny Fisher Maiden Lake's population of rainbow trout is restricted to youngsters and senior citizens only. Casting room is limited around this small pond.

Findlay Creek (BC)
cutthroat trout to 50 cm (1.5 kg)
bull trout to 70 cm (4.0 kg)
whitefish to 40 cm

A major tributary of the Kootenay River, Findlay Creek joins the Kootenay approximately 5 km south of Canal Flats. Although several kilometres of Findlay Creek are protected by a deep canyon, there are many accessible stretches which offer fine fishing. Cutthroat trout averaging 20-30 cm in length predominate, with bull trout and whitefish present in fair numbers as well. A gravel-dirt road beginning at Thunder Hill Campground above Columbia Lake leads up the Findlay Creek drainage.

Lavington Creek (BC)
cutthroat trout to 35 cm

A tributary of Findlay Creek, Lavington Creek can be reached by following logging roads that branch south off of the main Findlay Creek Road. Lavington Creek holds small cutthroat trout mostly in the 15-25 cm range.

Copper Lake (BC)
cutthroat trout to 40 cm

Copper Lake at the head of Sandown Creek can be reached by a rough road up Sandown Creek, or by road and 4-wheel drive road/trail from the Lavington Creek drainage. The lake holds cutthroat trout averaging 20-30 cm in length.

Centaur Lakes (BC)
brook trout to 40 cm

The Centaur Lakes are a series of three lakes situated on the benches above the southwest corner of Columbia Lake. Although recent reports indicate poor fishing, they likely still hold a small population of brook trout.

INVERMERE

Set in the heart of the Rocky Mountain Trench, Lake Windermere serves as the focal point of the region. Invermere is the business centre of the valley and offers numerous services including several sporting goods stores. The main valley also harbors the small towns of Athalmer, Wilmer and Windermere and is linked by Highway 93/95 to the outside; north to Golden, east to Banff, and south to Cranbrook. Fifteen kilometre-long Lake Windermere is more renowned for its warm waters, boardsailing and water skiing than for its fishing. The Columbia River, flowing downstream from Lake Windermere, holds plenty of whitefish and some large bull trout while nearby Toby and Horsethief Creeks offer fine stream fishing. A series of lakes, of which Lake Lillian holds the most promise for fishermen, are located on the benches above Toby Creek west of Invermere. On the east side of Lake Windermere, tiny Blue, Twin and Lost Lakes are all situated in the upper Windermere Creek watershed.

Lake Windermere (BC)
bull trout to 70 cm (3.5 kg)
rainbow trout to 50 cm (1.5 kg)
cutthroat trout to 45 cm
brook trout to 45 cm
kokanee to 50 cm (1.5 kg)
whitefish to 40 cm

Despite the wide variety of fish available, Lake Windermere has never gained a good reputation for fishing, mainly due to the large population of suckers and squawfish that inhabit the lake. However, the kokanee population has grown by leaps and bounds in recent years and somewhat increased the lake's popularity. Rainbow can usually be taken in the spring in the weeks immediately after ice-out. During the summer, trolling a fly in the areas around the lake's many inlet creeks such as Goldie Creek and Windermere Creek will often produce trout. Fishermen can also catch the occasional ling cod, chub, or bass.

Columbia River (BC)
bull trout to 70 cm (3.5 kg)
whitefish to 40 cm

The Columbia River flowing north from Lake Windermere possesses numerous deep pools and offers fair fishing for bull trout and whitefish. Best spots are where major tributaries such as Toby and Horsethief Creeks join the Columbia. The Wilmer Sloughs, a series of large, shallow lakes approximately 5 km north of Lake Windermere, hold little in the way of fish and are best left to the ducks.

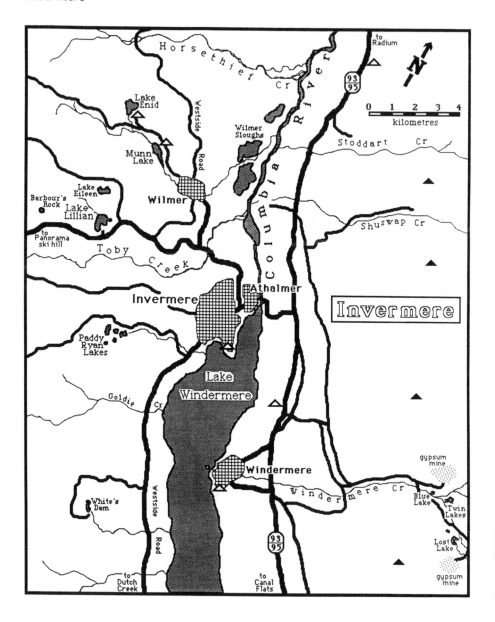

Windermere Creek (BC)

cutthroat trout to 25 cm

The small stream flowing from headwaters above Twin and Lost Lakes through the town of Windermere contains small cutthroat over its entire length. The upper portion of the creek can be accessed by the Westroc Mine Road (See note below.)

Blue Lake (BC)

cutthroat trout to 30 cm

A small but very deep lake of the most incredible colour, Blue Lake holds a few cutthroat in the 20-30 cm range. Roll casting ability will be required as a combination of steep banks and heavy forest surround the entire lake. *Note: To reach Blue Lake, Twin Lakes, and Lost Lake, the Westroc Mine Road must be driven. During working hours, the road is very dangerous due to the many large trucks that haul gypsum. Check with the mine office for hours of operation, and for procedure for driving mine road.*

Twin Lakes (BC)

cutthroat trout to 35 cm

Busy throughout the summer, Twin Lakes is a popular picnic spot and receives heavy fishing pressure. The cutthroat trout in the lakes average 20-25 cm in length, although bigger ones are often seen in the larger of the two lakes, an extemely deep body of water which is almost completely encircled by a high cliff making fishing difficult. There are a few locations to cast from, the most popular being the narrow channel between the two lakes.

Lost Lake (BC)

cutthroat trout to 40 cm

Accessed by a difficult-to-find trail that branches off the main road, Lost Lake often lives up to its name. Containing a small population of cutthroat trout averaging 20-30 cm in length, Lost will cause problems for most fly fishermen; steep banks are clogged with deadfall and heavy timber is the general nature of Lost's shoreline. Occasionally a flimsy raft may be available, courtesy of some enterprising fishermen.

White's Dam (BC)

cutthroat trout to 35 cm

Reached by following a veritable maze of logging roads on the west side of Lake Windermere, White's Dam retains little of its past glory. Cutthroat trout exceeding 80 cm in length were taken from this overgrown beaver pond in years past, but overfishing led to a severe decline in both number and size of trout taken. At present it holds a small population of cutthroat averaging 20-25 cm in length.

Paddy Ryan Lakes (BC)

brook trout to 30 cm
rainbow trout to 30 cm

Being the source of Invermere's water supply, many of the Paddy Ryan Lakes are closed to angling and are fenced off. The fifth and largest of the lakes is still open to fishing and holds brook trout averaging 20-25 cm in length as well as the occasional rainbow, remnant of past stockings. Most of the trees around the shoreline have been cut down so there is plenty of room for backcasting. Tiny Ben Abel Creek, the outlet creek for Paddy Ryan Lakes, contains small brook and rainbow trout and has long been a favourite of local youngsters.

Toby Creek (BC)

cutthroat trout to 40 cm
bull trout to 70 cm (3.5 kg)
whitefish to 35 cm

Access to the best stretches of Toby Creek which lie 2 to 10 km above its confluence with the Columbia River is generally difficult as the creek flows through a deep canyon. After run-off is complete, fishing is usually good for cutthroat and bull trout with excellent angling for whitefish in the fall.

Lake Lillian (BC)

rainbow trout to 60 cm (2.5 kg)
brook trout to 40 cm

Located just north of the Panorama ski hill road, Lake Lillian is popular with local anglers especially after ice-out. Lillian's pretty blue-green waters hold plenty of rainbow and brook trout in the 25-35 cm range, the zone dividing the deep water from the shallows usually holding the most fish, although trolling a fly through the deeper waters can also be productive at times. During low light periods, many of the larger fish make their way into the shallow waters to feed. A boat is strongly advised, as fishing from shore at Lake Lillian is difficult because of access problems due to private land and the few available locations offer little room for backcasting.

Barbour's Rock [Bluff Lake] (BC)

brook trout to 30 cm

Three kilometres beyond Lake Lillian and just to the north of the Panorama ski hill road, Barbour's Rock sits at the base of an impressive cliff face. Limited access, because of private land, has kept this lake virtually unfished in recent years so you can expect to find plenty of brook trout averaging 20-25 cm in length.

Lake Eileen (BC)
status: devoid of fish

Little more than an overgrown marsh, shallow Lake Eileen located 1 km north of Lake Lillian contains no fish.

Munn Lake [Wilmer Lake] (BC)
brook trout to 60 cm (2.5 kg)

Just west of the townsite of Wilmer lies the elongated form of Munn Lake. Popular in the spring soon after ice-melt, Munn's murky waters hold brook trout averaging 30-40 cm in length. Although fishing is possible from many locations along the shore, a boat is recommended.

Lake Enid (BC)
status: doubtful

Situated 2 km beyond Munn Lake, Lake Enid is a popular picnic spot and although brook trout were stocked here in the past, it is unlikely that any remain.

Horsethief Creek (BC)
cutthroat trout to 40 cm
bull trout to 70 cm (3.5 kg)
whitefish to 35 cm

Similar to all of the major creeks in the area that join the Columbia River from the west, Horsethief Creek offers good fishing in the late summer and early fall particularly during whitefish runs. The lower portion of Horsethief Creek is reached by taking the Westside Road north from Wilmer, while upper sections are accessed by numerous logging roads running through the region.

Stoddart Creek (BC)
cutthroat trout to 20 cm
bull trout to 25 cm

A small stream flowing west to join the Columbia, Stoddart Creek contains a few small cutthroat and bull trout. Access is from abandoned logging roads that intersect with Highway 93/95.

Shuswap Creek (BC)
cutthroat trout to 20 cm
bull trout to 25 cm

Old logging roads extending high into the Shuswap Creek drainage offer access to prospective anglers. Small bull trout are present in the upper reaches with small cutthroat predominant downstream.

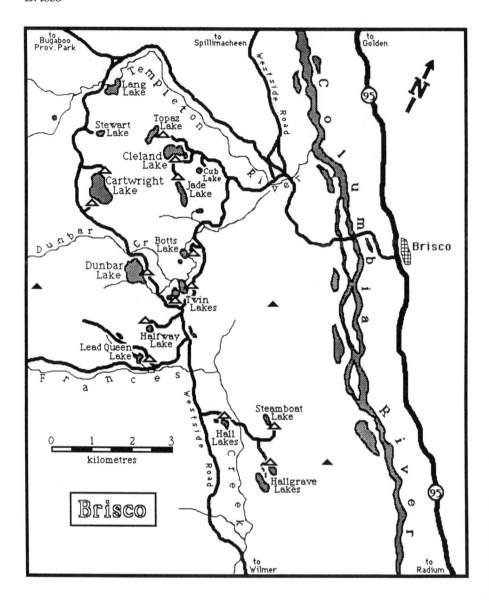

BRISCO

The district to the west of the small town of Brisco has many excellent trout lakes known collectively as the Fish Lakes. The main route through the area is the Westside Road, a gravel and dirt road which can be accessed from Brisco, Spillimacheen, Radium and Wilmer. Since all of the lakes can be reached by vehicle, they are very popular with local anglers and most spots are busy spring through fall. Cleland, Jade, Topaz and Cub Lakes, all lying within a few kilometres of each other, form one complex, while Dunbar, Twin and Botts Lakes, connected by Dunbar Creek, form another group farther south. Farther south still, Hall, Hallgrave and Steamboat Lakes are bunched together on the flank of Steamboat Mountain. Most of the other lakes of the area are solitary, and include Lead Queen, Halfway and Lang. Cartwright Lake, known for both the size and number of its rainbow trout, receives the heaviest fishing pressure of all lakes in the area.

Hall Lakes (BC)
cutthroat trout to 30 cm

These two shallow lakes lying just off the Westside Road contain a few cutthroat trout in small sizes. Most of the fish are concentrated in the larger lake, and are very spooky due to their shallow habitat. Although fly fishing from shore is possible from a number of locations, a boat is recommended.

Steamboat Lake (BC)
rainbow trout to 30 cm

Nestled high on the side of Steamboat Mountain, Steamboat Lake is reached by taking the Hall Lakes cutoff from the Westside Road. While most of the rainbow in Steamboat Lake are less than 25 cm in length, they are plentiful. Casting from shore is possible from quite a few spots, although a boat would definitely be a major asset.

Lead Queen Lake (BC)
cutthroat trout to 40 cm

Lead Queen Lake north of Frances Creek is a very shallow lake bordered by marsh on its west side. Little more than a very large beaver pond, Lead Queen contains cutthroat trout ranging from 25 to 35 cm in length. If fishing from shore, the best opportunities are found near the dam at the lake's outlet. From a boat, schools of fish can usually be seen in the main part of the lake: However, due to the shallow nature of the lake, the trout are very wary and many fly fishermen will no doubt be frustrated.

Hallgrave Lakes (BC)

cutthroat trout to 45 cm

A rough and muddy side road off the Steamboat Lake road leads to the shore of Upper Halgrave Lake. Shallows around the entire lake makes the use of a boat essential. Wet flies are particulartly effective in taking the lake's cutthroat which average 30-35 cm in length. A short trail of less than a kilometre in length leads from the north end of the lake over a ridge and down to Lower Halgrave Lake, a much larger body of water which also has a shallow margin making fly fishing from shore difficult. Carrying a canoe down to Lower Halg-rave increases the chances of catching fish manyfold, with large cut-throat in the 40 cm range taken regularly.

Frances Creek (BC)

cutthroat trout to 30 cm

Frances Creek, which parallels the Westside Road for several kilometres, is well-known by locals as an excellent trout stream. Cutthroat trout averaging 20-25 cm in length are abundant, es-pecially in the numerous pools and log jams along the creek.

Halfway Lake (BC)

rainbow trout to 40 cm

A rough road, much worse in bad weather, leads west from the West-side Road into seldom-visited Halfway Lake. Although a boat is preferable, fishing from shore can be very productive at times. Rain-bow trout in the 20-25 cm size are plentiful, and trolling a fly behind a boat or canoe is usually very effective, especially for novices who haven't mastered all the intricacies of casting.

Twin Lakes (BC)

cutthroat trout to 35 cm

Oddly named, the Twin Lakes actually consist of three lakes all joined by narrow channels. The small, shallow first lake usually has a few trout that congregate around one of the lake's several springs. The second lake is the deepest and holds the most trout, the majority ranging from 20 to 30 cm in length. The third lake is the largest but is very shallow, its best potential lying in its northeast corner where Dunbar Creek flows through. Although fishing from shore is possible, a boat is recommended for all of the lakes.

Dunbar Lake [Big Fish Lake] (BC)

cutthroat trout to 60 cm (2.5 kg)

Renowned in past years for its large cutthroat, Dunbar's reputation has been somewhat tarnished of late because of low productivity. A beautifully coloured lake, Dunbar holds cutthroat trout in small numbers ranging from 20-30 cm in length, although on occasion beauties of up to 60 cm are still caught. For those anglers without a boat, the best opportunities are found in the series of dams below the lake's outlet. If you're fishing from a boat, the margin separating the shallow water from the deep holds the best potential.

Botts Lake (BC)

cutthroat trout to 40 cm

Little more than a widening of Dunbar Creek, tiny marsh-rimmed Botts Lake holds plenty of cutthroat trout in the 20-35 cm range and usually produces well throughout the summer and fall. Fly fishermen will need a boat to reach fish-holding waters because of heavy reed growth around the lake. Generally favourable to fly fishing, trout can be taken on wet or dry lines with relative ease from most locations on the lake. Another small, deep lake located only a few hundred metres from the southwest corner of Botts across some boggy ground also holds cutthroat in fair numbers.

Dunbar Creek (BC)

cutthroat trout to 30 cm

Dunbar Creek, which connects Dunbar, Twin and Botts Lakes, has long stretches of fishable water holding small cutthroat trout. Loaded with dams, logjams and deep pools, Dunbar Creek is never more than a short hike from any road.

Cleland Lake (BC)

rainbow trout to 60 cm (2.5 kg)

As the largest of the Cleland-Jade-Topaz-Cub complex, Cleland receives the most attention from anglers. All four of the lakes are reached by taking the rough road that branches off the Westside Road just over 1 km above the Templeton River bridge. Cleland's translucent blue-green waters hold rainbow trout averaging 30-40 cm in length with larger ones taken regularly, and is best fished from a boat. During the day, most fish are taken from the shelf separating the shallows from the deep, but as daylight fades and many of the larger fish make their way into the shallow waters to feed, evenings becomes a prime time for dry fly fishermen.

Jade Lake (BC)
rainbow trout to 60 cm (2.5 kg)

Despite its difficult access on rough roads, long and narrow Jade Lake attracts many fishermen each summer. Restricted to fly fishing , Jade's waters holds plenty of hard-fighting rainbows averaging 35-45 cm in length. The extended shallows and heavy forest cover will deter most shore fishermen. From a boat, fish can generally be seen feeding in the shallows at both ends of the lake all during the day with increased activity in the shallows during low light periods. Patiently working the shallows with a wet line will usually produce positive results, whereas in the deep middle section of the lake, trolling a fly is generally an effective technique.

Topaz Lake (BC)
rainbow trout to 45 cm

Topaz Lake, located at the end of a rough and often muddy access road, is very shallow and has been prone in the past to winter kill. Recent reports indicate that rainbow trout still exist in good numbers, most averaging 30-35 cm in length. Long and narrow, Topaz is best fished from a boat, although fish can occasionally be taken from shore when feeding in the shallows.

Cub Lake (BC)
rainbow trout to 40 cm

A small, round, sinkhole lake ringed by marsh, Cub Lake does not overwhelm anyone with its beauty. Because fishing from shore is a near impossiblity due to forest cover and marsh, trolling or casting from a boat will produce better results. Cub does hold small rainbows in good numbers, most averaging 20-30 cm in length.

Cartwright Lake (BC)
rainbow trout to 70 cm (4.0 kg)

The most popular lake in the Brisco region, Cartwright is busy with fishermen from June through to October. Rainbows averaging 35-45 cm in length cruise the shallower water for food throughout the day, and from a boat a patient fly fisherman will get numerous opportunities to hook into a big fish. Trolling a fly slowly along the drop-off between the shallows and the deeper water can be extremely effective. Trolling the deep water with a wet line can also be productive at times. Extended shallows around the entire lake make fishing from shore very inefficient.

Stewart Lake (BC)

rainbows to 30 cm

Little more than a overgrown beaver pond, Stewart Lake can be reached by taking a short side road off the east side of the main road between Cartwright and Lang Lakes. Often murky, Stewart's waters hold small rainbow averaging 20-25 cm in length.

Lang Lake (BC)

rainbows to 40 cm

Lang Lake, largely cut off by private property, has little to offer anyone fishing from shore as much of its flooded shoreline is clogged with innumerable dead trees. Getting a boat onto Lang requires a short float down the Templeton River which flows right through the middle of the lake. The rainbow in Lang average 20-30 cm in length and are present in fair numbers. Trolling a fly can be very effective at times.

Templeton River (BC)

cutthroat to 25 cm
rainbow to 25 cm

The best fishing on the Templeton River is found in the area above Lang Lake where a seemingly infinite series of small beaver ponds exist. Cutthroat and rainbow in small sizes can be taken at most spots along the river, the area around the lower bridges on the Westside Road being particularly popular.

Columbia River (BC)

bull trout to 80 cm (7.0 kg)
whitefish to 40 cm

Running muddy for much of the year, the slow-moving Columbia contains plenty of bull trout and whitefish. Occasionally, rainbow or cutthroat trout are caught, as are suckers, ling and chub.

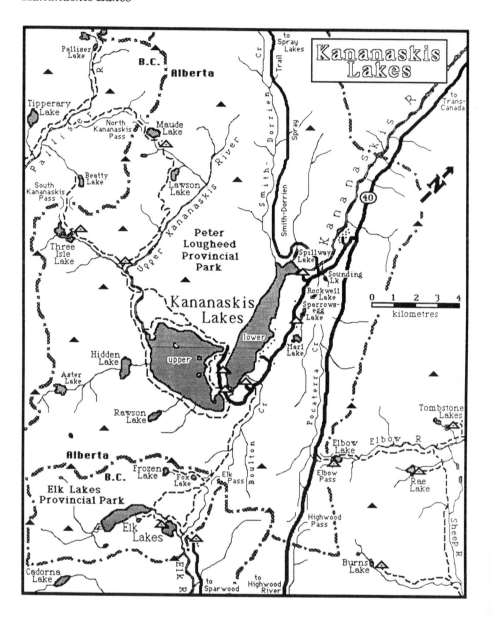

KANANASKIS LAKES

The magnificent Kananaskis Lakes in Peter Lougheed Provincial Park serve as the centerpiece of the region and are immensely popular with fishermen from June through September. Kananaskis Country and Peter Lougheed Provincial Park have several major frontcountry campgrounds in the area with limited tourist facilities. From Upper Kananaskis Lake a series of trails radiate out into the surrounding backcountry. To the northwest, hikers make their way to Three Isle and Maude Lakes, both popular destinations with fishermen, while to the west, more primitive trails lead to Hidden, Rawson and Aster lakes which are more noted for their scenery than for their angling. The Elk River, along with Fox, Frozen and Elk Lakes await hikers on the British Columbia side of Elk Pass in Elk Lakes Provincial Park. South of the Kananaskis Lakes off Highway 40, a short side trail leads to the ever-popular Elbow Lake, headwaters of the Elbow River. Ongoing trails along the upper Elbow River lead to Rae, Tombstone and Burns Lakes, all within a day's hike of Elbow Lake.

Kananaskis Lakes [Upper and Lower] (AB)
rainbow trout to 65 cm (3.0 kg)
bull trout to 75 cm (4.0 kg)
cutthroat trout to 60 cm (2.5 kg)
whitefish to 45 cm

Each summer, the Kananaskis Lakes with their impressive mountain background to the west attract hordes of fishermen and sightseers alike. Both lakes offer excellent fishing for rainbow trout which are stocked annually. In addition to the rainbows, which average 25-40 cm in length, large bull trout are also present in fair numbers (particularly in the Lower Lake) as well as limited numbers of cutthroat trout and whitefish. Due to the size of both lakes, trolling a fly is a popular technique, although casting a fly can be most effective if a school of rainbows is found surface feeding. On long, narrow Lower Lake, fishermen tend to have the most success at the south end in the area around the penstock, and at the far north end in the bay by Canyon Dam. On the Upper Lake, the area around the mouth of the Upper Kananaskis River is usually productive as are the waters around the lake's several islands. Shorebound fishermen tend to congregate along the numerous bays on the easily accessible northeast side and although this area often produces well, other less-fished areas of the Upper Lake are definitely worth a look. If boating on the Kananaskis Lakes, be aware of the strong winds that arise regularly.

Hidden Lake (AB)
status: devoid of fish

A muddy body of water that virtually dries up each fall, Hidden Lake is situated in heavy forest on the west side of Upper Kananaskis Lake. Attempts in the past to stock Hidden Lake have always failed.

Aster Lake (AB)
status: devoid of fish

An oversized glacial tarn, rockbound Aster Lake has never been stocked, and contains no fish.

Rawson Lake
cutthroat trout to 50 cm (1.5 kg)

Tucked away in a wooded valley south of Upper Kananaskis Lake, Rawson Lake was closed to angling for several years when the lake's healthy cutthroat trout population was used as brood stock by Fish and Wildlife. The lake was recently reopened to angling and rumours of large cutthroat in Rawson's waters have attracted plenty of fishermen.

Marl Lake, Sparrows-egg Lake, Rockwall Lake, Sounding Lake, Pocaterra Creek (AB)
cutthroat trout to 25 cm
bull trout to 30 cm

A series of shallow ponds and interconnecting beaver dams in the lower Pocaterra Creek drainage, Marl, Sparrows-egg, Rockwall and Sounding Lakes all contain scattered populations of small cutthroat and bull trout. Fishing is generally poor, and access is difficult due to the marshy nature of the valley bottom. Pocaterra Creek holds cutthroat and bull trout in small sizes and is a little more productive than the nearby lakes.

Spillway Lake (AB)
rainbow trout to 35 cm

Spillway Lake is located alongside the Smith-Dorrien--Spray Trail at the north end of Lower Kananaskis Lake. It's shallow waters generally hold a few schools of rainbow trout that have made their way in from Lower Kananaskis Lake and are unable to return. Although highly visible, Spillway's trout are very spooky and difficult to catch. Watch for cars on your backcast.

Elbow Lake (AB)

brook trout to 35 cm
cutthroat trout to 35 cm

Situated at the crest of Elbow Pass, less than 1 km by trail from Highway 40, the pretty blue waters of Elbow Lake attract numerous visitors every summer. Don't expect solitude. Brook trout predominate over cutthroat, most fish taken from the lake averaging 20-30 cm in length. Forest cover and extended shallows around much of the lake will deter many fly fishermen. However, fish can be taken very close to shore in many spots, particularly in the deeper waters off the scree slopes along the north side.

Elbow River [upper] (AB)

cutthroat trout to 30 cm
brook trout to 30 cm
bull trout to 35 cm

Flowing northeast from its source at Elbow Lake, the upper reaches of the Elbow River are overlooked by most fishermen despite a major hiking trail parallelling the river between the Elbow Pass region and Highway 66 (Elbow Falls Trail) at Little Elbow Campground. Cutthroat, brook and bull trout are all present in this upper section which near Elbow Lake resembles little more than a small creek. Rainbow trout become more prevalent in the heavily-fished lower reaches of the Elbow which is accessible via Elbow Falls Trail from Bragg Creek Village.

Tombstone Lakes (AB)

cutthroat trout to 35 cm (Lower Lake only)

Despite their ominous name, the Tombstone Lakes are set in a delightful basin located 1 km by trail northwest of the Elbow River at Tombstone Creek backcountry campground (8 km from Elbow Lake). The tiny Lower Lake, surrounded on three sides by forest, contains plenty of small cutthroat trout averaging 20-25 cm in length. Dramatically set beneath the towering east face of Tombstone Mountain, the shallow Upper Lake has never been stocked and contains no fish. Both lakes are listed as High Mountain Lakes in the fishing regulations.

Rae Lake (AB)
cutthroat trout to 50 cm (1.5 kg)

Ringed by a mix of forest and open meadows, the dark waters of Rae Lake lie tucked into the side of Mt. Rae's eastern outlier. Although only 2 km by ill-defined trail from Sheep trail over open slopes, Rae Lake to date has received little attention from anglers despite holding a good population of cutthroat trout in the 25-35 cm range. Back-casting room is available around much of the lake where meadows extend down to the shore. It's designated in the regulations as a High Mountain Lake.

Burns Lake (AB)
cutthroat trout to 40 cm

Located at the head of a minor tributary of the upper Sheep River, Burns Lake lies a distant 15 km by trail from Elbow Lake, and 10 km by trail from Highway 546 (Sheep River Trail). A steep scramble up a headwall protects Burns from all but the most enterprising hikers who will be rewarded by cutthroat trout in good numbers averaging 20-30 cm in length and surrounding meadows which afford plenty of room for backcasting.

Fox Lake (BC)
status: devoid of fish

A small lake located less than a kilometre west of Elk Pass, Fox Lake was rumoured in the past to contain both cutthroat and bull trout. However, this seems unlikely as Fox Lake annually dries up to the point of being incapable of holding fish.

Frozen Lake (BC)
status: doubtful

A particularly stunning lake set precariously on a lip high on Mount Fox, Frozen Lake remains a popular attraction for day hikers from the Elk Lakes and Peter Lougheed Provincial Parks. As its name suggests, Frozen Lake is very sheltered and generally remains ice-bound well into July. Both cutthroat and bull trout are thought to have at one time inhabited the deep waters, but poor results in recent years have prompted many fishermen to suggest that few or no trout remain in the lake.

Cadorna Lake (BC)
cutthroat trout to 50 cm (1.5 kg)

At the head of Cadorna Creek, pretty Cadorna Lake lies oblivious to the pressures of regular visitors, difficult access over poor trails from the Elk River assuring solitude for those reaching Cadorna. The lake holds cutthroat trout in the 25-35 cm range.

Elk Lakes (BC)

cutthroat trout to 50 cm (1.5 kg)
bull trout to 60 cm (2.5 kg)
whitefish to 40 cm

Set amid the spectacular glaciated peaks of the French Military Group, the Elk Lakes are becoming an increasingly popular destination for backbackers. Access is either via a 10 km trail from Peter Lougheed Provincial Park, or a long 130 km drive from Sparwood (the last 40 km are very rough), followed by a 2 km hike to the Lower Lake. Fishing is slow much of the summer in both the larger Upper and smaller Lower Elk Lakes due to heavy silting but as the lakes begin to clear in the later season and take on a distinctive green colouration, the fishing generally picks up, and cutthroat and bull trout averaging 25-35 cm in length can be taken in fair numbers. Thick with sunken deadfall, the area around the outlet of the Upper Lake is usually productive even when fishing is quiet elsewhere.

Elk River (BC)

cutthroat trout to 50 cm (1.5 kg)
bull trout to 80 cm (5.0 kg)
whitefish to 45 cm

From its source high in the glaciers at the head of Upper Elk Lake, the Elk River flows south and west for nearly 200 km before joining the Kootenay River as a major tributary. Cutthroat trout and whitefish predominate in all stretches of the river, with large bull trout also present in fair numbers especially in the upper reaches. Run-off usually lasts until mid-July when fishing starts to pick up. The entire Elk River below Elk Lakes Provincial Park is paralleled by road, dirt and gravel in the upper sections, and by Highway 3 west of Sparwood.

Three Isle Lake (AB)

cutthroat trout to 45 cm

A beautifully coloured body of water set less than a kilometre below South Kananaskis Pass, Three Isle Lake has long been a favourite of backcountry fishermen. A 12 km hike incorporating a steep head-wall immediately before the lake leads from the trailhead at Upper Kananaskis Lake to the lake which is not always "Three Isle", but occasionally "One Isle and Two Peninsulas" depending of water levels. Cutthroat trout averaging 25-35 cm are present in good numbers and can be taken from most locations around the lake. As the lake level has receded quite dramatically in recent years, there is plenty of casting room available, although rocks will undoubtedly cause problems for a few fly fishermen. Three Isle is listed in the regulations as a High Mountain Lake.

Beatty Lake (BC)

status: unknown

Completely encircled by forest, Beatty Lake lies just over a kilometre from the provincial boundary on the B.C. side of South Kananaskis Pass. Few reports on fishing in Beatty have ever made their way out, but it is possible the lake does contain a few cutthroat trout.

Tipperary Lake (BC)

status: unknown

Tipperary Lake, set in a narrow valley on the west side of the seldom visited upper Palliser River, remains a mystery to most fishermen, and is reached only by adventuresome individuals armed with map and compass. Although unconfirmed, it is likely that the lake holds cutthroat trout.

Lawson Lake (AB)

status: devoid of fish

A picturesque lake on the North Kananaskis Pass trail, Lawson was stocked in the early 1970's but the trout failed to reproduce. At present there are no fish in Lawson.

Maude Lake (AB)

cutthroat trout to 45 cm

Set in the alpine environs of North Kananaskis Pass, Maude Lake offers the fisherman the twin jewels of superb scenery and excellent fishing after a tiring 17 km hike-in from Upper Kananaskis Lake. Plenty of cutthroat trout mostly in the 25-35 cm range inhabit the lake's clear waters and can be caught from most locations around the shoreline. The larger fish tend to keep to the deeper waters off the north and west corners of the lake where steep terrain will generally limit backcasting. On calm evenings with insects about, a dry fly can be particulary effective. Maude is designated a High Mountain Lake in the fishing regulations.

SMITH-DORRIEN

The Smith-Dorrien—Spray Trail, a gravel road connecting Canmore and Peter Lougheed Provincial Park via the Spray Lakes Reservoir, provides access to this rugged area noted for its outstanding day and half-day hikes. Mud Lake and the Hogarth Lakes are located in a wide valley at the head of the Smuts and Smith-Dorrien watersheds which contains a virtual maze of abandoned logging roads offering easy access. Spur valleys to the west hold Commonwealth Lake and the Burstall Lakes, while to the east of the Smith-Dorrien valley, consecutive side valleys hold Rummel, Chester and Headwall Lakes.

Headwall Lakes (AB)
cutthroat trout to 45 cm

Located seven kilometres by trail from the Chester Lake parking area, the Headwall Lakes are set in rocky, windswept basins where a general lack of vegetation allows for backcasting without problem. Both the lower and upper lakes hold plenty of cutthroat trout averaging 25-35 cm in length which tend to keep to the area around the distinctive drop-off zone. Both lakes are designated in the fishing regulations as High Mountain Lakes.

Chester Lake (AB)
arctic char to 60 cm (2.5 kg)

Chester Lake and its appealing larch-filled valley, reached by a 6 km walk-in from the Smith-Dorrien—Spray Trail, attracts numerous day sightseers and anglers throughout the summer. Chester was stocked in 1974 with arctic char (a close relative of the bull trout) which are now reproducing naturally. The char tend to keep to the deeper waters and are generally caught in greater numbers by bait and spin fishermen, although patient and persistent fly fishermen will take their fair share. Casting is difficult from most spots due to either forest cover or scree slopes along the east and south shores. Chester Lake is listed in the regulations as a High Mountain Lake.

Rummel Lake [West Galatea Lake] (AB)
cutthroat trout to 40 cm

Although Rummel Lake is not accessed by trail, those anglers with a map and compass will have no problem reaching the lake either from the west via old logging roads along the Smith-Dorrien—Spray Trail or from the south via the Chester Lake trail. Set in an atttractive basin, Rummel's clear waters hold cutthroat trout in the 20-30 cm range. It's designated as a High Mountain Lake in the fishing regulations.

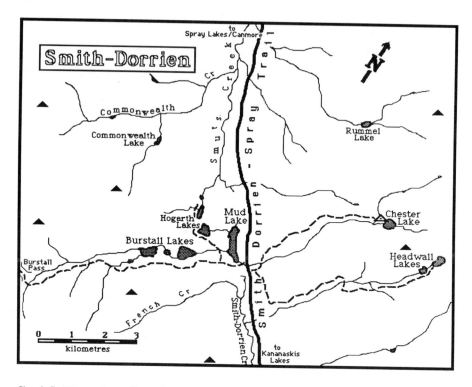

Smith-Dorrien Creek (AB)

rainbow trout to 25 cm

Flowing south as it parallels the Smith-Dorrien--Spray Trail, Smith-Dorrien Creek is very accessible to anglers. Stocked in the past with rainbow trout, the creek still contains rainbow in small sizes, while French Creek, a major tributary of the Smith-Dorrien, has few or no trout.

Mud Lake (AB)

cutthroat trout to 35 cm
bull trout to 50 cm (1.5 kg)
whitefish to 30 cm

Fed by the meltwaters of Robertson Glacier, Mud Lake, true to its name, remains chocolate-coloured for most of the year. Accordingly, fishing is usually slow for cutthroat, bull trout and whitefish which inhabit Mud's roadside waters. Much of the shoreline is marshy, and there are few locations that offer adequate backcasting room.

Burstall Lakes (AB)

status: doubtful

This series of fine lakes in a meadowed valley 2 km west of Mud Lake have never been stocked, and reports indicate they are devoid of fish. There is a chance Burstall Creek between Burstall Lake and Mud Lake may contain a few small cutthroat and bull trout.

Hogarth Lakes (AB)

cutthroat trout to 40 cm

These two emerald-green bodies of water located 2 km by trail from the Mud Lake Parking area receive surprisingly little attention from anglers despite their proximity to the Smith-Dorrien—Spray Trail. Both lakes contain cutthroat trout averaging 20-30 cm in length, the extreme water clarity allowing the angler to see fish cruising about. Casting room is adequate around the larger of the two lakes, but somewhat restricted around the smaller, narrower one. Both are designated as High Mountain Lakes in the fishing regulations.

Commonwealth Lake [Lost Lake] (AB)

cutthroat trout to 40 cm

Commonwealth Lake, situated in a secluded side valley off Commonwealth Creek, receives few visits from anglers each season probably because of access requiring bushwhacking. Listed as a High Mountain Lake, Commonwealth holds cutthroat in the 20-30 cm range and is encircled by forest which makes casting difficult from most locations. Nearby Commonwealth Creek contains small cutthroat trout, and can be reached along abandoned logging roads from the Smith-Dorrien—Spray Trail.

Smuts Creek (AB)

cutthroat trout to 25 cm
bull trout to 40 cm
whitefish to 25 cm

Flowing alongside the Smith-Dorrien Trail from Mud Lake to the Spray Lakes Reservoir, Smuts Creek offers a few stretches of good stream fishing. Small cutthroat predominate with the odd bull trout or whitefish also present.

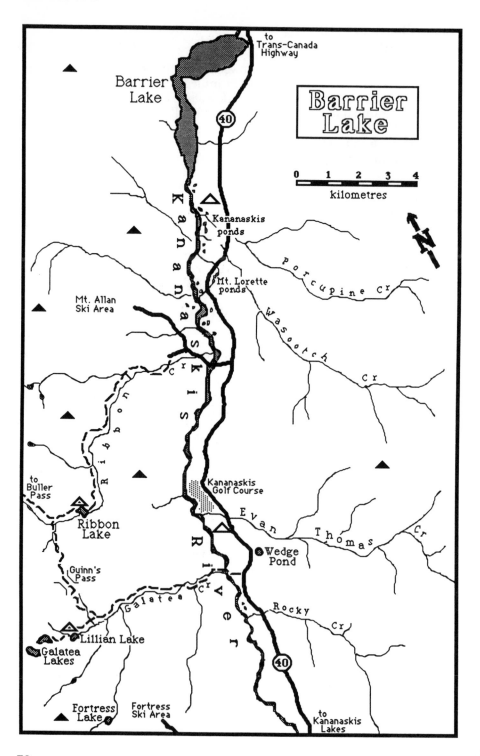

Barrier Lake

to
Trans-Canada
Highway

40

Barrier
Lake

**Barrier
Lake**

0   1   2   3   4
kilometres

N

Kananaskis
ponds

Porcupine Cr

Mt. Lorette
ponds

Wasootch

Mt. Allan
Ski Area

Cr

Ribbon

Kananaskis

Cr

to
Buller
Pass

Kananaskis
Golf Course

Ribbon
Lake

Evan   Thomas
Cr

Wedge
Pond

Guinn's
Pass

River

Galatea   Cr

Rocky

Lillian Lake

Cr

Galatea
Lakes

40

Fortress
Lake

Fortress
Ski Area

to
Kananaskis
Lakes

BARRIER LAKE

Highway 40 (Kananaskis Trail) runs through the core of the region from the Trans-Canada Highway in the north to Peter Lougheed Provincial Park in the south. En route, limited supplies of gas, food and fishing equipment are available at Fortress Junction, Ribbon Creek Alpine Village and Mt. Kidd R. V. Park. The area has several major frontcountry camprounds as well as a Travel Alberta Information Centre at Barrier Lake. Winding its way north to the Bow River, the beautiful Kananaskis River and its multitude of accompanying beaver ponds are within easy walking distance of Highway 40 for most anglers. Barrier Lake, formed by a dam on the Kananaskis River, is one of only a handful of lakes in the Canadian Rockies that contain brown trout and for this reason attracts many fishermen. Travelling south along Highway 40 you pass the Mt. Lorette Ponds and Wedge Pond which both offer good roadside fishing and are stocked annually. The Ribbon Creek-Galatea Creek loop presents a challenging hike with some fine backcountry fishing en route in Ribbon, Galatea and Lillian Lakes.

Barrier Lake (AB)
brown trout to 50 cm (1.5 kg)
rainbow trout to 50 cm (1.5 kg)
whitefish to 40 cm

Barrier Dam on the Kananaskis River creates Barrier Lake, a beautiful green-coloured body of water that fluctuates in size with the seasons. Late in the fall and early in the spring, the area around the inlet of the Kananaskis River becomes one large mud flat intersected by the river winding back and forth but as the dam fills with meltwater, so the mudflats disappear and the lake gains almost 2 km in length. Barrier holds plenty of brown trout and whitefish in the 25-35 cm range as well as a few rainbow trout, while on rare occasions, a brook or bull trout may also be taken. Fishing is best from a boat, although there are a few locations where shore-bound fishermen do well. Any one of a number of points that jut out into the lake hold good possibilities, as does the area around the inlet and the main bay near Barrier Dam.

Kananaskis River (AB)

brook trout to 40 cm
cutthroat trout to 40 cm
rainbow trout to 40 cm
whitefish to 40 cm
bull trout to 60 cm (2.5 kg)

Flowing from the Kananaskis Lakes to the Bow River, the Kananaskis River with its deep pools attracts plenty of anglers. Readily accessible from Highway 40, the Kananaskis River's deep pools hold a variety of fish with brook trout predominating, although cutthroat, rainbow, bull trout and whitefish are all present in fair numbers as well. Hiking a few hundred metres up or downstream, even on busy days, will usually bring a fisherman to a pool of his own. Be aware that the release of water from the dam on Lower Kananaskis Lake can cause changes in water levels over a few hours which usually disrupts fishing.

Kananaskis ponds (AB)

brook trout to 35 cm
rainbow trout to 35 cm

A seemingly endless maze of beaver ponds parallel the Kananaskis River between Barrier Lake and Ribbon Creek. Although some are subject to winter kill, most hold small rainbow, or more likely, brook trout averaging 20-30 cm in length. The ponds closest to the highway are generally overfished and reaching the more productive ponds usually means working through a tangle of brush and deadfall. Wet feet are a sure bet. Major clusters of ponds are found along the river south of Barrier Lake (including Beaver Ponds Picnic Area) and near the junction of the Kananaskis River with Porcupine, Wasootch and Rocky Creeks.

Mount Lorette Ponds (AB)

rainbow trout to 40 cm

A series of small man-made lakes, the Mount Lorette Ponds were built to provide handicapped and elderly persons the opportunity to fish. A network of paved trails leads from the parking lot past a picnic area to all the ponds where rainbow trout in the 20-30 cm range is the normal catch. The ponds are stocked annually.

Wedge Pond (AB)

rainbow trout to 40 cm

A man-made lake situated alongside Highway 40, Wedge Pond attracts hordes of fishermen because of its ease of access. Stocked each year, Wedge contains rainbow trout averaging 20-30 cm in length, and plenty of backcasting room is available around the entire lake.

Evan-Thomas Creek (AB)

brook trout to 25 cm
bull trout to 30 cm
rainbow trout to 25 cm

A major tributary of the Kananaskis River, Evan-Thomas Creek has fair angling in its lower sections. Brook, bull and rainbow trout in small sizes predominate with the occasional cutthroat or whitefish also taken.

Ribbon Creek (AB)

cutthroat trout to 25 cm

The lower reaches of Ribbon Creek hold a few small cutthroat trout and may also hold the odd rainbow or bull trout. Fishing is best restricted to the waters within a kilometre or two of the Kananaskis River which includes a number of beaver ponds.

Ribbon Lake (AB)

cutthroat trout to 45 cm

Ribbon Lake, an exquisite body of water set on a lip above Ribbon Falls, is guarded by cliffs making access very difficult. The first 11 km of the 13 km trail are a straightforward walk up Ribbon Creek at a very moderate grade to the delightful Ribbon Falls, but once past the falls, the trail rises steeply, soon coming to a series of exposed ledges and cliff faces to which chains have been attached to aid climbing. Even so, it is still a dangerous section, particularly in wet weather, and those faint-of-heart are strongly advised to pass on this lake or to use the longer Guinn's Pass or Buller Pass access routes. Ribbon holds cutthroat averaging 25-35 cm in length. Casting a fly is difficult around much of the shoreline due to heavy brush, although there are enough suitable locations to keep fly fishermen happy. A distinctive drop-off can be seen around the entire lake and fishing this zone where the shallow meets the deep is usually very productive. Ribbon is designated as a High Mountain Lake in the regulations.

Fortress Lake (AB)

cutthroat trout to 40 cm

A small dark-blue lake set beneath the imposing north wall of The Fortress, Fortress Lake is reached by a 4 km hike from Fortress Ski Area. Designated a High Mountain Lake, Fortress holds cutthroat trout averaging 20-30 cm in length. Scree slopes from The Fortress make up of half of the lake's shore, with the rest a mixture of forest and meadow allowing for reasonable backcasting.

Lillian Lake (AB)
cutthroat trout to 50 cm (1.5 kg)

A very popular backcountry destination, Lillian Lake is crowded with hikers and anglers throughout the summer. Located 6 km by trail from Highway 40, the shallow, olive-coloured waters hold cutthroat averaging 20-30 cm in length. Due to water clarity, fish can be seen far out into the lake and casting ahead of cruising fish will produce positive results even though heavy forest cover around much of the shore will inhibit backcasting. Under low light conditions, fish can very often be taken by keen-eyed fishermen within a few metres of shore. It is listed in the fishing regulations as a High Mountain Lake.

Galatea Lakes (AB)
cutthroat trout to 45 cm

Little more than a kilometre by ill-defined trail above the Lillian Lake campsite lie the twin gems of Lower and Upper Galatea Lakes. Both of these turquoise bodies of waters hold cutthroat in the 20-30 cm range, the lower lake containing the larger population. Their setting in basins at tree line ensure plenty of backcasting room around both lakes which are very clear and drop off rather quickly, and a wet fly fished deep generally gets strikes. Galatea lakes are designated as High Mountain Lakes in the regulations.

Galatea Creek (AB)
cutthroat trout to 25 cm
bull trout to 30 cm
brook trout to 25 cm

The lower 2 km of Galatea Creek contain a few small cutthroat, bull and brook trout.

> *Time is but the stream I go a-fishing in.*
> *Henry David Thoreau.*

CANMORE

Serving as the centre of the area is the town of Canmore which offers complete tourist facilities. The Trans-Canada Highway, leading east to Calgary and northwest to Banff, parallels the Bow River throughout the entire region. The Bow, in particular the stretch near the Trans-Canada bridge, receives heavy fishing pressure. The 1-A Highway which branches north of the Trans-Canada just east of Canmore offers alternate access to the Bow River as well as to Gap Lake, Grotto Mountain Pond, Canmore beaver ponds and the Steele Brothers Ponds. From Canmore, the gravelled Smith-Dorrien--Spray Trail which heads directly west through Whiteman Gap leads in short order to Goat Pond and the Spray Lakes Reservoir, a very popular spot with local anglers and busy all summer long. Spray Lakes West campground, accessible by car, is located along the west side of the reservoir on a rough road which continues on to the Assiniboine/Marvel hiking trailhead at Canyon Dam. The Smith-Dorrien--Spray Trail which follows the eastern shoreline of the Spray Lakes Reservoir leads to Peter Lougheed Provincial Park, eventually intersecting with the Kananaskis Lakes Trail.

Spray Lakes Reservoir (AB)

lake trout to 85 cm (8.0 kg)
cutthroat trout to 60 cm (2.5 kg)
whitefish to 45 cm

Measuring over 20 km in length, Spray Lakes Reservoir is located southwest of Canmore in a deep valley between the Goat and Kananaskis Ranges and is accessed by the Smith-Dorrien--Spray Trail running between Canmore and the Kananaskis Lakes. The area is very popular with campers and fishermen and campsites along the west shore are inevitably filled each weekend throughout the summer. Due to the lake's size, a boat is essential for fishing, but boaters should be aware that very strong winds are common and often keep all crafts off the water for days at a time. Huge lake trout inhabit the lake, with whitefish also present in good numbers as well as the occasional cutthroat trout. Although bait fishermen generally have a distinct advantage over fly fishermen when pursuing lake trout, a streamer trolled deep can be effective at times. For those shore-bound anglers, areas around the many inlet creeks often hold trout, the upper end of the lake near the inflow of the Spray River being particularly productive although a 6 km hike-in is required beyond Canyon Dam. There are special limits on lake trout taken from Spray Lakes Reservoir, so check regulations.

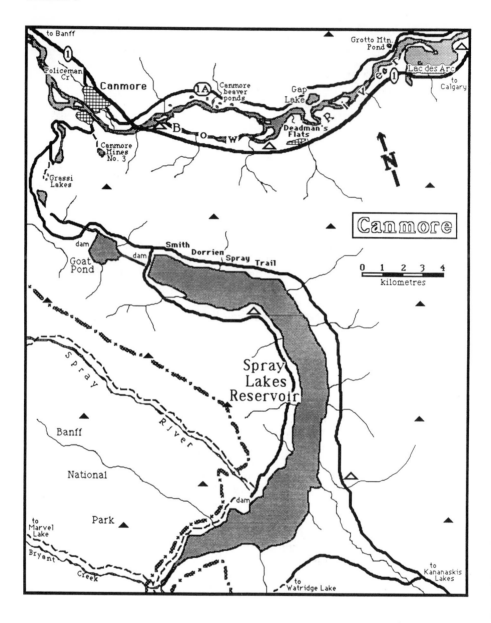

Goat Pond (AB)

rainbow trout to 50 cm (1.5 kg)

Part of the reservoir/power complex, Goat Pond is a man-made lake 2 km northwest of Spray Lakes Reservoir alongside the Smith-Dorrien--Spray Trail. Most of the shoreline and lake is cluttered with deadfall and although rainbow trout averaging 25-35 cm in length are there for the catching, most fishermen will likely catch more snags than fish.

Grassi Lakes (AB)

status: devoid of fish

Two tiny charming lakes of exquisite color, the Grassi Lakes are set in the basin immediately beneath Whiteman Gap. Although they contain no fish the lakes are a popular hiking destination.

Canmore Mines No. 3 (AB)

rainbow trout to 40 cm

Canmore Mines No. 3 is a small man-made pond located approximately 1 km south of the Spray-Smith--Dorrien Trail just outside of Canmore. Stocked regularly, it contains plenty of rainbow trout mostly in the 20-30 cm range.

Bow River (AB)

rainbow trout to 70 cm (4.0 kg)
brown trout to 75 cm (4.5 kg)
brook trout to 50 cm (1.5 kg)
bull trout to 70 cm (4.0 kg)
whitefish to 45 cm

The stretch of the Bow River flowing from the Banff National Park boundary to Lac Des Arc receives heavy angling pressure during the summer. Readily accessible from either the Trans-Canada or the 1-A Highways, this section of the Bow offers some excellent river fishing for rainbow and brown trout , with large individuals in the 2-3 kg range taken regularly. Bull and brook trout as well as whitefish are also present although their numbers are somewhat limited. The area around the Trans-Canada Highway bridge and the old C.P.R. bridges seem inordinately popular and are heavily overfished, even though other excellent pools are waiting just around the bend both upstream and downstream. Fishing slows dramatically during run-off which lasts from June through late-July. Early season fishing from mid-April to late-May is usually very productive, the action picking up again in August through October.

Policeman Creek (AB)

brown trout to 30 cm
rainbow trout to 30 cm

Flowing directly through Canmore, Policeman Creek is very popular with local youngsters, particularly the area around the bridge that leads to Canmore's business centre. Both brown and rainbow trout in small sizes averaging 15-25 cm in length can be taken.

Canmore Beaver Ponds (AB)

rainbow trout to 35 cm
brown trout to 35 cm

Interconnected with various channels of the Bow River, the Canmore beaver ponds are located alongside the 1-A Highway 4 km east of Canmore. The ponds contain rainbow trout along with a few brown trout, few exceeding 25 cm in length.

Gap Lake (AB)

brown trout to 50 cm (1.5 kg)
brook trout to 40 cm
whitefish to 40 cm

Gap Lake is sandwiched between the 1-A Highway and the C.P.R. mainline 8 km east of Canmore. Brown and brook trout in the 25-35 cm range predominate with whitefish present in fair numbers as well. Casting room is available around most of the shoreline, although heavy underbrush may present problems.

Grotto Mountain Pond (AB)

rainbow trout to 35 cm

Grotto Mountain Pond and its nearby picnic area are situated on the north side of 1-A Highway just west of Lac Des Arc. Stocked regularly, the pond is populated by rainbow trout averaging 20-30 cm in length. Casting room is available around the entire pond.

Lac Des Arc (AB)

status: doubtful

Merely an overflow basin for the Bow River, Lac Des Arc is no more than 1-2 m deep and dries up completely on occasion. Accordingly, any fish population will tend to keep near the river on the north side, although the odd whitefish might be taken from the shallow waters that make up the main part of the lake.

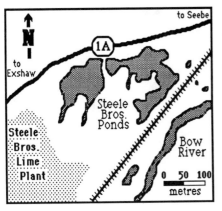

Steele Brother's Ponds (AB)

rainbow trout to 40 cm
brown trout to 40 cm

This series of large, interconnected beaver ponds immediately east of the Steele Brother's lime plant on the 1-A Highway contain good numbers of both rainbow and brown trout. As with most beaver dams, the surrounding vegetation growth is heavy and finding a spot to cast from effectively may prove difficult.

We may say of angling as Dr. Boteler said of strawberries. Doubtless God would have made a better berry, but doubtless God never did, and so (if I may be judge) God never did make a more calm, quiet, innocent recreation than angling.

Izaak Walton.

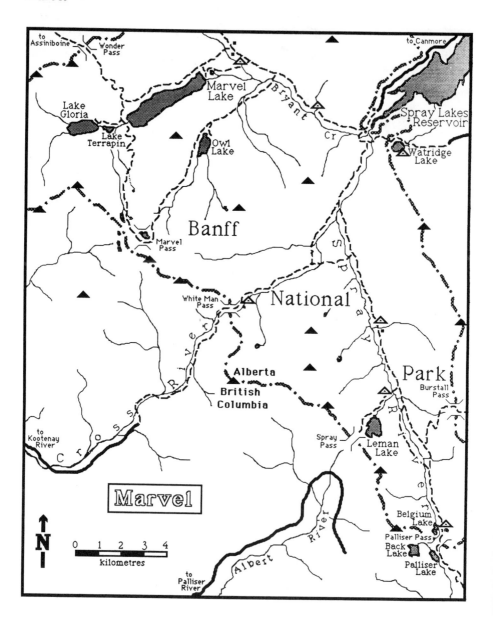

MARVEL

Always close to the peaks of the continental divide, the Marvel area possesses some outstanding scenery. The northern portion of the area is dominated by appropriately named Marvel Lake with its beautiful translucent blue-green waters, and although Marvel receives the majority of the attention, Owl, Gloria and Terrapin offer just as much for those anglers willing to make the effort to reach their shores. Main access to Marvel Lake is along Bryant Creek via a trail that begins on the west side of Spray Lakes Reservoir 40 km west of Canmore. In recent years, the Watridge Lake trailhead, reached via the Watridge logging road from the Smith-Dorrien--Spray Trail, has increased in popularity. The upper Spray River, with its long stretches of fishable water, and Leman Lake, noted for its large cutthroat trout, annually attract hikers to this less-renowned but nonetheless impressive section of Banff National Park. The trio of Belgium, Palliser and Back Lakes are bunched together at the crest of Palliser Pass which constitutes the southern boundary of Banff National Park.

Marvel Lake (PC)
cutthroat trout to 75 cm (5.0 kg)

Set in a long, narrow valley and over 4 km in length and 75 m in depth, Marvel Lake holds some immense cutthroat trout. Due to the lake's size, however, fishing from shore is often a frustrating proposition, fishermen generally having the most success at the east end of the lake, although those willing to expend the energy will find fish all around the lake including the west end which is very productive at times. Fishing the deep, clear waters of Marvel Lake, you would be strongly advised to use a sinking fly line. In addition to its size, Marvel's heavily forested shoreline poses an additional problem for fly fishermen. One worthwhile although difficult solution is to carry in a rubber raft or float tube. Be aware that the waters around the massive log jam at the outlet creek on the northeast end are closed to fishing year-round, as is Marvel Creek from Marvel Lake to Bryant Creek.

Lake Terrapin (PC)
cutthroat trout to 40 cm

Sandwiched between Marvel Lake to the east and Lake Gloria to the west and reached via a short spur trail off the Marvel Pass trail, the silty blue waters of Lake Terrapin hold a small number of cutthroat trout for which the angling is generally poor. Tall grass along the shoreline inhibits access (wet feet are a certainty) and makes backcasting very difficult.

Lake Gloria (PC)
cutthroat trout to 50 cm (1.5 kg)

One of the most exquisitely coloured lakes in the Rockies, Gloria's rich blue waters hold some fine cutthroat trout. Because fish will tend to keep near shore because of the silted nature of the water, fishing near one of the many inlet streams can be particularly effective. The quality of trails diminishes rapidly beyond the area of the outlet stream and those anglers travelling along the shoreline will encounter heavy brush.

Marvel Pass lakes (PC)
status: devoid of fish

Situated in the alpine meadows of Marvel Pass, these promising looking waters have never been stocked and contain no trout.

Owl Lake (PC)
brook trout to 35 cm

Located 10 km from Spray Lakes Reservoir by trail, Owl Lake's sparkling blue-green waters sit in a quiet subalpine valley. Differing opinions exist as to whether or not trout reproduce in Owl Lake, the most recent reports indicating that very few brook trout remain thus effectively diminishing the lake's popularity among anglers. For those willing to try, there is ample backcasting room around the entire lake.

Bryant Creek (PC)
cutthroat trout to 35 cm

A noisy companion to hikers travelling to either Marvel Lake or Assiniboine Pass, Bryant Creek's clear waters hold a fair number of cutthroat trout. The creek is very popular in its lower reaches within a kilometre or two of the Spray Lakes Reservoir. In the meadow section upstream from the Bryant Creek Warden Cabin, there are several kilometres of slow, fishable water as well as numerous beaver ponds.

Spray River (upper) (PC)
cutthroat trout to 30 cm

The upper Spray River, which flows from the Palliser Pass region down to the Spray Lakes Reservoir, has many stretches of excellent fishing. From the first crossing 4 km above Spray Lakes to a point 8 km upstream at the Leman Lake cut-off, the Spray River winds its way back and forth across a wide, flat valley, forming innumerable pools each holding plenty of pan-sized cutthroat trout. Although heavy brush may be a hinderance in spots, most fishermen will have little difficulty casting into trout-holding waters.

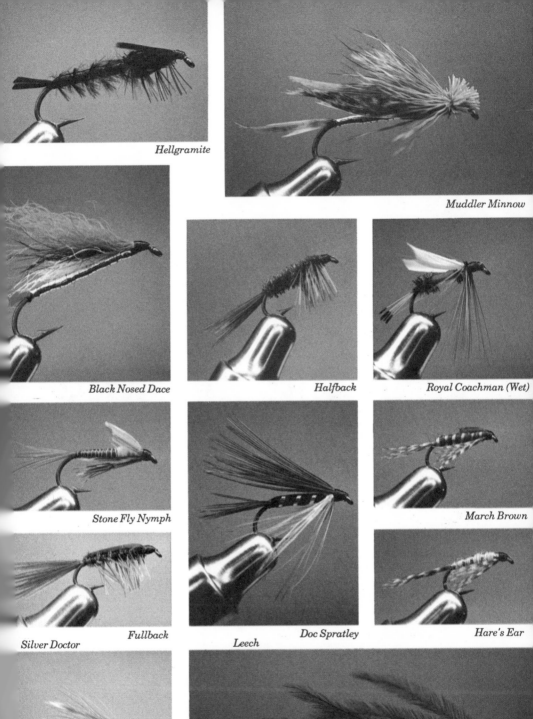

Hellgramite

Muddler Minnow

Black Nosed Dace

Halfback

Royal Coachman (Wet)

Stone Fly Nymph

March Brown

Silver Doctor   Fullback

Leech   Doc Spratley

Hare's Ear

Grasshopper

Black Gnat

Cahill (light)

Adams

Black Ant

Mayfly

Tom Thumb

Cahill (dark)

Midge

Royal Coachman (Dry)

Mosquito

Elk Hair Cadd

Alderson Lake, Waterton

Lower Twin Lake, Tamarack

Headwall Lake, Smith-Dorrien

Lundbreck Falls Crowsnest River, Crowsnest

Picklejar Lake, Oldman-Highwood

Twin Lake, Brisco

Lake Gloria, Marvel

Top left:
Lillian Lake, Barrier La

Left: *Lower Galatea Lo*
Barrier Lake

Right:
Lake Magog, Assiniboi

Top: *Marvel Lake, M*

Bottom:

Sunburst Lake, Ass

Watridge Lake (AB)
cutthroat trout to 50 cm (1.5 kg)

Situated just outside the boundary of Banff National Park in Kananaskis Country, Watridge Lake is very popular with local anglers who fish its clear, green waters for cutthroat trout averaging 25-35 cm in length. The 2 km-long Watridge Lake trail, which ultimately joins the Spray River/Bryant Creek trail complex, has become increasingly popular with hikers since the upgrading of the Smith-Dorrien—Spray road and as a result, fishing pressure has increased at Watridge Lake in recent years. Although casting room is limited around much of the lake, there are enough breaks in the vegetation cover to satisfy fly fishermen. Watridge is listed in the fishing regulations as a High Mountain Lake.

Leman Lake (PC)
cutthroat trout to 70 cm (4.0 kg)

Very popular in years past due to its large trout, Leman Lake has suffered badly through a period of overfishing. With a consequent dramatic decline in the quality of fishing, the number of anglers also declined, so that while Leman still holds some truly outstanding cutthroat, their numbers are limited and most anglers will return home empty-handed. Most fish taken average 45-50 cm in length, although larger ones are taken occasionally. Standard access to Leman is either via the 14 km trail from the Spray Lakes Reservoir or the 13 km Burstall Pass trail. A seldom used 2 km access route begins on the B.C. side from logging roads on the upper Albert River and alternates between following game trails and bushwhacking. A topographic map is strongly recommended for this route.

Belgium Lake (PC)
cutthroat trout to 35 cm

Set in the alpine environs of Palliser Pass, shallow Belgium Lake has a small population of cutthroat trout which face the ever-present threat of winter-kill. The lake's alpine surroundings provides ample backcast room for fly fishermen.

Palliser Lake (BC)
status: devoid of fish

Palliser Lake, an appealing body of water on the B.C. side of Palliser Pass, has never been stocked and contains no fish.

Back Lake (BC)
status: devoid of fish

Never stocked, algae-infested Back Lake sits in a rocky basin less than a kilometre above Palliser Lake.

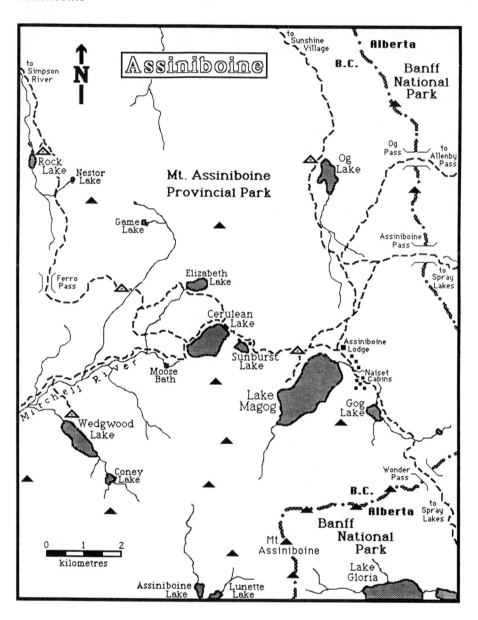

ASSINIBOINE

One of the true gems in the Canadian Rockies, the Assiniboine area has been a favourite of backcountry travellers since the turn of the century. Despite lengthy access routes, incredible scenery and outstanding fishing ensure that the Assiniboine area will be crowded each summer. Lake Magog, set beneath the awe-inspiring summit of Mt. Assiniboine, represents the heart of the region. The main campground is located on the bench above Magog's northwest shore, while Assiniboine Lodge (reservations only) and the government-run Naiset Cabins (first come-first serve) are found on the lake's northeast corner. Sunburst, Cerulean, Elizabeth and Gog Lakes all lie within the Assiniboine core area, while Wedgwood and Og Lakes are easy half-day trips from Lake Magog.

Four main trails lead to Assiniboine, the shortest and most popular of which begins at Spray Lakes Reservoir, 40 km west of Canmore. At the halfway point along Bryant Creek the main trail branches and hikers can choose from either the Assiniboine Pass (19 km) or the Wonder Pass (20 km) options. A 27 km route begins at Sunshine Village in Banff National Park, crosses Sunshine Meadows to Citadel Pass, and works through Golden Valley and Valley of the Rocks before emerging in the Assiniboine meadows at Og Lake. A more strenuous 32 km hike begins at the confluence of the Simpson and Vermilion Rivers in Kootenay National Park and follows the Simpson River and Surprise Creek past Rock Lake, eventually crossing Ferro Pass before swinging east into the Assiniboine core area. The fourth alternative is a seldom-used 30 km trail which follows the course of the Mitchell River from Magnesite Creek. The trailhead for the Mitchell River route is reached by driving Settler's Road beginning in Kootenay National Park and following spur roads up the Cross and Mitchell Rivers.

Gog Lake (BC)
cutthroat trout to 35 cm

Located just over 1 km south of the Naiset Cabins in a quiet basin on the trail to Wonder Pass, Gog Lake holds a good number of trout and is popular among novices and experts alike. Much of Gog's shoreline is excellent for backcasting and its sheltered setting usually protects it from the strong winds that prevail on other lakes of the region. Although the trout only average 25-30 cm, which is small by Assiniboine standards, their numbers and their willingness to hit a fly make up for their size. The fish seem to be evenly distributed throughout the lake, but most fishermen will choose to work from the accessible north and east shores despite the prospect of wet feet.

Lake Magog (BC)
cutthroat trout to 65 cm (3.0 kg)

Magog, over 2 km in length, is the largest lake of the Assiniboine area. Its treeless shoreline offers ample room to backcast and it waters hold some fine cutthroat trout which, although not as plentiful as in years past, average better than 40 cm in length. As with most lakes in the area, water clarity dictates that low light periods (early morning and late evening) will be the most productive as this is the time fish enter the shallower water to feed. High winds are often a problem for fly fishermen on Magog during the daytime. Magog has no outlet stream, but the area around the several inlet creeks often hold fish. Around the lake, those able to send out 30 m of line can fish the deeper water, but fishermen with lesser casting prowess can settle for the tactic of "patrolling" the shoreline and keeping a keen eye out for rising fish. This method is particularly effective late in the evenings when the lake is very calm, and fish can be seen rising within a few metres of shore. Because of its high elevation, ice-out on Magog doesn't usually occur until late June, and spawning until mid-July.

Og Lake (BC)
status: devoid of fish

Located at the south end of the appropriately named Valley of the Rocks, Og Lake was stocked many years ago with cutthroat trout. Unfortunately, the trout failed to reproduce and there has been no trout in Og Lake for a number of years now.

Sunburst Lake (BC)
cutthroat trout
status: closed at present

Located just over 1 km west of Lake Magog by trail, Sunburst Lake was long regarded as one of the premier fly fishing lakes in the Rockies. Closed for study for a number of years, Sunburst may be reopened in the near future. Those fishermen planning a trip to the area are advised to contact the B.C. Parks Branch for updated information. Cutthroat trout of monumental proportions have been taken in the past from this diminutive lake, and even today, just sighting one of these 5 kg monsters will make any fisherman's heart pound and palms sweat.

Cerulean Lake (BC)
cutthroat trout to 85 cm (7.0 kg)
rainbow trout to 85 cm (7.0 kg)

Located only 300 m west of Sunburst Lake, Cerulean Lake attracts many fishermen with its reputation for trophy-sized trout. Although small in number, some extremely large cutthroat and rainbow trout along with cutthroat-rainbow hybrids inhabit the lake's deep, blue-green waters, few less than 45 cm in length. The shoreline offers few opportunities for backcasting, so roll casting ability is a must. As Cerulean has no inlet creek and only a tiny outlet, fish in the lake tend to keep to boundary which separates the shallow water from the deep. At most locations around the shore this zone is within casting distance, and if wind and light conditions are right, fish can be sighted from shore. Be forewarned, however, that only patience and a good amount of luck will produce a trophy fish from Cerulean.

Elizabeth Lake (BC)
status: doubtful

The remarkably clear waters of Elizabeth Lake once held cutthroat trout reaching 2.0 kg in weight. Over time it became apparent that the fish in Elizabeth did not reproduce naturally, and not having been stocked in recent years, it is highly doubtful if Elizabeth contains any trout nowadays. For those fishermen wishing to test its waters, Elizabeth Lake is found in a small larch-filled basin less than 1 km north of Cerulean Lake.

Wedgwood Lake (BC)
cutthroat trout to 50 cm (1.5 kg)

Forest-enclosed Wedgwood Lake is located in a side valley south of the Mitchell River some 4 km by trail below Cerulean Lake. Less heavily fished than other lakes in the Assiniboine area because of its location, Wedgwood holds cutthroat trout averaging 30-35 cm in length. With the exception of a few isolated openings, casting is difficult due to the proximity of the forest cover to the lakeshore. A very distinctive dropoff dividing the shallow water from the deep is visible from shore, this zone usually holding fish although both the outlet and inlet areas can also be very productive at times. The fish in Wedgwood tend to travel in schools and because of the clarity of the water, it is often more useful to walk along the shore keeping an eye on the water than to cast into an area where no fish can be seen.

Coney Lake (BC)

status: doubtful

Situated in a rocky amphitheatre half a kilometre upstream from the inlet of Wedgwood Lake, tiny Coney Lake is algae-infested and it is doubtful whether it holds fish.

Moose Bath (BC)

status: devoid of fish

A small, shallow pond below the west end of Cerulean Lake, Moose Bath has long been rumoured to contain trout. Despite the rumours, Moose Bath dries up in summer to the point of being incapable of holding trout.

Mitchell River (BC)

cutthroat trout to 35 cm
bull trout to 70 cm (4.0 kg)
whitefish to 30 cm

Flowing westward from Assiniboine to its confluence with the Cross River, the Mitchell River possesses numerous fine pools that hold fish. Access is easy along a horse trail which parallels the Mitchell River downstream of Wedgwood Lake, eventually reaching logging and mining exploration roads in the Magnesite Creek vicinity. Seldom fished, the Mitchell River is generally productive by mid-summer after the spring runoff is complete.

Game Lake (BC)

status: unknown

This small tarn at the head of Nestor Creek, a tributary of the Mitchell River, may contain small populations of cutthroat trout that have entered from Nestor Creek. No trails to the lake exist; simply follow Nestor Creek from the Ferro Pass trail. Set in an enclosed basin, Game Lake remains frozen until mid-July.

Nestor Lake (BC)

status: unknown

The headwaters of Surprise Creek, Nestor Lake receives few or no visitors each year. The lake likely holds a few cutthroat trout that have made their way in from Surprise Creek.

Rock Lake (BC)

cutthroat trout to 20 cm

Situated halfway along the increasingly hiked Ferro Pass access to Assiniboine, Rock Lake is becoming popular as a stopover point. Ideal for novice fly fishermen, Rock Lake holds lots of small cutthroat in the 15-20 cm range (none larger). The shoreline is forgiving in terms of backcasting from most locations, although wet feet are likely on the east side of the lake. The rockslide on the west side allows casting without wet feet, but be aware that rocks will claim the hooks of those anglers with sloppy backcasts. Even though tiny, the eager trout in Rock Lake will give pleasure to beginners as casting distance and technique are not important. Surprise Creek, which is the outlet for Rock Lake, holds trout for a kilometre or so downstream from the lake before becoming too steep and rapid on its descent to the Simpson River.

Assiniboine Lake / Lunette Lake (BC)

status: unknown

Two small, remote lakes accessible by trail from logging roads on the Mitchell River may contain populations of cutthroat trout. An ill-defined trail leads east along Aurora Creek (a tributary of the Mitchell River) before turning north at Assiniboine Creek into the basin containing Assiniboine and Lunette Lakes. Be forewarned that this is very rugged and isolated country.

When listening to fishing stories, always remember that the size of the fish increases proportionally with the number of times the story has been told.

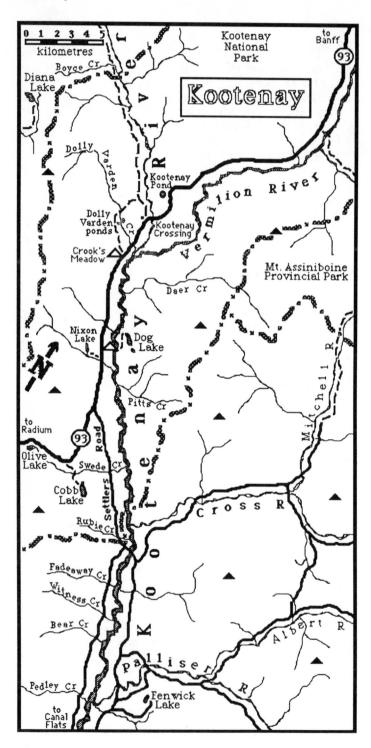

KOOTENAY

The upper Kootenay River serves as the main artery for this region which includes the southern half of Kootenay National Park and is paralleled south for 15 km from Kootenay Crossing by Highway 93 (Banff-Windermere Highway). Settlers Road, a gravelled logging road, parallels the river beyond the southern boundary of Kootenay National Park and offers access to major tributaries of the river including the Palliser, Albert, Cross and Mitchell Rivers. From Highway 93, short side trails lead to Dog, Nixon and Cobb Lakes, while pretty Olive Lake lies alongside the highway at the crest of Sinclair Pass.

Kootenay River (PC-BC)

cutthroat trout to 50 cm (1.5 kg)
bull trout to 75 cm (5.0 kg)
whitefish to 40 cm

The Kootenay River, which flows south from headwaters in the Vermilion Range, offers many kilometres of fine stream fishing. Cutthroat trout in the 25-35 cm range predominate, with both whitefish and bull trout also present in good numbers. The upper reaches of the Kootenay north of the Kootenay Park boundary is characterized by slow water and numerous marshy areas. Still relatively small as it crosses the park boundary, the river begins to drop in elevation and loses most of its marshy features until, after joining the Vermilion River (which is larger than the Kootenay at the confluence), it possess enough volume to genuinely be given river status. Flowing back and forth across the wide Kootenay Valley, the river develops into a series of pools and riffles. The junctions of the Kootenay with major rivers such as the Vermilion, Cross and Palliser are always productive, as are the areas around the confluence of minor tributaries. Within Kootenay National Park these minor tributaries include Dolly Varden, Daer, Pitts, Swede and Rubie Creeks and outside the park boundary, Fadeaway, Witness, Bear and Pedley Creeks.

Palliser River (BC)

cutthroat trout to 45 cm
bull trout to 70 cm (4.0 kg)
whitefish to 40 cm

A major tributary of the Kootenay River, the Palliser River joins the Kootenay approximately 30 km south of Kootenay Crossing. Access to the Palliser watershed is provided by Settlers Road which begins in Kootenay National Park, and then by a series of logging roads which give relatively easy access to most prospective fishing spots. The river holds plenty of cutthroat and bull trout as well as whitefish.

Albert River (BC)

cutthroat trout to 40 cm
bull trout to 70 cm (4.0 kg)
whitefish to 35 cm

The Albert River, a major tributary of the Palliser, is accessible from logging roads branching off the Palliser River. A fast-flowing river much like the Palliser, the Albert likewise holds cutthroat and bull trout and the occasional whitefish in its many pools. From roads on the upper reaches of the Albert, a short but ill-defined trail leads to Leman Lake and the upper Spray River.

Fenwick Lake (BC)

rainbow trout to 40 cm

Visited by few fishermen, Fenwick Lake is located 4 km west of Settlers Road along a rough but passable track. Set in marshy surroundings, Fenwick contains rainbow trout averaging 20-30 cm in length.

Cross River (BC)

cutthroat trout to 45 cm
bull trout to 70 cm (4.0 kg)
whitefish to 40 cm

Joining the Kootenay River just outside the Kootenay National Park boundary, the Cross River offers some excellent fishing particularly in its lower reaches where a series of falls and pools within 2 km of the Cross' confluence with the Kootenay usually produce well. Although both bull trout and whitefish are present, cutthroat averaging 20-35 cm in length are taken in greater numbers.

Olive Lake (PC)

brook trout to 25 cm

A delightful little lake of a particularly pleasing shade of green, Olive sits alongside Highway 93 at the summit of Sinclair Pass. Although stocked in the past with rainbow and cutthroat trout, only brook trout are present today and most of the fish are small, few reaching 25 cm in length. Casting is difficult around most of the shoreline due to the proximity of the forest cover. Because Olive is a very shallow and clear lake and fish can easily be seen swimming about, casting ahead of cruising fish is generally very effective.

Cobb Lake (PC)

brook trout to 45 cm

Located 3 km by trail from the Highway 93, Cobb Lake lies in a quiet opening in the forest where a marshy shoreline will ensure that most anglers end up with soggy feet. Cobb's dark waters hold brook trout averaging 20-30 cm in length. Casting is difficult with the exception of the few locations where forest cover opens up slightly. As the lake's bottom drops off quickly, one of the better tactics for this lake is to use a wet fly and let it sink deep before retrieval.

Dog Lake (PC)

brook trout to 40 cm

Dog Lake, 3 km by trail from McLeod Meadows campground, is one of the region's more popular fishing spots with its plentiful supply of brook trout in the 25-35 cm range. Backcasting is difficult along Dog's west shore due to forest cover, while heavy weed growth in the lake makes a dry line preferable. The small beaver ponds at the lake's outlet usually hold a few trout.

Nixon Lake (PC)

status: devoid of fish

This small, shallow pond located less than a kilometre west of Highway 93 by trail has never been stocked and contains no fish.

Dolly Varden Creek and Ponds (PC)

cutthroat trout to 30 cm
bull trout to 30 cm

Despite its name, Dolly Varden Creek holds far more cutthroat trout than bull trout (formerly Dolly Varden). Approximately 2 km upstream from the Kootenay River lies an extensive series of beaver dams where cutthroat in the 15-25 cm range are numerous. These ponds can be reached by either following the creek upstream, or by following the fire road that connects Kootenay Crossing with Crook's Meadow.

Kootenay Pond (PC)

status: doubtful

A popular location in the past, Kootenay Pond produced only as long as regular stocking occurred. Although trout were taken as late as. the mid-1970's, it is highly doubtful if any fish remain today.

Diana Lake (BC)

cutthroat trout to 50 cm (1.5 kg)

Set in the Brisco Range, lovely Diana Lake and its accompanying basin is generally overlooked by most anglers because of awkward access. The most common access is via logging roads east of the town of Edgewater in the Columbia Valley followed by a 4 km hike up Diana's outlet creek. An alternate route requiring map and compass leads from Boyce Creek just outside the Kootenay Park boundary. Seldom ice-free until early July due to its sheltered location, Diana Lake holds plenty of cutthroat trout averaging 25-35 cm in length.

High Lake / Dainard Lake (BC)

cutthroat trout to 40 cm

These two lakes, hidden high in the Vermilion Range near the headwaters of the Kootenay River, receive little attention other than from the occasional outfitter's party. Located just outside the western boundary of Kootenay National Park, High and Dainard contain cutthroat trout averaging 25-35 cm in length in good numbers. Access is via a combination of fire road, logging road and trail for which a map and compass are strongly recommended.

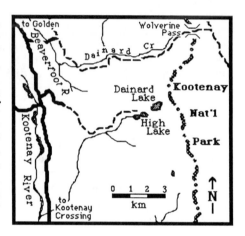

Nothing grows faster than a fish from the time he bites until he gets away.

VERMILION

Encompassing the northern half of Kootenay National Park, this region holds limited possibilities for anglers. The Vermilion River, which parallels Highway 93 (Banff-Windermere Highway), is silted for much of the year and has never been noted for good fishing. Trying some of the Vermilion's small tributaries, or taking a short hike to the Simpson River, represent much more worthwhile ventures in terms of fishing potential, the most popular spots in the area being Kaufmann Lake and Floe Lake, both of which offer good backcountry fishing and superb scenery.

Kaufmann Lake (PC)
brook trout to 40 cm

Fourteen kilometres by trail from Marble Canyon on Highway 93, Kaufmann Lake lies tucked away in a hanging valley beneath the towering peaks of the continental divide. Very popular with backpackers, Kaufmann Lake is busy throughout the summer. This long, narrow lake contains brook trout ranging from 20-30 cm in length which can be taken from most locations around the lakeshore, but casting may be a problem due to the proximity of the forest cover. The area around the inlet creek at the far end of the lake usually holds fish and offers plenty of backcasting room.

Tokumm Creek (PC)
bull trout to 40 cm
cutthroat trout to 30 cm

Paralleling the Kaufmann Lake trail for almost its entire distance, Tokumm Creek appears to have plenty of potential as a trout stream. Unfortunately, fish cannot make it upstream past the falls in Marble Canyon, so the only fishing in Tokumm Creek is in the last half kilometre before it joins the Vermilion River.

Vermilion Pond (PC)
cutthroat trout to 20 cm
brook trout to 20 cm

Tiny Vermilion Pond, lying just off Highway 93 north of Vermilion Crossing, contains small brook and cutthroat trout in its shallow waters. Most of the fish tend to keep to the middle of the pond beyond the reach of all but the most expert fishermen.

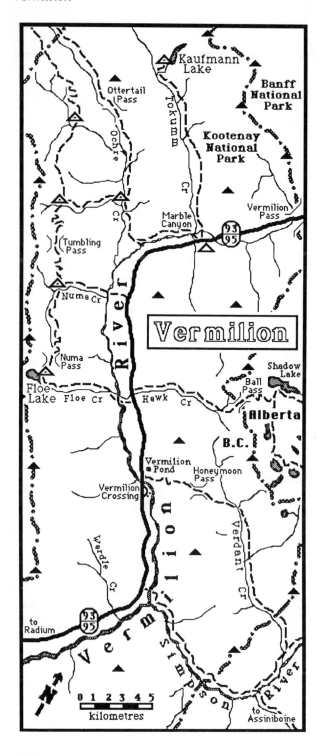

Vermilion River (PC)

bull trout to 60 cm (2.5 kg)
cutthroat trout to 35 cm
whitefish to 35 cm

Very accessible as it flows alongside Highway 93 (Banff-Windermere Highway), the Vermilion River remains very silty for much of the year. However, the Vermilion does possess some fine holes and for a few brief weeks late every summer it clears enough to allow reasonable fishing. Bull and cutthroat trout and whitefish in the 20-30 cm range are normally taken, although large bull trout to 60 cm can also be caught on occasion. The best fishing spots tend to be where one of the innumerable tributaries join the Vermilion, particularly if the side creeks are clearer than the main river.

Ochre Creek, Numa Creek, Floe Creek, Hawk Creek, Wardle Creek (PC)

bull trout to 25 cm
cutthroat trout to 20 cm

Once their waters have cleared after run-off, all of the major tributaries of the Vermilion River contain small cutthroat and bull trout in their lower reaches within a kilometre of their confluence with the river.

Floe Lake (PC)

cutthroat trout to 50 cm (1.5 kg)

Dwarfed by the immense face of the Rockwall, its pretty blue waters dotted with ice floes, Floe Lake is one of the most beautiful spots in all the mountain parks and certainly one of the most popular. All summer long, the surrounding alpine meadows are active with hikers who have packed in along the 10 km trail from Highway 93. Floe's waters hold a small population of cutthroat trout, but their size, averaging 35-40 cm in length, and their fighting ability makes up for their numbers. Casting room is available around most of the shoreline. If wind and light conditions are right, fish can be seen in Floe's clear waters, but they are usually very wary and flee to deep water at the slightest disturbance.

Simpson River (PC-BC)

cutthroat trout to 40 cm
bull trout to 75 cm (4.0 kg)
whitefish to 30 cm

The Simpson River, which flows from the Golden Valley in Mount Assiniboine Provincial Park to the Vermilion River in Kootenay Park, has long stretches of fishable waters. The 8 km stretch above its confluence with the Vermilion River is within the boundaries of Kootenay National Park (national park license required) and contains many large pools home to cutthroat and whitefish and usually a large bull trout or two. Above the 8 km-mark (signs mark the boundary), the Simpson lies inside Mount Assiniboine Provincial Park (B.C. license required) and is characterized by faster waters and less pools. Because no glaciers feed the Simpson River, it is generally very clear and the spring run-off usually short-lived.

Verdant Creek (PC-BC)

cutthroat trout to 25 cm
bull trout to 40 cm

A major tributary of the Simpson River, Verdant Creek can be reached by trails on the upper Simpson River or by the Honeymoon Pass trail which begins just north of Vermilion Crossing. The many pools on Verdant Creek are home to cutthroat and bull trout generally running about 20-25 cm in length.

There are two periods when fishing is good - before you get there and after you leave.

BANFF

Centered on the world-renowned tourist resort of Banff, this area is one of the most heavily fished regions within the mountain parks. Services of all types, including the sale of fishing tackle, can be obtained in Banff where you'll also find park warden offices and park information centres. Nearby Lake Minnewanka has long been a favourite of anglers who come in search of its huge lake trout. Reached by the Lake Minnewanka Road, Two Jack and Johnson Lakes also attract plenty of fishermen. Readily accessible, the Bow River is always active with canoeists and fishermen throughout the summer as are the Vermilion Lakes, while the adjacent Echo Creek and Whiskey Creek beaver pond complexes usually provide a little solitude.

Lake Minnewanka (PC)

lake trout to 120 cm (20.0 kg)
bull trout to 80 cm (6.0 kg)
rainbow trout to 65 cm (3.0 kg)
splake to 60 cm (2.5 kg)
whitefish to 45 cm

Almost 20 km in length and one of the largest lakes in the Rockies, Minnewanka's depths hold lake trout of immense proportions which each year tempt innumerable fishermen to test their skills against these monsters. The first weeks after ice-out is generally the most productive as the lakers keep to the areas near inlet creeks and feed actively. Trolling a fly, especially in the areas around inlet creeks at this time, can be very productive. As summer progresses, the lake trout tend to move out to deeper waters and fishing slows noticably. Although lakers in the 15-20 kg range are taken on occasion, most average 2-3 kg in weight. Aside from lake trout, Minnewanka holds rainbow trout, bull trout, splake and whitefish in good numbers. Boats are available for rent at Minnewanka. Due to the size and location of the lake, boaters should be very aware of changing weather conditions and of the strong winds that can appear suddenly.

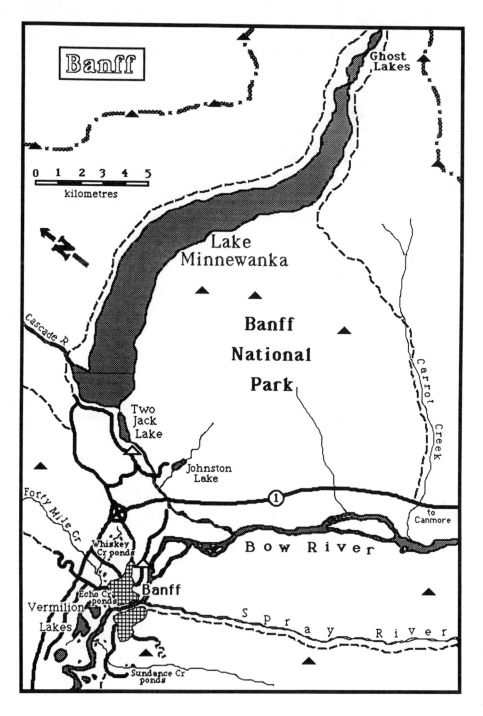

Ghost Lakes (PC)

lake trout to 75 cm (5.0 kg)
bull trout to 70 cm (4.0 kg)
rainbow trout to 60 cm (2.5 kg)
splake to 55 cm (2.0 kg)
whitefish to 45 cm

An extension of the extreme eastern end of Lake Minnewanka, the Ghost Lakes vary in size and number with fluctuating water levels. The variety of fish is identical to those in Minnewanka, although generally available in slightly smaller sizes. Reaching the Ghost Lakes requires either a long boat trip down the entire length of Minnewanka, or an 8 km hike-in from the Ghost River Road. If fishing from shore, the best areas tend to be those where the lakes are at their narrowest point.

Two Jack Lake (PC)

rainbow trout to 60 cm (2.5 kg)
lake trout to 70 cm (4.0 kg)
splake to 50 cm (1.5 kg)

Located less than 1 km south of Lake Minnewanka, Two Jack Lake offers a pleasant respite for those fishermen overwhelmed by the size of Minnewanka. Rainbow averaging 30-45 cm in length predominate over lake trout and splake. The nearby campground ensures that Two Jack's shores will be busy all summer long.

Johnson Lake (PC)

rainbow trout to 50 cm (1.5 kg)
brook trout to 50 cm (1.5 kg)

Two kilometres south of Two Jack Lake, Johnson Lake has received far fewer visitors in recent years since the closing of the alternate access to Lake Minnewanka from the Trans-Canada Highway. As anglers are restricted to shore at Johnson Lake, the lake's population of rainbow and brook trout has remained plentiful. The shallow areas around the shoreline can be very productive for fly fishermen, especially during low light conditions when fish enter the shallows to feed.

Vermilion Lakes (PC)

rainbow trout to 70 cm (3.5 kg)
brook trout to 70 cm (3.5 kg)
cutthroat trout to 50 cm (1.5 kg)
bull trout to 75 cm (5.0 kg)
whitefish to 40 cm

These three shallow lakes located west of Banff alongside the Bow River have gained a reputation over the years for fine fishing. The two most easterly lakes have extended shallows and are of little value to fishermen relegated to shore. From a boat, fishing is most productive in the deeper water which is accentuated by its darker colouration. The most westerly lake is the deepest of the three, but still not deep by normal standards being seldom more than 4-5 m in depth. Fishing is possible from a number of shoreline locations although getting there will require getting a little soggy. While large brook and rainbow trout are taken on occasion, most fish taken average 25-35 cm in length.

Echo Creek ponds (PC)

brook trout to 25 cm
rainbow trout to 25 cm

A network of beaver ponds connecting the Vermilion Lakes with the Bow River holds the promise of solitude due to difficult access and the guarantee of wet feet. Small brook and rainbow trout predominate, although cutthroat and bull trout are also present.

Whiskey Creek ponds (PC)

brook trout to 25 cm
rainbow trout to 25 cm
cutthroat trout to 25 cm

Located between Banff townsite and the Trans-Canada Highway, the maze of beaver ponds along Whiskey Creek receive plenty of attention from anglers each season. The ponds hold small brook, rainbow and cutthroat trout.

Forty Mile Creek (PC)

brook trout to 25 cm
cutthroat trout to 25 cm
bull trout to 25 cm

Forty Mile Creek joins the Whiskey Creek pond complex north of Banff after crossing the Trans-Canada Highway just west of the Buffalo Paddock. It holds brook, cutthroat and bull trout as well as the odd rainbow. Be aware that the creek is closed to angling in the vicinity of the Banff townsite water intake.

Sundance Creek ponds (PC)

brook trout to 25 cm

The series of beaver dams that extend along Sundance Creek for 3 km above its confluence with the Bow are readily accessible from the Cave and Basin road. Small brook trout predominate with cutthroat and rainbow present as well.

Bow River (PC)

bull trout to 70 cm (5.0 kg)
rainbow trout to 60 cm (2.5 kg)
brook trout to 60 cm (2.5 kg)
cutthroat trout to 50 cm (1.5 kg)
brown trout to 50 cm (1.5 kg)
whitefish to 40 cm

The section of the Bow that flows in and around the town of Banff is characterized by slow water and deep pools. Canoeists frequent the river throughout the summer and fishermen can always be seen working the shoreline for a wide variety of trout, including rainbow, brook, cutthroat and bull, most in the 25-40 cm range. Downstream from Bow Falls, the occasional brown trout is also caught. Along with the numerous deep pools, areas where tributaries join the Bow are also generally productive.

Spray River (lower) (PC)

brook trout to 50 cm (1.5 kg)
brown trout to 45 cm
rainbow trout to 50 cm (1.5 kg)
cutthroat trout to 45 cm
bull trout to 70 cm (5.0 kg)

A major tributary of the Bow River, the Spray River joins the Bow just west of Banff. Accessible by the Spray River Fire Road for the entire distance to the Spray Lakes Reservoir, the Spray offers good fishing for cutthroat trout in its upper reaches. In the lower reaches, brook, rainbow and brown trout in the 25-35 cm range are the normal catch. Large bull trout are taken on occasion along all stretches of the river.

Carrot Creek (PC)

brown trout to 25 cm
bull trout to 30 cm

tCarrot Creek joins the Bow River 3 km west of the Banff Park Boundary. In its lower reaches, it holds bull, brown and rainbow trout in small sizes.

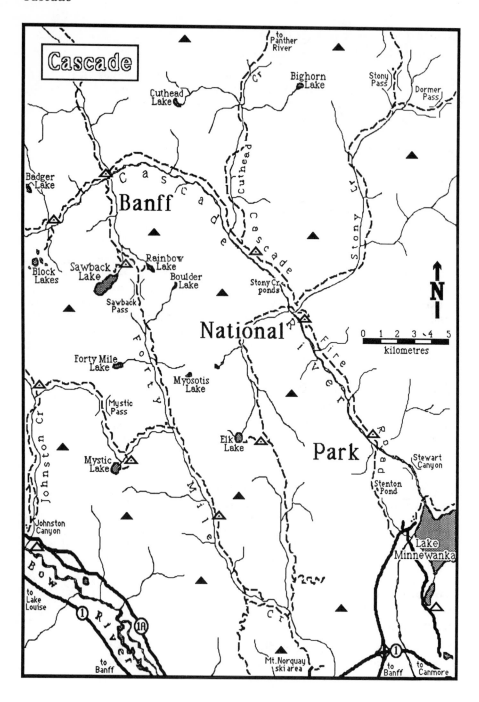

CASCADE

The Cascade River and its accompanying fire road run directly through the heart of the Front Ranges. The southern end of the fire road meets the Lake Minnewanka Road approximately 1 km west of the lake itself and 5 km east of the Trans-Canada Highway overpass. Although the upper Cascade is very popular with outfitters, the area receives relatively few hikers each year because of the huge distances involved. However, in the past few summers, more and more mountain bikers are making their way up the Cascade Fire Road and should be well aware as should all those fishermen entering the area that the Cascade Valley contains one of the highest concentration of grizzly bears anywhere in the Rocky Mountains.

In the upper Cascade, Sawback Lake receives the most angling pressure, while Block, Badger, Cuthead, Bighorn and Rainbow Lakes see relatively few visitors each season. From the Mt. Norquay ski hill parking area, trails offer alternate access into the upper Cascade and to Mystic Pass where Mystic Lake attracts plenty of attention during the summer. Lakes in the upper Forty Mile drainage are seldom fished, and include Myosotis, Boulder and Forty Mile. Elk Lake, which also has its trailhead at the Mt. Norquay parking lot, is set in the valley between the Cascade River and Forty Mile Creek and is very popular with day hikers and backpackers alike.

Cascade River (PC)

cutthroat trout to 35 cm
brook trout to 35 cm
rainbow trout to 30 cm
bull trout to 60 cm (2.5 kg)
whitefish to 30 cm

Flowing for over 35 km from headwaters to Lake Minnewanka, the Cascade River with its innumerable excellent pools offers good fishing along its entire length for cutthroat and brook trout and the occasional rainbow, bull trout and whitefish. The Cascade Fire Road, closed to vehicular travel, parallels the river for much of the distance and offers easy access. The lower sections of the river are heavily fished while the headwaters area is visited only by outfitters and intrepid backpackers.

Stenton Pond (PC)
brook trout to 20 cm

Stenton Pond is actually several small, shallow interconnected beaver ponds located alongside the Cascade Fire Road just over 2 km from the road's southern terminus on the Lake Minnewanka Road. The ponds hold small brook trout, few larger than 15 cm in length. Due to the shallow water, the fish are very wary and an abundance of shoreline vegetation and deadfall make fly fishing a difficult but interesting proposition.

Stony Creek (PC)
cutthroat trout to 20 cm
bull trout to 25 cm

A major tributary of the Cascade River, Stony Creek enters the Cascade approximately 15 km upstream from Lake Minnewanka. Fast-flowing Stony Creek holds both cutthroat and bull trout in small sizes and numbers.

Stony Creek ponds (PC)
brook trout to 25 cm

The Stony Creek ponds are located just over 2 km north of the bridge over Stony Creek on the Cascade Fire Road. Set in somewhat marshy surroundings between the fire road and the Cascade River, these beaver ponds hold a fair number of small brook trout. Reaching the ponds without getting wet will take some skill, as will casting to the easily spooked trout. Backcasting room is generally available except around the odd deadfall.

Cuthead Lake (PC)
cutthroat trout to 40 cm
bull trout to 60 cm (2.5 kg)

Six kilometres north of Flint's Park junction, the route to Cuthead Lake leaves the Cascade Fire Road and ascends the Cuthead Creek drainage westward, alternating between bushwhacking and game trails for the final 4 km to the lake whose silted waters hold cutthroat trout averaging 25-30 cm in length as well as a few bull trout. Sparsely treed meadows around the lake offer ample room for back-casting.

Cuthead Creek (PC)

cutthroat trout to 20 cm
bull trout to 25 cm

The Cascade Fire Road follows the course of Cuthead Creek which enters the Cascade River approximately 20 km upstream from Lake Minnewanka. The most fishable waters are in the lower reaches of Cuthead Creek where it holds some small bull and cutthroat trout.

Bighorn Lake (PC)

brook trout to 30 cm

Bighorn Lake is located in a barren cirque 4 km east of Cuthead Creek along an ill-defined trail which begins on the Cascade Fire Road opposite Cuthead Lake valley. Winding through heavy timber, the trail emerges above treeline and works its way steeply alongside Bighorn's tiny outlet creek, finally reaching the small basin holding the lake. The brook trout in Bighorn are small, most in the 20-25 cm range.

Block Lakes (PC)

cutthroat trout to 40 cm

Located near the headwaters of the Cascade River, the Block Lakes are set in a basin gouged high into the side of Block Mtn. Guarded by a 150 m-high cliff face, the lakes are only accessible to skilled climbers who register with the warden service before attempting the climb. At one time the Block Lakes were stocked with Quebec Red Trout which flourished for a short period of time but failed to reproduce. At present, cutthroat trout averaging 25-35 cm in length are caught regularly.

Badger Lake (PC)

brook trout to 30 cm

Three kilometres of bushwhacking in a northerly direction from the upper Cascade River/ Block Lakes campsite leads to isolated Badger Lake. Since the final half kilometre into Badger's rockbound surroundings requires negotiating a 150 m cliff, registration with the warden service is mandatory. Difficult access, along with recent reports indicating few trout remain in Badger keep it off most fishermen's "must-visit" list.

Sawback Lake (PC)
cutthroat trout to 55 cm (2.0 kg)

Long renowned for its fine fishing, Sawback Lake receives many visitors each year despite its lengthy access. Located almost 30 km from Mt. Norquay via Forty Mile Creek or 40 km from Lake Minnewanka via the Cascade Fire Road, Sawback Lake is most popular with outfitters, although determined hikers will be equally rewarded for their efforts. Set in a beautiful basin just below Sawback Pass (Forty Mile Summit), the translucent green waters of Sawback Lake hold a large population of cutthroat trout averaging 25-35 cm in length with larger ones taken quite regularly. While forest cover prevents adequate backcasts from many spots along the shore, a number of small peninsulas jutting out into the lake offer ideal locations for fly fishing.

Rainbow Lake (PC)
rainbow trout to 35 cm

Rainbow Lake sits in a prominent bowl a little over a kilometre north and east of Sawback Pass. As its name suggests, the lake contains rainbow trout, and although fairly plentiful, are small in size with few larger than 30 cm. Backcasting room is available around much of the shoreline as the lake is located near treeline.

Forty Mile Creek (upper) (PC)
cutthroat trout to 25 cm
brook trout to 25 cm
bull trout to 30 cm

The upper sections of Forty Mile Creek flowing between Sawback Pass (Forty Mile Summit) and Mt. Norquay hold plenty of trout in small sizes. Trails parallelling Forty Mile Creek for its entire length offer easy access to the numerous pools.

Boulder Lake (PC)
status: doubtful

Diminutive Boulder Lake sits in a desolate cirque at an elevation of nearly 2400 metres and can be reached by following game trails along its outlet creek from the south side of Sawback Pass (Forty Mile Summit). The cutthroat trout once stocked in the lake either no longer exist, or are present in very small numbers.

Forty Mile Lake (PC)

brook trout to 30 cm

Nestled in a high subalpine valley west of the main Forty Mile Creek valley, Forty Mile Lake sees very few human visitors each year. Easiest access is is via ill-defined and often nonexistent game trails that work up the small outlet creek which enters Forty Mile Creek approximately 3 km above the Mystic Pass junction. The lake itself contains a small population of brook trout few larger than 25 cm in length.

Myosotis Lake (PC)

rainbow trout to 30 cm

Tiny Myosotis Lake is set in a barren cirque 2 km east of the upper Forty Mile Creek valley. The lake was stocked a number of years ago with rainbow trout and reports indicate that a few still exist, maintaining themselves through natural propogation. Access is for route finders armed with map and compass.

Mystic Lake (PC)

cutthroat trout to 45 cm
bull trout to 60 cm (2.5 kg)

Mystic Lake is located 17 km from Johnston Canyon and 19 km from Mt. Norquay near the midway point on the Mystic Pass trail. Fisherman who annually make their way to these fine trout waters set in a sheltered basin 3 km below Mystic Pass are seldom disappointed for Mystic holds plenty of cutthroat averaging 25-35 cm in length as well as a few large bull trout. Casting is difficult around much of the shoreline, and those anglers not adept at roll casting should try the outlet area. Despite the lake's relatively remote location, numerous hikers and horse parties make their way in to Mystic each year.

Elk Lake (PC)

cutthroat trout 50 cm (1.5 kg)

The impressive east face of Mt. Brewster towers over the pretty larch-filled basin containing Elk Lake. Located 14 km by trail from the Mt. Norquay parking area, Elk Lake has long been a favourite with local fishermen with its abundance of casting room along the shore and plentiful supply of good-sized cutthroat trout which keep anglers returning year after year. Ten kilometres north of Elk Lake, the trail joins the Cascade Fire Road at Stony Creek.

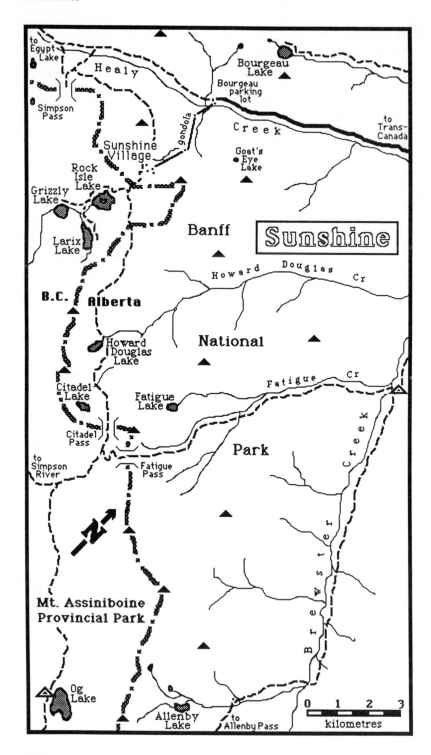

SUNSHINE

The hub of the region, Sunshine Village and its surrounding flower-filled meadows, is accessed by gondola from Borgeau Parking Lot which in turn is reached by taking the Sunshine access road 9 km west of Banff along the Trans-Canada Highway. Most day hikers make their way through the Sunshine Meadows to nearby Rock Isle, Larix and Grizzly Lakes, although return trips to Howard Douglas and Citadel Lakes are well within a day's limit of most hikers. Sunshine Village is also the trailhead for the Citadel Pass route to Assiniboine (with Lake Magog some 27 km distant) and a round-about route which heads westward to join the main Egypt Lake trail in the Simpson Pass/Healy Pass vicinity. Farther afield, extended hikes into the headwaters of Brewster Creek lead to isolated Fatigue and Allenby Lakes. Bourgeau Lake, a steep 7 km hike, begins at a signed parking area along the Trans-Canada Highway 2 km north of the Sunshine turnoff.

Bourgeau Lake (PC)
Brook trout to 50 cm (1.5 kg)

Set in a deep, rocky amphitheatre just over 7 km by trail from the Trans-Canada Highway, Bourgeau Lake is home to a particularly feisty breed of brook trout. In years past when numerous large trout were taken from Bourgeau, the lake became very popular with anglers which inevitably led to a decline in the quality of fishing. Some large trout still inhabit its waters, but most fish taken will only average 20-30 cm in length. Backcasting room is adequate along much of the shoreline, although rocks will take the barb off the hook of many a disgruntled fly fisherman.

Goat's Eye Lake (PC)
status: unknown

A small tarn hidden high on the flank of Goat's Eye Peak, tiny Goat's Eye Lake was stocked in the past with rainbow trout. As so few people make their way to the lake, no confirmed reports exist as to whether or not trout are still present in the lake. A difficult scramble up the side of Goat's Eye Peak generally deters most fishermen.

Rock Isle Lake
brook trout
status: closed

Located in the beautiful Sunshine Meadows just over a kilometre from Sunshine Village, picturesque Rock Isle Lake is at present closed to angling due to its use as water supply for the Village.

Larix Lake (BC)

brook trout
status: closed

Recently closed to angling, Larix Lake lies in a quiet, meadowed basin less than a kilometre below Rock Isle Lake.

Grizzly Lake (BC)

brook trout
status: closed

Angling is not permitted in Grizzly, a small, round body of water which is reached by following the outlet stream of Larix Lake.

Howard Douglas Lake (PC)

brook trout to 40 cm

Located on the Citadel Pass trail 6 km from Sunshine Village, Howard Douglas Lake is often overlooked by fishermen passing through on their way to the more renowned waters of Assiniboine. Encircled by meadows and a few stands of larch, the waters of Howard Douglas hold a fair number of brook trout, most ranging from 15-25 cm, although trout reaching 40 cm are caught regularly. The fish seem to be equally distributed throughout the lake with the majority of larger fish taken from the south end.

Citadel Lake [Sunset Lake] (PC)

rainbow trout to 40 cm

Lying less than half a kilometre south of the Citadel Pass trail over a small knoll, Citadel Lake is seldom seen, much less visited by most hikers. The lake is set in a small basin with half its shoreline comprised of scree and half of meadow, the latter offering an abundance of backcasting spots. The majority of rainbow trout caught exceed 25 cm.

Brewster Creek (PC)

bull trout to 30 cm
cutthroat trout to 25 cm

Paralleled by horse trails for its entire length, Brewster Creek possesses many kilometres of fishable waters. Small bull and cutthroat trout can be taken from most stretches with brook, cut-throat and rainbow trout also taken occasionally.

Fatigue Lake (PC)

rainbow trout to 35 cm

Set in a basin beneath Fatigue Peak, Fatigue Lake is reached by following ill-defined game trails up a tributary branching west off the Fatigue Pass trail. Rarely visited due to its isolated location, Fatigue Lake holds rainbow trout averaging 20-30 cm in length in good numbers.

Allenby Lake (PC)

rainbow trout to 35 cm

Set in a hanging valley 2 km west of the Brewster Creek-Allenby Pass route to Assiniboine, Allenby Lake is overlooked by most fishermen passing through the region despite the fact that Allenby's waters hold good numbers of rainbow trout in the 20-30 cm range. Casting room is available around the entire lake.

Lord, grant that I may catch a fish
So large that even I,
When telling of it afterwards,
May have no need to lie.

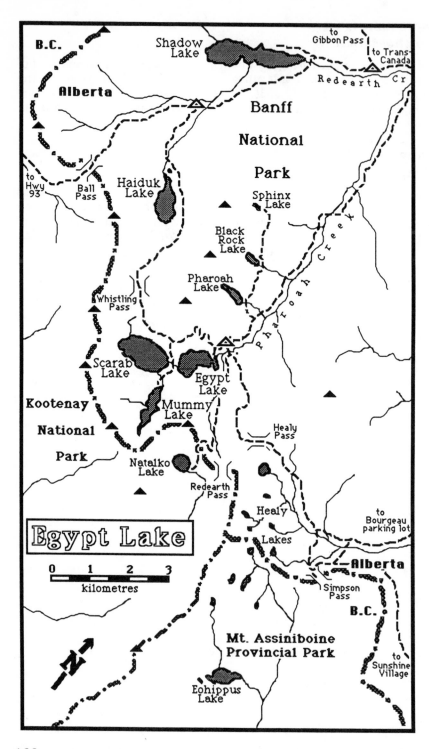

B.C.

Alberta

Shadow
Lake

to
Gibbon Pass

to Trans-
Canada

R e d e a r t h   Cr

Banff

National

Park

to
Hwy
93

Ball
Pass

Haiduk
Lake

Sphinx
Lake

Black
Rock
Lake

P h a r o a h   Creek

Pharoah
Lake

Whistling
Pass

Scarab
Lake

Egypt
Lake

Kootenay

National

Mummy
Lake

Healy
Pass

Park

Natalko
Lake

Redearth
Pass

Healy

to
Bourgeau
parking lot

Healy

Lakes

Alberta

Egypt Lake

Simpson
Pass

B.C.

0   1   2   3
kilometres

N

Mt. Assiniboine
Provincial Park

to
Sunshine
Village

Eohippus
Lake

EGYPT LAKE

Egypt Lake, located at the core of one of Banff National Park's most popular backpacking destinations, is crowded with hikers and fishermen from mid-June through the end of September. The main access into this superb region begins at the Bourgeau Parking Lot and follows the Healy Creek trail to Healy Pass before dropping down to Egypt Lake. The Healy Lakes and Eohippus Lake are reached via side trails off the main Egypt Lake trail on the east side of Healy Pass. Lakes within the immediate Egypt Lake complex include Egypt, Scarab, Mummy, Pharoah, Black Rock and Sphinx, while both Natalko and Haiduk are within easy reach of day hikers based at the main Egypt Lake campground. Shadow Lake at the northern end of the Egypt Lake area is accessed by a 14 km trail that begins at Redearth Creek Parking Lot on the Trans-Canada Highway and which also serves as longer access to the Egypt Lake complex.

Egypt Lake (PC)
cutthroat trout to 40 cm
brook trout to 35 cm

Located less than 1 km from the shelter and campground, Egypt Lake is the most heavily fished lake of the area, its deep, clear waters holding a good number of trout few of which exceed 30 cm in length. The deep waters off the rockslide along the north shore generally hold the larger trout. Brook trout are in the majority, but both cutthroat and brookies can be taken from most spots, particularly around the area of the inlet creek which falls from Scarab Lake. The outlet pond and the outlet stream usually hold a few trout which can be spotted from shore but due to their shallow habitat, the fish are very wary. Backcasting room is at a premium, so roll casting will be the order of the day from many locations.

Scarab Lake (PC)
cutthroat trout to 50 cm (1.5 kg)

Situated in a large basin above Egypt Lake, Scarab Lake is reached by following the steep trail that winds its way up the cliff band above Egypt's northwest corner. Silt from snowmelt accounts for Scarab's striking blue-green colour and although the lake does not hold a large number of trout, trout taken will often exceed 30 cm in length. Its location near treeline ensures ample backcasting room. Due to the lake's high elevation and shaded position beneath Haiduk Peak, Scarab is often ice-covered well into July and spawning often occurs later that month.

Mummy Lake (PC)
cutthroat trout to 50 cm (1.5 kg)

Mummy Lake can be reached either by the ill-defined and rocky trail from nearby Scarab Lake (cross outlet of Scarab on makeshift bridge), or by a route which crosses the low pass northwest of Natalko Lake (there is no trail, but the way is straightforward). Long and narrow, Mummy Lake is set in a rocky, windswept valley located a few hundred metres above Scarab Lake, its high elevation and absence of vegetation allowing for backcasting around most of the shoreline. Because the lake is usually ice covered until mid-July, spawning can occur as late as early August. Relatively few in number, the trout in Mummy Lake average 30-40 cm in length.

Pharoah Creek (PC)
cutthroat trout to 30 cm
brook trout to 25 cm

The upper waters of Pharoah Creek hold a fair number of cutthroat in the 15 - 20 cm range as well as a few brook trout downstream of the Egypt Lake outlet where, for several kilometres, the creek winds its way back and forth across open meadows. Casting ability is not important, a factor which may appeal to many novices.

Pharoah Lake (PC)
cutthroat trout to 45 cm

Fishermen heading north from the Egypt Lake shelter and campsite on the trail on the west bench above Pharoah Creek will encounter within 1 km a marked side trail leading to Pharoah, Black Rock and Sphinx Lakes. The side trail winds its way up the flank of Pharoah Peak for just over a kilometre to the notch containing Pharoah Lake which is set beneath the sheer cliffs of the Pharoah Peaks and has a very dark and deep appearance. Scree slopes make up much of the shoreline, there being few spots which permit a reasonable backcast. Although there is not a large number of fish in Pharoah, most are good-sized with the average in the 35-40 cm range.

Black Rock Lake (PC)
cutthroat trout to 35 cm

One kilometre beyond Pharoah Lake and set in a very similar basin lies Black Rock Lake, named for the dark cliffs above. It holds a large number of cutthroat trout averaging 20-25 cm in length which can be seen well out into the lake due to the clarity of the water. Backcasting room is adequate along much of the shoreline, although a few rocks in the shallows along the north shore may tempt a few fishermen to wade out in search of a better casting position.

Sphinx Lake (PC)
status: doubtful

Situated in a small basin 2 km beyond Black Rock Lake, tiny Sphinx Lake at one time had a breeding population of cuttroat trout, but recent examination tends to indicate that no trout presently exist. A very poor and ill-defined trail leads past Black Rock Lake for those hardy souls wishing to check the lake out for themselves.

Natalko Lake [Talc Lake] (PC)
brook trout to 30 cm

Natalko Lake is reached by following a trail south from the Egypt Lake warden's cabin along the east bank of Pharoah Creek for approximately 2 km to a junction where a side trail heads west into the Natalko Lake basin 2 km distant. The lake itself is situated just within the boundary of Kootenay National Park. Its waters are incredibly clear, even for a mountain lake, and as a result fish are easily spooked. Meadow along much of the shoreline allows for backcasting while rockslides on the far side of the lake will test roll casting abilities. Although the lake holds plenty of brook trout averaging 25-30 cm, the wariness of the fish will surely try most fishermen's patience.

Healy Lakes (PC)
cutthroat trout to 20 cm

This series of interconnected ponds and small lakes set in the meadows beneath the Monarch Ramparts southwest of Healy Pass contain small cutthroat trout. The size and number of trout varies with each lake, but few fish are larger than 15 cm in length. The Simpson Pass trail leads past many of the ponds and the main Egypt Lake trail also passes close by. Although there is ample casting room at most of the lakes, the marshy nature of the shorelines will result in wet feet for most fishermen.

Eohippus Lake (BC)
cutthroat trout to 40 cm

This seldom visited lake nestled beneath the prominent east face of The Monarch and lying completely within Mt. Assiniboine Provincial Park contains cutthroat trout in the 25-30 cm range. The most straightforward access involves hiking the crest of the Ramparts south from Healy Pass and dropping down to the lake from above. However, be aware that lingering snowpack and dangerous cornices on the Ramparts prevent the use of this route until mid-summer. The other approach requires working your way southward through meadows and larch stands from the Healy Lakes/Simpson Pass area. Named for its resemblance to a prehistoric species of horse this uniquely shaped lake is completely surrounded by open meadows which ensures plenty of backcasting room.

Haiduk Lake (PC)

cutthroat trout to 50 cm (2.0 kg)

Situated 4 km northwest of Scarab Lake through Whistling Pass, and also accessible from Shadow Lake and Ball Pass, secluded Haiduk Lake contains some fine cutthroat trout. Fishing is best along the scree slope on the western side of the lake, but you should also check the several inlet creeks. Shaded much of the day by the high wall to the west, Haiduk is often frozen into early July and access trails snowbound. Late season fishing is often productive until freeze-up which usually occurs in September.

Shadow Lake (PC)

cutthroat trout to 45 cm
brook trout to 40 cm
rainbow trout to 40 cm

A strikingly beautiful lake set in a forested valley beneath the east face of Mt. Ball, Shadow Lake is reached via the 14 km trail from Redearth Creek trailhead on the Trans-Canada Highway. Although it is the largest of the lakes in the Egypt/Sunshine complex, and in turn holds some good-sized trout, Shadow Lake has never gained a reputation for outstanding fishing, and in recent years, continued fishing pressure has further reduced both the number and size of the trout taken. Cutthroat and brook trout are caught with more regularity than rainbow, the areas around inlet creeks being some of the better waters. The outlet bay also holds fish, particularly during the low light periods of early morning and late evening when fish enter the shallower waters to feed.

Redearth Creek (PC)

cutthroat trout to 20 cm
brook trout to 20 cm

Redearth Creek, flowing from Shadow Lake to the Bow River, holds both cutthroat and brook trout although small and relatively few in number. Best fishing opportunities exist in the few kilometres of slow water below Shadow Lake, and in the last half kilometre before Redearth Creek flows into the Bow.

CASTLE

Centered on the impressive form of Castle Mountain (formerly Mt. Eisenhower) and the junction of Highway 93 with the Trans-Canada Highway, this region has many popular fishing spots within easy hiking distance. Altrude, Vista, Boom, Arnica and Twin Lakes can all be reached by trails originating from Highway 93 (Banff-Windermere Highway), while Copper and Smith Lakes are located just east of Castle Junction along the Trans-Canada Highway. Trails to Taylor and O'Brien Lakes start at the Taylor Creek picnic area along the Trans-Canada Highway 8 km west of Castle Junction. Rockbound and Tower Lakes, hidden behind Castle Mountain, have their trailhead at the Eisenhower Warden Station on the 1-A Highway. Luellen Lake is the only major backpacking destination in the Castle area, its access trail beginning farther south along the 1-A Highway at Johnston Canyon. Paralleled by both the Trans-Canada and the 1-A Highways, the Bow River is very accessible to anglers.

Taylor Lake (PC)

cutthroat trout to 45 cm

Nestled in a high side valley 6 km by trail from the Trans-Canada Highway, beautifully-coloured Taylor Lake is a popular destination for day hikers throughout the summer months. Its icy waters hold cutthroat generally ranging from 25-35 cm in length. The area around the outlet is the most popular with fly fishermen as there is suitable backcasting room, but you should not be dissuaded by heavy brush along the shoreline as you work along the trail towards the head of the lake since fish can often be seen feeding within a few metres of shore. Keeping a sharp eye out for trout is one of the keys to fishing Taylor Lake. For those willing to make the effort, the waters off the scree slopes on the south side of the lake are usually productive.

O'Brien Lake [Larch Lake] (PC)

cutthroat trout to 50 cm (1.5 kg)

Although located only 2 km by trail from the outlet of Taylor Lake, O'Brien Lake is overlooked by most hikers visiting the area despite feisty cutthroat trout in good numbers averaging 30-40 cm and pleasant surroundings which make O'Brien one of the gems of the entire region. Sparse forest cover around much of the lake allows plenty of room for backcasting. Fish can be taken from most spots around the lake, although larger ones seem to prefer the deeper water off the scree slopes along the west shore. Much of the shoreline in the vicinity of the outlet creek is marshy causing most dry-foot enthusiasts to avoid the area.

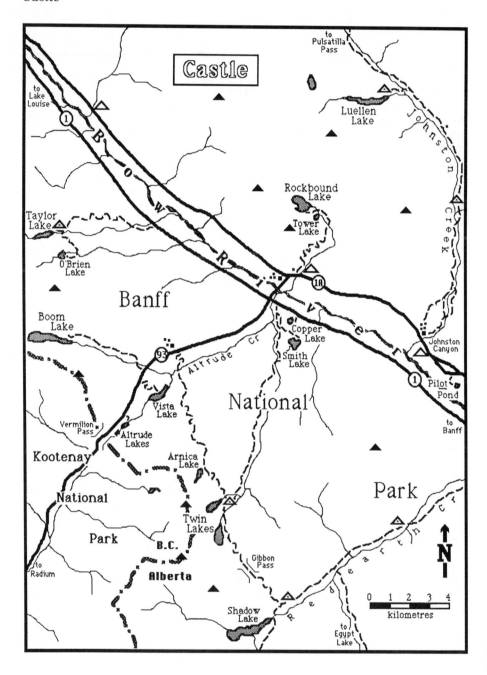

Boom Lake (PC)
cutthroat trout to 50 cm (1.5 kg)

A large body of water set beneath the impressive cliffs of Boom Mountain, Boom Lake holds cutthroat trout averaging 25-35 cm in length. Although overfishing has reduced the number of trout in Boom during recent years, patient fishermen willing to work the shoreline will usually be rewarded. During low light periods trout can often be seen feeding among the logs in the shallow waters around the outlet. Boom Creek between the lake and Highway 93 contains a limited number of small cutthroat.

Altrude Lakes (PC)
cutthroat trout to 35 cm

Passed daily by hundreds of vehicles, the Altrude Lakes sits unnoticed alongside Highway 93 just east of the continental divide separating Banff and Kootenay Parks. The Upper Lake which is visible from the highway holds a dwindling population of cutthroat trout with recent reports indicating that few or none remain. The Lower Lake, located a few hundred metres off the highway, offers relatively poor fishing for cutthroat averaging 20-30 cm in length, the best potential lying in the area along the distinctive drop-off zone.

Vista Lake (PC)
cutthroat trout to 40 cm
brook trout to 40 cm

Vista Lake sits at the bottom of a deep valley south of Highway 93, and is reached by a short, steep 1.5 km trail. Brook trout are the dominant species, although cutthroat are taken regularly. Looking down from the highway you'll notice Vista's two-toned colouration and those fishermen making the trek down to the lake's shore are advised to fish this zone along the drop-off. Backcasting room is limited.

Altrude Creek (PC)
brook trout to 25 cm
cutthroat trout to 25 cm
bull trout to 35 cm

Altrude Creek, which flows from the Altrude Lakes through Vista Lake before entering the Bow River, contains brook, cutthroat and bull trout in small sizes. Fish can be taken along the entire course of the creek which is most heavily fished in the lower reaches near the confluence with the Bow.

Arnica Lake (PC)
cutthroat trout to 50 cm (1.5 kg)

Set beneath the ominous cliffs of Storm Mountains's north shoulder, little Arnica Lake is often overlooked by fishermen heading into Twin Lakes, yet despite its size, some fine cutthroat inhabit Arnica's blue waters with most trout taken averaging 30-40 cm in length. Back-casting is a problem around much of the shoreline, so roll casting ability will be necessary. Arnica Lake is usually frozen into early July because of its sheltered location.

Twin Lakes (PC)
cutthroat trout to 40 cm

The striking east face of Storm Mountain which rises above Twin Lakes keeps the area in shadow much of the time. As a result, the lakes thaw late and area trails are usually snowbound well into July. Access is via two 8 km-long hiking trails beginning across the highway from Storm Mountain Lodge on Highway 93 and from the Altrude Creek picnic site near Castle Junction. A third trail also leads from the Shadow Lake campsite over Gibbon Pass to Lower Twin Lakes 6 km distant. Both lakes contain cutthroat trout in good numbers averaging 20-30 cm in length. The Lower (south) Lake holds better potential for the fly fisherman as it offers more back-casting room along its shoreline than the Upper Lake. For those fishermen having problems casting, the Upper Lake's outlet creek is worth a look.

Copper Lake (PC)
rainbow trout to 40 cm

A small lake set in a sink hole less than a hundred metres from the busy Trans-Canada Highway, Copper Lake is popular with anglers because of its ease of access and its plentiful amounts of rainbow trout averaging 20-25 cm in length. Although casting conditions are not ideal because of the vegetation and the sloped terrain near the shoreline, Copper's trout usually feed fairly close to shore and tend to be very willing to strike at a fly. Keeping a close eye on the water for cruising fish or for riseforms will greatly enhance opportunities.

Smith Lake (PC)

cutthroat trout to 35 cm
brook trout to 35 cm

Located less than 2 km by trail from the Altrude Creek picnic site, tranquil Smith Lake sits amid forested surroundings which will be a source of consternation for most fly fishermen as heavy tree cover makes its way down to the water's edge around much of the lake. The marshy nature of the lakeshore presents an additional barrier when trying to cast to the fishable water. Cutthroat trout predominate, although the occasional brook trout may also be present.

Tower Lake (PC)

cutthroat trout to 30 cm

Located eight kilometres by steep trail from the Eisenhower Warden Station on the 1-A Highway, Tower Lake lies hidden behind the massive turrets of Castle Mountain. It holds a small population of cutthroat trout (most under 25 cm in length) which can generally be seen from shore, but because of shallow waters the fish are wary and will be spooked by most casts. The terrain is favourable for fly casting, and the best tactic here is to cast well ahead of fish as they cruise the shoreline for food.

Rockbound Lake (PC)

brook trout to 40 cm
cutthroat trout to 40 cm

Lying less than 1 km above Tower Lake, appropriately named Rockbound Lake sits in a rugged amphitheatre at tree line where the sparse vegetation allows for plenty of backcasting room although rocks will undoubtedly remove a few flies. Brook trout far outnumber cutthroat trout, with most fish taken averaging 20-30 cm. From many locations along the shore fish can be seen in Rockbound's extremely clear waters.

Luellen Lake (PC)

cutthroat trout to 55 cm (2.0 kg)

Set in a long, narrow valley 18 km by trail from Johnston Canyon, Luellen Lake has long been popular with backcountry fishermen on account of its plentiful supply of good-sized cutthroat, most averaging 30-40 cm in length. The lake is ringed by forest so roll casting will be the order of the day from most potential fishing spots. Fishermen, working up either the north or south side of the lake can generally sight schools of fish from shore and should try working a wet fly which can be very productive at times.

Johnston Creek (PC)

cutthroat trout to 20 cm
bull trout to 30 cm

Small cutthroat trout are plentiful in the upper creek above Johnston Canyon where many fine pools are easily reached from the Luellen Lake/Pulsatilla Pass trail which parallels Johnston Creek for its entire length. In the lower reaches of the creek, bull trout predominate between Johnston Canyon and the Bow River which receives heavy fishing pressure.

Pilot Pond (PC)

rainbow trout to 50 cm (1.5 kg)
brook trout to 45 cm
cutthroat trout to 45 cm

Pilot Ponds sits in a quiet forest-encircled basin half a kilometre below the 1-A Highway. Its clear waters hold both rainbow and brook trout averaging 30-40 cm in length as well as the odd cutthroat, though this may be doubtful. At the distinctive drop-off zone, fish tend to keep to the deeper waters most of the day, only venturing into the shallows to feed during low light periods. With heavy forest cover around the shore and extended shallows, Pilot will not be a shore-bound fly fisherman's favourite lake. However, a boat will dramatically improve fishing potential.

Bow River (PC)

cutthroat trout to 40 cm
brook trout to 40 cm
rainbow trout to 40 cm
bull trout to 70 cm (5.0 kg)
whitefish to 35 cm

The section of the Bow River flowing between Baker Creek and Johnston Creek holds many kilometres of fishable waters with its numerous deep pools. Cutthroat are usually taken in greater numbers by fly fishermen than other species, although brook trout and whitefish are caught regularly along with the occasional rainbow. Also present are some large bull trout which bait fishermen will generally have greater success in taking than fly fishermen. Although the river is overfished in the most readily accessible areas, fishermen willing to work upstream or down to an out-of-the-way hole will usually be rewarded.

SKOKI

Skoki and its network of sparkling lakes and alpine meadows have been popular with fishermen and hikers alike for over 50 years. The main access into the area starts from Temple Lodge on the back side of Lake Louise ski area. After 4 km of road walking from the trailhead at Fish Creek, you follow a trail across Boulder Pass (holding Ptarmigan Lake) and Deception Pass into Skoki Lodge, a backcountry chalet (reservations only) located in the heart of the region. Hidden, Redoubt, Baker, Skoki, Merlin, Castilleja and Red Deer Lakes are all reached by short side trails en route to the lodge. Although both cutthroat and rainbow are present in good numbers, most anglers come in pursuit of the large brook trout inhabiting Redoubt, Baker and Ptarmigan Lakes. Many longer distance trails radiate out from Skoki, extending deep into the backcountry of Banff National Park along the Red Deer and Pipestone Rivers and Baker Creek.

Baker Lake (PC)

brook trout to 55 cm (2.0 kg)
cutthroat trout to 45 cm

Baker Lake, the largest lake in the Skoki region is very popular with fly fishermen. Set in a wide basin near treeline, it holds both cutthroat and brook trout ranging from 30-40 cm in length with brook trout being caught more often than cutthroat although both species inhabit all areas of the lake. The west end of the lake is usually productive, particularly near the inlet creek and wet flies fished deep here tend to attract more brook trout, whereas cutthroat are more favourable to dry flies. Due to its high elevation and lack of tree cover around the shore, Baker is susceptible to strong winds.

Little Baker Lake (PC)

brook trout to 30 cm

Situated less than a kilometre from Baker Lake, Little Baker has held small numbers of brook trout in the past, though recent surveys tend to indicate that very few trout remain. Backcasting room is adequate along much of the shoreline.

Tilted Lake (PC)

brook trout to 30 cm

Set in the same basin as Little Baker Lake, Tilted Lake reportedly has a small population of brook trout, although few fish have been taken recent years. General lack of tree cover allows for backcasting.

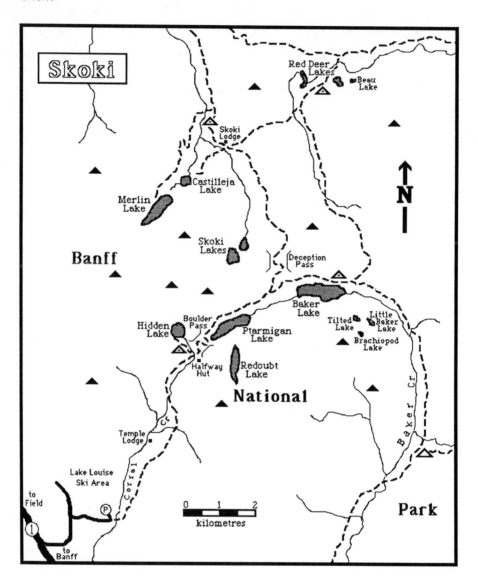

Brachiopod Lake (PC)

status: devoid of fish

Despite rumours to the contrary, Brachiopod Lake contains no fish and dries up completely on occasion.

Baker Creek (PC)

cutthroat trout to 25 cm
brook trout to 25 cm
bull trout to 30 cm
whitefish to 25 cm

Best in its upper reaches, particularly in the meadows below Baker Lake, Baker Creek holds a variety of fish with cutthroat and brook trout predominant in the upper sections and bull trout more numerous downstream. Baker Creek is accessible from a trail that parallels the creek over its entire course.

Ptarmigan Lake (PC)

brook trout to 40 cm
cutthroat trout to 40 cm

Set in windswept Boulder Pass 9 km from the trailhead, the sparkling waters of Ptarmigan Lake hold both brook and cutthroat trout averaging 25-30 cm in length with brook trout being the dominant species. Although backcasting room is available around the entire lake, this advantage is offset by frequent strong winds which make life miserable for most fly fishermen. A drop-off zone within casting distance tends to hold most of the fish.

Redoubt Lake (PC)

brook trout to 60 cm (2.5 kg)
cutthroat trout to 40 cm

Redoubt Lake is perched in a high, alpine basin less than a kilometre south of Ptarmigan Lake by trail. Very popular with anglers following ice-out which generally occurs in mid-July, Redoubt has earned a reputation for holding large brook trout which dominate in both number and size over the cutthroat. Redoubt's tundra-like setting allows for backcasting from all locations around the lake.

Hidden Lake (PC)

cutthroat trout to 30 cm

Set in a rocky amphitheatre located less than a kilometre along a side trail from Halfway Hut, Hidden Lake likely holds a very limited number of small cutthroat trout. A general lack of success by fishermen over the past few years has tended to produce rumours proclaiming the final demise of fish in Hidden but for those fishermen willing to put this rumour to the test, the best potential lies in the deep waters along the rocky north shore.

Corral Creek (PC)

cutthroat trout to 25 cm
brook trout to 25 cm

Corral Creek has a small population of brook and cutthroat trout in its upper reaches and also at its lower end near its confluence with the Bow River. The fast waters in the middle section hold very few fish.

Skoki Lakes [Zigadenus Lake] (PC)

status: devoid of fish

Skoki Lakes [Myosotis Lake] (PC)

rainbow trout to 30 cm

The beautifully coloured Skoki Lakes, Zigadenus and Myosotis, are located high on the west side of Skoki Valley beneath the east face of Ptarmigan Peak. Visible to the west as you descend the north side of Deception Pass, the lakes can be reached either by leaving the trail and working across the valley, or by following a rough trail that begins half a kilometre south of Skoki Lodge. Both lakes are heavily silted which accounts for their striking green colour. Zigadenus, the upper lake, was once stocked with rainbow trout which failed to re-produce, while Myosotis has a dwindling population of rainbows. Recent reports indicate poor fishing.

Castilleja Lake (PC)

status: doubtful

A small lake encountered en route to Merlin Lake, Castilleja was at one time stocked with rainbows but evidence over the past years indicates that the fish failed to take hold. There is a possibility some cutthroat may have entered the lake from the Pipestone drainage.

Merlin Lake (PC)

rainbow trout to 30 cm
brook trout to 30 cm

Set in a hanging valley above Castilleja Lake, and protected by a small cliff band requiring scrambling ability, lies picturesque Merlin Lake which has a small population of rainbow and brook trout. Its alpine setting allows for good casting along much of its shoreline. Due to its elevation and sheltered location, Merlin is usually icebound until mid-July with freeze-up occuring early in the fall.

Red Deer Lakes (PC)

brook trout to 50 cm (1.5 kg)
cutthroat trout to 40 cm
rainbow trout to 40 cm

The two Red Deer Lakes are set in a wide, open valley 4 km by trail from Skoki Lodge. The Upper Lake, the larger of the two, lies west of the trail and contains cutthroat trout as well as smaller numbers of rainbow and brook trout. Although room for backcasting is available, the lake is very shallow for a fair distance out from shore which makes it difficult for fly fishermen to reach deeper waters holding the fish. Best opportunities for fly fishermen are in the areas around the inlet and outlet streams. The Lower Lake, found just east of the main trail, has both rainbow and brook trout. However, the marshy nature of the area almost ensures wet feet and the abundance of bullrushes makes casting difficult. Several channels, most of which hold trout, wind back and forth across the marshy flats around the Lower Lake.

Beau Lake (PC)

brook trout to 30 cm
rainbow trout to 30 cm

This small lake just east of Lower Red Deer Lake holds both brook and rainbow trout in small numbers. Beau's swampy surroundings will provide ample opportunity to test waterproof boots.

You can't tell - maybe the fish goes home and brags
about the size of the bait he stole.

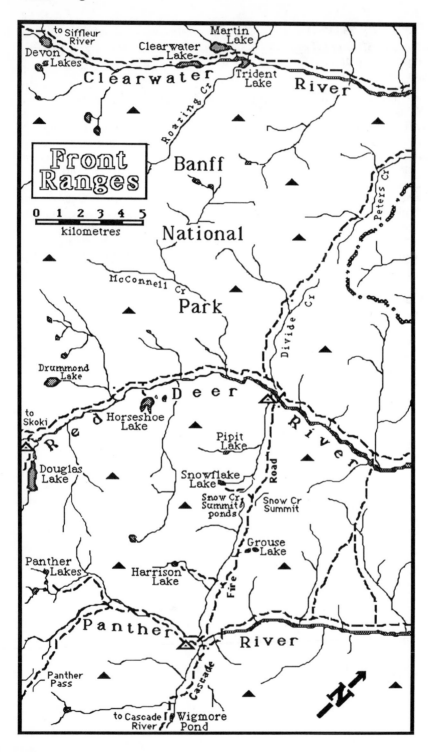

FRONT RANGES

Covering the watersheds of the upper Red Deer, Panther and Clearwater Rivers, this area lies deep within the Front Ranges of Banff National Park which is home to many a grizzly bear. Visitors entering the region are generally limited to horse parties and a few enterprising hikers who should be aware that major river fords are to be expected on most trails in the region and that there are no easy escape routes back to civilization. From the upper Red Deer River, which can be accessed from Skoki Valley, side trails branch to Douglas and Horseshoe Lakes. The Cascade Fire Road, although lengthy, provides an alternate approach. By following the fire road south from the Red Deer River into the Panther River drainage, you come to short spur trails leading to Pipit, Snowflake, Grouse and Harrison Lakes. The Panther Lakes are located at the headwaters of the Panther River. To the north, the Clearwater River flows east from its source at the Devon Lakes through Clearwater and Trident Lakes and passes close by Martin Lake on its journey towards the plains.

Clearwater River (PC)
bull trout to 75 cm (5.0 kg)
whitefish to 40 cm
brook trout to 35 cm

Flowing eastwards from humble beginnings at the Devon Lakes on Clearwater Pass, the Clearwater River eventually joins the North Saskatchewan River at Rocky Mountain House as a major tributary. The section of the Clearwater within the boundaries of Banff National Park is seldom fished due to long approach routes, all of which require a minumum of two days travel. In its upper reaches the river holds bull trout and whitefish, with brook trout becoming more plentiful downstream from Trident Lake. Horse trails parallel the Clearwater for its entire length. A dangerous ford of Martin Creek above Trident Lake will cause problems for most hikers.

Trident Lake (PC)
bull trout to 75 cm (5.0 kg)
whitefish to 40 cm
Two kilometres downstream from Clearwater Lake the Clearwater River again widens, this time into the form of Trident Lake whose waters hold bull trout averaging 40-50 cm and whitefish averaging 20-30 cm in length. As with Clearwater Lake, bait fishermen will have an advantage over fly fishermen. Fishing is best near the major inlets on Trident Lake which include the Clearwater River, Martin and Roaring Creeks.

Clearwater Lake (PC)

bull trout to 75 cm (5.0 kg)
lake trout to 75 cm (5.0 kg)
whitefish to 40 cm

Set in wide valley 10 km downstream from Clearwater Pass, Clearwater Lake is merely a widening of the river and along with Trident and Martin Lakes is visited by few fishermen each season. The lake holds large bull and lake trout, many in the 40-60 cm range, as well as a fair number of whitefish. Fly fishermen will generally have a difficult time in Clearwater, both bull and lake trout favouring bait fishermen, but despite this, both species can be taken on a fly if conditions are right. Work the area around the inlet and outlet for best results.

Devon Lakes (PC)

lake trout to 75 cm (5.0 kg)
bull trout to 75 cm (5.0 kg)
cutthroat trout to 60 cm (2.5 kg)
brook trout to 50 cm (1.5 kg)
whitefish to 40 cm

Set in alpine surroundings immediately east of Clearwater Pass, the Devon Lakes are one of the region's most popular fishing destinations. The main and largest lake contains plenty of lake and bull trout in large sizes together with a number of whitefish. The two smaller lakes, located in a basin just to the south of the main lake, have both been stocked in the past. Cutthroat were planted in the upper lake and reports indicate that they have taken hold with most fish taken averaging 30-40 cm in length. The lower lake was stocked with brook trout and although their reproductive success has not been determined, fishing is generally reported as poor. Backcasting room is plentiful around all three lakes due to lack of tree cover.

Martin Lake (PC)

brook trout to 55 cm (2.0 kg)

Martin Lake is located less than a kilometre above Trident Lake on Martin Creek. Stocked in the past with brook trout, Martin offered good fishing for a number of years before a steady decline. At present, it is likely a small population of brook trout still exist, maintaining their numbers through natural reproduction.

Red Deer River (PC)

brook trout to 35 cm
bull trout to 70 cm (4.0 kg)
whitefish to 40 cm

From its source at Red Deer Lakes, the Red Deer River offers fine river fishing as it flows east to the Banff National Park boundary. While the main river is often very silty until mid to late summer due to glacial run-off, many of the side channels and ponds provide excellent opportunities to catch trout at this time. Brook trout predominate in the upper sections with bull trout and whitefish becoming more plentiful downstream. In the vicinity of Red Deer Lakes, the occasional rainbow or cutthroat may also be caught. Horse trails along the upper Red Deer connect with the Cascade Fire Road which continues east from Scotch Camp to the park boundary.

Douglas Lake (PC)

cutthroat trout to 55 cm (2.0 kg)

This relatively large lake set in a wide valley to the south of the main Red Deer River Valley usually attracts a few eager fishermen each season despite a tricky ford of the Red Deer prior to reaching the Douglas Lake spur trail. Cutthroat trout averaging 30-40 cm in length inhabit the lake's silty waters in good numbers. Although brook trout were also stocked at one time in Douglas, reports indicate that few or none remain. The areas around the lake's inlet and outlet are generally the most productive, although cutthroat can be taken from most spots along the shore, the trout tending to keep fairly close to the shore in search of food due to silted waters. Because of the proximity of the forest cover around much of the shore, casting is difficult except at the inlet end where broad marshy meadows extend down to the lake.

Horseshoe Lake [Skeleton Lake] (PC)

rainbow to 40 cm
brook trout 40 cm

Located 6 km downstream from Douglas Lake, Horseshoe Lake is protected by a dangerous ford of the Red Deer River. Although horse parties will have little trouble with the river crossing, most hikers will likely avoid the ford and bypass Horseshoe altogether which is unfortunate since this distinctly U-shaped lake holds plenty of rainbow and brook trout averaging 25-35 cm in length. Casting room is available from many locations around the lake.

Drummond Lake (PC)
status: devoid of fish

Hidden in a side valley northwest of the Red Deer River, Drummond Lake has never been stocked and contains no fish.

Pipit Lake (PC)
rainbow trout to 40 cm

This small, isloated lake lying west of the Cascade Fire Road as it ascends the north side of Snow Creek Summit receives very few visitors each summer. A map and compass are recommended as no trails lead to the lake, although the route is fairly obvious. Recent reports indicated that Pipit holds a small population of rainbow trout averaging 20-30 cm in length.

Snowflake Lake (PC)
status: doubtful

Set in an beautiful alpine basin west of Snow Creek Summit, Snowflake Lake has been unable to maintain a population of trout. Both rainbow and brook trout have been unsuccessfully planted in the past and reports now indicate that the lake is likely barren.

Snow Creek Summit ponds (PC)
bull trout to 40 cm

This series of beaver ponds on the western side of Snow Creek Summit is overlooked by most parties passing through, despite the fact the ponds hold plenty of small bull trout averaging 20-30 cm in length.

Grouse Lake (PC)
status: devoid of fish

Grouse Lake lies hidden in a narrow side valley just east of the Cascade Fire Road. The brook trout stocked in the past failed to reproduce and the lake is now devoid of fish.

Harrison Lake (PC)
cutthroat trout to 45 cm
bull trout to 50 cm (1.5 kg)

Harrison Lake, nestled high on the flank of an unnamed peak at the south end of the Vermilion Range, is accessed by a 3 km side trail west of the Cascade Fire Road. Visited by few fishermen each season, Harrison is one of the region's hidden treasures for cutthroat and bull trout averaging 25-35 cm in length which make it worth the long distances travelled.

Panther River (PC)

bull trout to 70 cm (4.0 kg)
whitefish to 40 cm

Flowing east to its junction with the Red Deer River, the Panther River offers average stream fishing at best. Bull trout and whitefish are found in pockets along the entire length of the river but never in great numbers. As you progress downstream, the fishing generally picks up, and nearing the park boundary, the odd brook trout and rainbow can also be caught. Horse trails parallel the Panther and the Cascade Fire Road intersects the river at Wigmore Creek.

Panther Lakes (PC)

status: doubtful

This series of lakes set amid spectacular scenery at the head of the Panther River have never been stocked. It is possible, although unlikely, that a few bull trout have worked their way into the lakes.

Wigmore Pond (PC)

bull trout to 40 cm
rainbow trout to 30 cm
brook trout to 30 cm

Tiny Wigmore Pond sits alongside the Cascade Fire Road just north of Wigmore Summit. Although rainbow and brook trout have been stocked in the past and reports indicate they are still present, bull trout is the predominate species. Casting room is available around the entire lake, although fly fishermen may be plagued with strong winds that rush through the pass at nearby Wigmore Summit.

How far a fisherman will stretch the truth depends on the length of his arms.

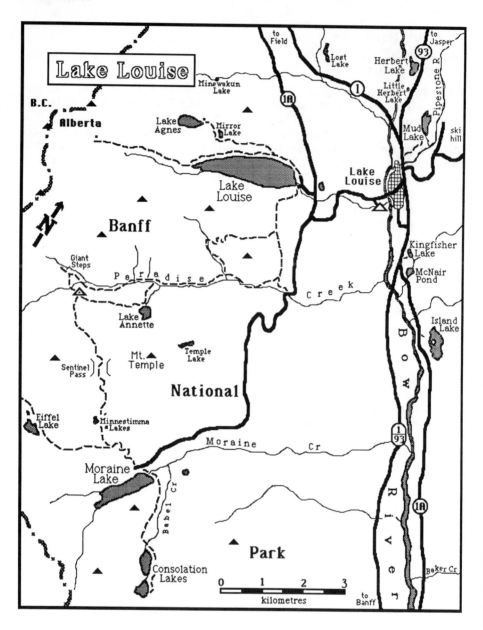

LAKE LOUISE

Fishing amid some of the most exquisite settings anywhere in the mountain world will tend to distract many anglers. Although more renowned for its scenery than for its fishing, the Lake Louise region does possess a small number of good fishing spots. The Trans-Canada Highway heading west to Field and southeast to Banff is the area's main thoroughfare together with Highway 93 (Icefields Parkway) to Jasper which branches north off the Trans-Canada just west of Lake Louise, a tiny village offering the basics of gas, food and lodging. As for fishing, the ever popular Bow River can be reached from many locations along both highways. Despite the relatively poor angling offered by the twin jewels of Lake Louise and Moraine Lake, numerous fishermen are attracted to their shores each summer. Better fishing exists at lakes situated along the Bow Valley such as Mud, Lost, Kingfisher and Island which are all accessible by short trails from the Trans-Canada Highway.

Moraine Lake (PC)
bull trout to 70 cm (4.0 kg)
cutthroat trout to 55 cm (2.0 kg)
splake to 60 cm (2.5 kg)

Well known as "the lake on the back of the Canadian twenty dollar bill," Moraine Lake has suffered a dramatic decline over the years in its quality of fishing and nowadays only small numbers of cutthroat and splake in the 30-40 cm range and the occasional bull trout of 50 cm or more are taken from the lake's appealing turquoise waters. Canoes are available for rent at the lake during summer months. Fishing in Moraine tends to be best during low light conditions, and slowly trolling a wet fly behind a canoe during these times is generally regarded as the best tactic.

Consolation Lakes (PC)
cutthroat trout to 40 cm [lower lake only]
brook trout to 35 cm

Located 3 km by trail from the Moraine Lake parking lot, the Consolation Lakes are set in a secluded subalpine valley beneath Mt. Babel. Both lakes contain brook trout averaging 20-30 cm in length, the lower lake also holding cutthroat trout in the same size range. Ample backcasting room is available from scree slopes which make up much of the shoreline. The clarity of the water in both lakes makes early morning and late evening the prime time for fishing.

Eiffel Lake (PC)
status: devoid of fish
Eiffel Lake, 6 km from the Moraine parking area by trail, sits in the middle of barren Desolation Valley. Eiffel has never been stocked and contains no fish.

Minnestimma Lakes (PC)
status: devoid of fish

This series of shallow tarns in Larch Valley have never been stocked and are devoid of fish.

Moraine Creek (PC)
brook trout to 25 cm
cutthroat trout to 25 cm
bull trout to 30 cm

The outlet for Moraine Lake contains brook and cutthroat trout which are most plentiful in the vicinity of the confluence with Babel Creek. On the lower part of Moraine Creek, within a kilometre of the Bow River, limited numbers of small brook and cutthroat as well as bull trout can be taken.

Temple Lake (PC)
rainbow trout to 30 cm

Located on the eastern flank of magnificent Mt. Temple, and reached only by route finders armed with map and compass, diminutive Temple Lake is seldom visited by hikers or fishermen. The lake was stocked in the past with both rainbow and brook trout and reports indicate that a small population of rainbow trout still exists, the result of natural reproduction.

Lake Annette (PC)
cutthroat trout to 35 cm
rainbow trout to 35 cm

In the heart of Paradise Valley, Lake Annette sits directly below the foreboding north face of Mt. Temple, its deep, dark waters holding a limited number of cutthroat and rainbow trout in the 20-30 cm range and likely some cutthroat-rainbow hybrids as well. Heavy brush around much of the shoreline inhibits backcasting, although there are a few adequate locations.

Paradise Creek (PC)

cutthroat trout to 25 cm
bull trout to 25 cm

Paradise Creek, flowing through the entire length of Paradise Valley, contains small cutthroat in the middle section between Giant Steps and the Moraine Lake Road and small cutthroat and bull trout in the lower reaches near its confluence with the Bow River.

Lake Louise (PC)

whitefish to 35 cm
bull trout to 60 cm (2.5 kg)

With Mts. Victoria and Lefroy providing a dazzling backdrop, Lake Louise's brilliant emerald-coloured waters has gained a world-wide reputation for scenic excellence. Unfortunately, Lake Louise's fishing is worthy of little acclaim. Whitefish in the 20-30 cm range and the occasional bull trout are all that are taken from Louise. Stocked in the past with splake, rainbow, cutthroat, and brook trout, it is possible, although unlikely, that very limited numbers of some of these species still exist. Canoes are available for rent during the summer.

Mirror Lake (PC)

status: devoid of fish

This small lake along the trail from Lake Louise to Lake Agnes contains no fish and has never been stocked.

Lake Agnes

splake
status: closed

Lake Agnes, nestled in a hanging valley behind the Beehives, serves as the water supply for the Chateau Lake Louise and is therefore closed to angling.

Minewakun Lake (PC)

status: unknown

Tiny Minewakun Lake sits in a secluded basin beneath the north face of Mt. St. Piran 2 km northwest of Lake Louise. The reproductive success of brook trout stocked in the lake has never been determined and because there are no access trails, few anglers make their way into Minewakun, thus giving it an air of mystery.

Bow River (PC)

cutthroat trout to 40 cm
brook trout to 40 cm
rainbow trout to 40 cm
bull trout to 70 cm (4.0 kg)
whitefish to 35 cm

Cutthroat and brook trout predominate in this section of the Bow River flowing between the Highway 1/93 junction in the north and Baker Creek in the south. Accessible from both the Trans-Canada and the 1-A highways, the Bow contains some really fine stretches of fishable water.

Island Lake (PC)

status: doubtful

Located just east of 1-A Highway, shallow Island Lake has been stocked in the past with a variety of trout, none of which have been able to take hold. Most reports indicate that Island Lake is devoid of fish.

McNair Pond (PC)

cutthroat trout to 30 cm
rainbow trout to 30 cm
brook trout to 30 cm

Readily accessible, McNair Pond is situated alongside the 1-A highway just east of the Trans-Canada—1-A junction. Created by the construction of the highway and the damming of a small creek, much of McNair's shoreline consists of dead trees which allow for little backcast room. Cutthroat and rainbow from 15-25 cm in length predominate with the occasional brook trout taken as well.

Kingfisher Lake (PC)

rainbow trout to 40 cm
brook trout to 35 cm

Reached by a short 300 m trail from the Trans-Canada Highway, Kingfisher Lake is visited by many anglers each summer. Rainbow trout averaging 20-30 cm in length are caught in greater number than brook trout. A wide margin of shallow water along with heavy forest cover around the shore makes Kingfisher unpopular with most fly fishering enthusiasts. However, casting distance is significantly reduced during low light conditions when trout enter the shallower waters to feed.

Mud Lake (PC)

brook trout to 45 cm
cutthroat trout to 50 cm (1.5 kg)
rainbow trout to 40 cm

Located west of the Trans-Canada Highway in the Pipestone River drainage, Mud Lake sits amid forested surroundings. Holding both cutthroat and brook averaging 30-40 cm in length and perhaps the odd rainbow, Mud's character presents a number of problems for fly fishermen. Due to extended shallows, fishermen require long casts to reach fish holding waters while the thick vegetation around Mud's shoreline is not conducive to fly casting.

Herbert Lake (PC)

brook trout to 50 cm (1.5 kg)
splake to 60 cm (2.5 kg)

A popular roadside picnic spot along Highway 93 (Icefields Parkway), Herbert Lake's crystal clear waters attract many fishermen after splake and brook trout averaging 30-40 cm. Remnants of cutthroat and rainbow populations from previous stockings may also be present, although unlikely. Fishing from shore requires long casts to reach deeper water where the fish hold for most of the day due to water clarity. Working around to the side of the lake opposite the highway offers slightly better access to deeper waters. Fishing from a canoe is the best plan.

Little Herbert Lake (PC)

rainbow trout to 30 cm

Little more than a roadside pond, Little Herbert Lake is located less than a kilometre south of Herbert Lake on the west side of Highway 93. It contains a limited population of small rainbow trout. Because long casts are not required, Little Herbert is a favourite of novices.

Lost Lake (PC)

status: doubtful

Lost Lake is an infrequently-visited body of water located on the north side of the Trans-Canada Highway 2 km east of Kicking Horse Pass. A very shallow lake completely rimmed with forest, Lost has been stocked in the past with cutthroat and brook trout, both of which have failed to reproduce. As it has not been stocked in recent years, it is highly doubtful if any fish remain.

O'HARA

O'Hara's scenery of pristine mountain lakes set beneath the spectacular peaks of the continental divide is equal to that of any area in the Rockies. Although the O'Hara vicinity has long been renowned for hiking and climbing and not for fishing, prospective anglers coming to this corner of Yoho National Park will not be disappointed. Lake O'Hara, the focal point of the region, is reached via a 13 km limited access fire road from the Trans-Canada Highway. Arrangements can be made with Lake O'Hara Lodge to reserve a space on the shuttle bus which runs several times a day during summer months. Both Lake O'Hara Lodge and the Alpine Club of Canada's Elizabeth Parker Hut require reservations as does the park campground located a half kilometre below Lake O'Hara alongside Cataract Brook. From the shores of beautiful lake O'Hara, trails radiate out to nearby lakes, including Mary, Schaeffer, McArthur, Morning Glory, Linda, Vera and Oesa.

Lake O'Hara (PC)
cutthroat trout to 45 cm

Situated beneath the same impressive peaks that form the backdrop for Lake Louise, the emerald green waters of Lake O'Hara is a favourite destination of backcountry visitors. Unfortunately, Lake O'Hara's fishing has never been able to match its beauty. Containing cutthroat in the 20-25 cm range, O'Hara may also hold the odd rainbow, although most have been absorbed over time into the cutthroat population. On occasion, cutthroat upwards of 40 cm in length are taken. There are numerous locations along the shoreline where reasonable casting room is available. The tangle of sunken logs in the area of the lakes outlet is a popular spot which usually holds trout, albeit small. Canoes can be rented from the Lake O'Hara Lodge, but fishing from a boat is not usually a great aid here as the fish tend to stay close to shore due to the silted nature of the water.

Lake Oesa (PC)
status: devoid of fish

Ice-covered ten months a year, Lake Oesa was once stocked with rainbow trout which failed to take hold.

Yukness Lake, Lake Victoria, Lefroy Lake (PC)
status: devoid of fish

Three small, silted bodies of water alongside the trail to Lake Oesa have never been stocked and contain no fish.

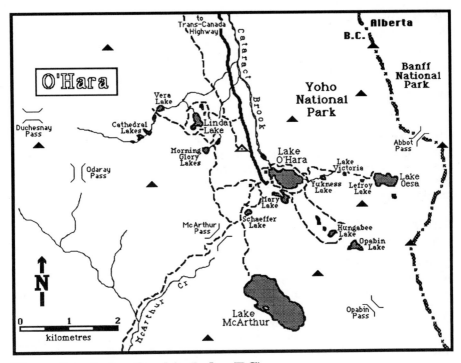

Hungabee Lake, Opabin Lake (PC)

status: devoid of fish

Set in the alpine environs of the Opabin Plateau, neither Hungabee nor Opabin Lake have ever been stocked.

Lake McArthur (PC)

brook trout to 35 cm

The largest lake of the region lies hidden in a hanging valley 3 km south of Lake O'Hara and is noted for its exceptional blue colouration, a result of heavy silting from nearby glaciers. Although the lake holds brook trout averaging 25-30 cm in length, fishermen at McArthur have not enjoyed great success in recent years. Reports tend to indicate that a very small number of trout still exist in McArthur and a few fish are taken each year.

Schaeffer Lake (PC)

status: doubtful

Although stocked in the past with both rainbow and cutthroat trout, no reproductive success has ever been recorded and Schaeffer Lake is very likely devoid of fish.

Mary Lake (PC)
status: devoid of fish

Located on a bench just south of Lake O'Hara, Mary Lake has never been stocked and contains no fish.

Morning Glory Lakes (PC)
cutthroat trout to 30 cm

The Morning Glory Lakes are a series of three shallow lakes situated beneath the impressive north face of Mt. Odaray. All three contain limited populations of small cutthroat trout which spook easily due to the clear, shallow nature of the water. Plenty of backcasting room is available around all three lakes.

Linda Lake (PC)
cutthroat trout to 50 cm (1.5 kg)

Linda Lake, set in a quiet subalpine basin northwest of Lake O'Hara, offers the best potential of any lake in the region. Its clear blue waters hold plenty of cutthroat trout in the 20-30 cm range with larger fish taken regularly. Numerous openings in the forest cover along the shoreline allow for backcasting. No one area seems to be best, and fishermen are advised to keep a close eye on the water while working around the lake.

Vera Lake (PC)
cutthroat to 35 cm

Vera Lake, a little over 4 km by trail from Lake O'Hara, is seldom visited by fishermen most of whom do not venture beyond nearby Linda Lake. Its placid waters hold a small population of cutthroat trout averaging 20-25 cm in length which are usually found in the areas around the inlet and outlet creeks.

Cathedral Lakes (PC)
status: unknown

Located half a kilometre above Vera Lake, the diminutive Cathedral Lakes have never been stocked with trout. However, since it's possible that fish could have migrated upstream over time from Vera Lake, the lakes are worth a look for anyone in the area.

Cataract Brook (PC)
cutthroat trout to 25 cm

Paralleling the Lake O'Hara Fire Road, Cataract Brook, as its name indicates, contains numerous falls and rapids. The creek holds small cutthroat trout in its upper section particularly in the 2 km stretch below Lake O'Hara where several large pools just below the lake's outlet are generally productive.

KICKING HORSE

Flowing west, the Kicking Horse River forms a deep valley bounded on the north and south by the imposing peaks of Yoho National Park. The Trans-Canada Highway parallels the river, cutting through the middle of the region between Golden to the west and Lake Louise to the east. En route, the village of Field, housing the headquarters for Yoho National Park, offers little in the way of services beyond the essentials of gas and food. Sink, Summit and Ross Lakes are located within a kilometre of Kicking Horse Pass and the continental divide. Farther west, Wapta Lake lies alongside the Trans-Canada Highway, while Sherbrooke and Narao Lakes are only a short hike away. At the western end of the region, the Ottertail and Otterhead Rivers join the Kicking Horse.

Kicking Horse River (PC)

bull trout to 60 cm (2.5 kg)
brook trout to 40 cm
whitefish to 35 cm

The Kicking Horse River forms the main artery of Yoho National Park, its tributaries extending to the far corners of the park. Paralleled by the Trans-Canada Highway, the river is readily accessible to anglers, but unfortunately offers only mediocre fishing even on its best days. It is heavily silted most of the year, clearing up only in the late summer-early fall when bull trout and whitefish along with a few brook trout can be taken. Most fish are in the 20-30 cm range, although large bull trout to 60 cm can be caught on occasion. Fishing is best around the Kicking Horse's confluence with its tributary streams, particularly the larger ones such as the Emerald, Amiskwi, Ottertail and Otterhead Rivers.

Ross Lake (PC)

brook trout to 35 cm

The small tree-fringed lake clogged with sunken deadfall lying less than a kilometre south of 1-A Highway receives little fishing pressure due to its secluded location. Ross' green waters hold brook trout averaging 20-30 cm in length with the best angling opportunities to be found along the scree slopes on the south side of the lake.

Narao Lakes (PC)

brook trout to 35 cm

Set amid marshy surroundings 2 km by trail south of Wapta Lake, the Narao Lakes are seldom visited by fishermen since wet feet are unavoidable and few fish are present. Although the lakes were stocked in the past with brook trout, their reproductive success is suspect at best.

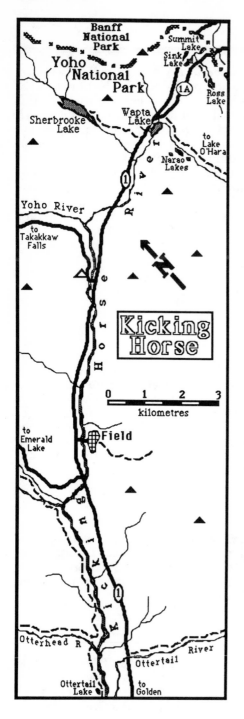

Summit Lake (PC)
status: doubtful

This shallow lake located alongside the 1-A Highway just west of Kicking Horse Pass is no longer of much interest to fishermen since its ability to hold fish is entirely dependent on regular plantings, a practice which no longer occurs in Summit. Rainbow, cutthroat and brook trout have all been stocked in Summit in years past and all have failed to reproduce. Due to winter kill, it is doubtful if any are still present.

Sink Lake (PC)
status: doubtful

Sink Lake possesses many of the same characteristics as its sister lake Summit, with winter kill being a major factor in the demise of fish in the lake over the years. Rainbow, brook and cutthroat trout, as well as splake have all been planted in Sink, but failed to take hold. Although unlikely, some remnants of rainbow and brook trout plantings may still exist.

Wapta Lake (PC)
lake trout to 60 cm (2.5 kg)
rainbow trout to 40 cm
brook trout to 40 cm
splake to 40 cm

Wapta Lake receives relatively little fishing pressure despite its proximity to the Trans-Canada Highway. Rainbow, brook and lake trout, along with the occasional splake are all present with most fish averaging 25-35 cm.

Right:
Floe Lake, Vermilion

Cuthead Lake, Cascade

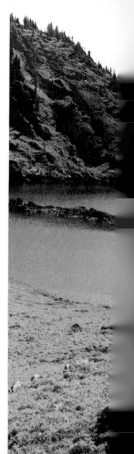

Top left:
Taylor Lake, Castle

Top right:
Rockbound Lake, Castle

Bottom left:
Merlin Lake, Skoki

Bottom right:
Rock Isle Lake, Sunsh

Yoho Lake, Yoho-Emerald

Scarab Lake, Egypt Lake

Baker Lake, Skoki

Black Rock Lake, Egypt Lake

Pinto Lake, North Saskatchewan

Top: Kingfisher Lake, Lake Louise   *Bottom: Upper Brazeau River, Brazeau*

Princess Lake, North Boundary

Amethyst Lake, Tonquin

Fish Lake, Bow Lake

Cavell Lake, Tonquin
Moose River, Robson

As the lake is silted in nature, the area around the inlet and outlet generally produce the best. If fishing from a boat, a wet fly fished deep can often be very effective.

Sherbrooke Lake (PC)
rainbow trout to 50 cm (1.5 kg)
lake trout to 55 cm (2.0 kg)

The narrow valley between Paget Peak and Mount Ogden holds the elongated form of Sherbrooke Lake. With tributaries flowing from the Daly and Niles Glaciers, the lake is very silty most of the year and fishing is understandably slow for rainbow and lake trout ranging from 20-35 cm in length. Fishermen working around the shore can usually take rainbows in the shallow water, particularly in the area of the outlet which is strewn with deadfall. Although streamers often work on the lake trout, bait fishermen usually have an advantage over fly fishermen.

Otterhead River (PC)
bull trout to 40 cm
brook trout to 30 cm
whitefish to 30 cm

The Otterhead River joins the Kicking Horse River as a major tributary approximately 5 km west of Field and can be reached from a fire road along the north side of the Kicking Horse. It contains bull and brook trout along with whitefish in its lower reaches and bull trout in its upper waters. Most fish taken are small, averaging only 15-25 cm in length.

Ottertail Lake (PC)
brook trout to 35 cm

Ottertail Lake is located on the north side of the Kicking Horse River just over a kilometre west of the river's confluence with the Otter-head. Seldom fished, the lake holds brook trout in the 15-25 cm range

Ottertail River (PC)
bull trout to 40 cm
brook trout to 30 cm
whitefish to 30 cm

Whitefish, brook and bull trout all inhabit the lower stretches of the Ottertail River while only small bull trout are present in the upper reaches. A fire road branching off the Trans-Canada Highway leads up the Ottertail drainage where trails carry on to Lake O'Hara and Kootenay National Park.

YOHO-EMERALD

Encompassing the northern half of Yoho National Park, this area possesses an abundance of superb scenery and a scarcity of good fishing opportunities. The main access is via the Yoho Valley Road or the Emerald Lake Road, both of which branch north off the Trans-Canada Highway. Exquisitely coloured Emerald Lake is a favourite with sightseers and fishermen alike and is the hub of hiking trails leading to Hamilton Lake and Yoho Lake which is located near the summit of Yoho Pass. From the terminus of the Yoho Valley Road at 380 m-high Takakkaw Falls, the main Yoho Valley trail leads past Celeste, Duchesnay and Marpole Lakes, none of which hold much promise for fishermen.

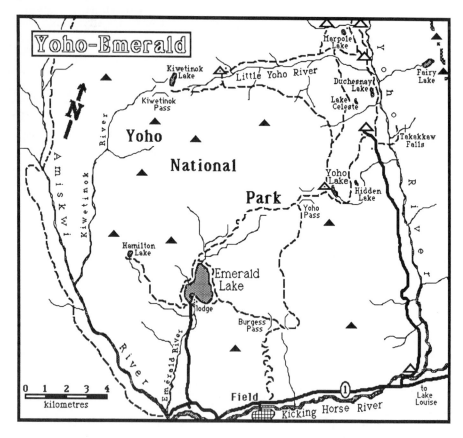

Emerald Lake (PC)

brook trout to 50 cm (1.5 kg)
rainbow trout to 50 cm (1.5 kg)

Emerald Lake's dazzling setting attracts hordes of vistors each summer, and its shoreline always seems to be busy with hikers, photographers and anglers. Although Emerald is not an outstanding fishing lake, its rich green waters contain fair numbers of both brook and rainbow trout averaging 25-35 cm in length, the former in the majority. The occasional bull trout may also be present. As the water is silted, fish can generally be taken close to shore, particularly in the area around the outlet and bridge to Emerald Lake Lodge. From a canoe, which can be rented from the lodge, the best tactic is to keep fairly close to shore while trolling a fly.

Hamilton Lake (PC)

status: devoid of fish

Delightful Hamilton Lake, 5 km by trail above Emerald Lake and set in a rocky cirque beneath Mount Carnarvon, has never been stocked and contains no trout.

Emerald River (PC)

brook trout to 35 cm
rainbow trout to 35 cm
bull trout to 40 cm

Flowing from Emerald Lake to the Amiskwi River, the Emerald River possesses long stretches of fishable water which are only a short walk away from the Emerald Lake Road. Small brook and rainbow trout seldom exceeding 30 cm in length predominate with a few bull trout present as well.

Amiskwi River (PC)

brook trout to 35 cm
bull trout to 55 cm (2.0 kg)

*t*The Amiskwi River receives little attention from anglers, particularly in the upper sections, because of long access along a seldom-hiked fire road which parallels the Amiskwi over its entire length. Small brook and bull trout in the 15-25 cm range are the normal catch, although larger bulls are taken on occasion. Due to high, muddy water, the river river is generally unfishable until late July.

Kiwetinok River (PC)
bull trout to 40 cm

The Kiwetinok River, a tributary of the Amiskwi River, contains bull trout in small numbers and sizes but is generally not worth the effort of a long approach up the Amiskwi Fire Road.

Yoho River (PC)
status: doubtful

With its headwaters the Wapta and Yoho Glaciers, the Yoho River is extremely silted throughout the year. In addition to heavy silting, the river is excessively torrential over most of its course and it is very unlikey that trout would survive under these conditions. It is possible, however, that small bull trout may live in some pockets near the confluence of clearer running tributary streams.

Little Yoho River (PC)
status: devoid of fish

Flowing through much-hiked Little Yoho Valley, the Little Yoho River is too torrential and silty to hold trout.

Yoho Lake (PC)
brook trout to 35 cm

Situated less than a kilometre east of Yoho Pass, lovely Yoho Lake is very popular with hikers and fishermen throughout summer months. The lake contains plenty of brook trout in smaller sizes, averaging 20-25 cm in length which can usually be seen cruising a few metres off shore, so crafty fishermen should have no problem catching fish. However, if wind conditions prevent fish sightings, a wet fly fished deep generally produces well. Casting room is limited to the areas where meadows extend down to the shore.

Hidden Lake (PC)
status: doubtful

Located on the east side of the Yoho Lake-Takakkaw Falls trail, tiny Hidden Lake has been stocked in the past with both brook and rainbow trout. However, the fish failed to reproduce and it is very doubtful if any remain.

Fairy Lake (PC)

status: devoid of fish

Nestled high on the flank of Trolltinder Mountain, Fairy Lake is protected by a 300 m high cliff. Fortunately for fishermen, Fairy Lake has never been stocked and contains no fish.

Duchesnay Lake (PC)

status: doubtful

Forest-rimmed Duchesnay Lake is situated on the west side of the Yoho Valley trail 4 km from the Takakkaw Falls trailhead. This shallow lake was stocked in the past with brook trout, but it is likely the fish succumbed to winter kill.

Lake Celeste (PC)

status: devoid of fish

This small, shallow body of water lying less than a kilometre due west of Duchesnay Lake has never been stocked and contains no fish.

Marpole Lake (PC)

status: doubtful

Located just south of Twin Falls Chalet, diminutive Marpole Lake has been stocked several times in the past with brook, cutthroat and rainbow trout. In recent years, fishing has been very poor in Marpole, leading to speculation that there are no longer trout in the lake. Aside from reproductive failure, winter kill is also likely a major factor limiting numbers.

Kiwetinok Lake (PC)

status: devoid of fish

Set in the harsh alpine environs of Kiwetinok Pass, Kiwetinok remains ice-covered much of the year. No fish are present.

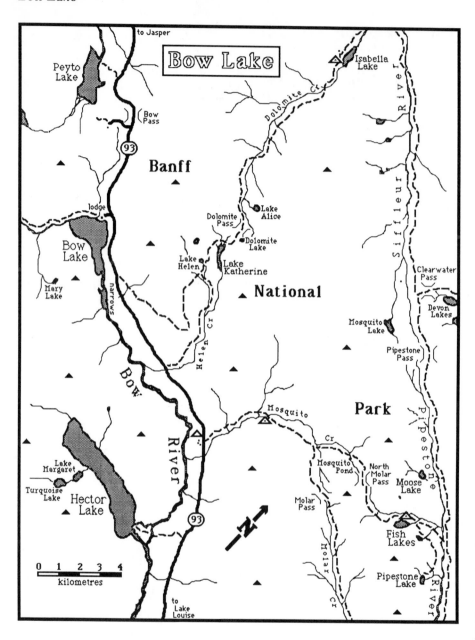

Bow Lake

Peyto Lake

to Jasper

Isabella Lake

Bow Pass

Dolomite Cr

Siffleur River

93

Banff

lodge

Bow Lake

narrows

Mary Lake

Dolomite Pass

Lake Alice

Dolomite Lake

Lake Helen

Lake Katherine

National

Mosquito Lake

Clearwater Pass

Devon Lakes

Pipestone Pass

Helen Cr

Bow

River

Mosquito

Park

Pipestone

Lake Margaret

Turquoise Lake

Hector Lake

Mosquito Pond

Mosquito Cr

North Molar Pass

Moose Lake

Molar Pass

Fish Lakes

Molar Cr

Pipestone Lake

Pipestone River

93

N

0 1 2 3 4
kilometres

to Lake Louise

BOW LAKE

Some excellent backcountry fishing opportunities exist in this area characterized by glaciers and rugged mountains. Highway 93 (Icefields Parkway) runs through the middle of the region paralleling the Bow River and passing close to popular Bow Lake. Farther south, a short spur trail leads down from the Parkway to Hector Lake, beyond which lie Margaret and Turquoise Lakes. The Fish Lakes area including nearby Moose and Pipestone Lakes is a favourite of backpackers as is the nearby Dolomite Pass region which contains Helen, Katherine and Dolomite Lakes. Isabella Lake, located 15 km beyond Dolomite Pass in the Siffleur River drainage, is a seldom visited lake with outstanding potential.

Bow River (PC)
cutthroat trout to 40 cm
brook trout to 40 cm
bull trout to 70 cm (4.0 kg)
whitefish to 35 cm

The section of the Bow River flowing between Bow Lake and the junction of the Trans-Canada Highway and the Icefields Parkway offers fair fishing at best. Fishing starts to pick up after run-off is is complete which usually occurs in late-July. Then, cutthroat and brook trout in the 20-30 cm range as well as whitefish and a few large bull trout can be taken. Although this stretch of the Bow possesses an abundance of fine pools, the fish population is much smaller than farther downstream and many anglers will be disappointed after working likely looking waters for hours on end without positive results.

Bow Lake (PC)
lake trout to 75 cm (5.0 kg)
bull trout to 75 cm (5.0 kg)
cutthroat trout to 50 cm (1.5 kg)
whitefish to 40 cm

A long-time favourite of fishermen due to its roadside location, the appealing blue waters of Bow Lake have consequently suffered a decline in the quality of fishing over the years. However, large lake and bull trout are still present in good numbers and patient fishermen are usually rewarded with fish averaging 35-45 cm in length. Cutthroat trout in the 25-35 cm range along with whitefish are also present in the lake and attract the attention of fly fishermen. Areas around inlet creeks usually produce well as do the "narrows" where Bow Lake tapers down to Bow River width. Num-ti-jah Lodge, its bright red roof visible from the highway, provides lakeside accomodations and canoe rentals.

Mary Lake (PC)
status: unknown

The small tarn hidden behind Crowfoot Mountain and 5 km distant from Bow Lake remains a mystery to most anglers due to its isolated location. Stocked in the past with both cutthroat and brook trout, reproductive success has never been determined and few reliable reports are available.

Hector Lake (PC)
lake trout to 75 cm (5.0 kg)
bull trout to 75 cm (5.0 kg)
splake to 55 cm (2.0 kg)
cutthroat trout to 50 cm (1.5 kg)
brook trout to 50 cm (1.5 kg)
whitefish to 40 cm

Although only 2 km by trail from the Icefields Parkway and noted for its splendid setting, Hector Lake receives relatively little pressure from visitors each summer as access includes a ford of the Bow River. A large lake by mountain standards, Hector is an imposing sight to shore-bound anglers. Its silted waters hold a variety of fish including large lake and bull trout plus splake, cutthroat and brook trout and whitefish. Areas around major inlet creeks and the lake's outlet hold the most potential for anglers. Carrying a boat or canoe down from the highway will aid fishing immensely.

Lake Margaret (PC)
cutthroat trout to 50 cm (1.5 kg)
brook trout to 40 cm

Lake Margaret lies hidden in a quiet side valley south of Hector Lake. Difficult access, including a ford of the Bow River and a tedious hike along the wooded south shore of Hector Lake, keeps the number of anglers to a minimum each season. The lake holds plenty of cutthroat and brook trout in the 25-35 cm range with the cutthroat predominating.

Turquoise Lake (PC)
status: unknown

Set in a rocky basin guarded by high cliffs, the beautifully-coloured waters of Turquoise Lake are seldom seen by fishermen. Those fishermen attempting to reach Turquoise from Lake Margaret are required to register out with the warden service due to the dangerous nature of the climb. The lake was stocked in the past with splake and although it is likely that fish still exist, very few accurate details concerning the lake are available.

Mosquito Pond (PC)

rainbow trout to 30 cm

This small pond just below North Molar Pass on the Fish Lakes trail generally serves as a watering hole for thirsty hikers. It was stocked in the past with rainbow trout which presently maintain their small population through natural reproduction. The few remaining trout average 15-20 cm in length.

Fish Lakes (PC)

cutthroat trout to 55 cm (2.0 kg)

Located 15 km by trail from the Icefields Parkway, the Fish Lakes are set in an open subalpine valley below North Molar Pass and are very popular with backpackers who crowd the Fish Lakes campsite during summer months. Both the larger and smaller of the two Fish Lakes contain cutthroat trout in good numbers in the 25-35 cm range. The water is extremely clear, and casting room is plentiful around both shorelines. Nymphs are productive under most conditions but when there is activity on the water a dry fly is most effective.

Pipestone Lake [Lower Fish Lake] (PC)

cutthroat trout to 50 cm (1.5 kg)

Pipestone Lake, located 2 km southeast of little Fish Lake along an ill-defined trail is an easy half-day excursion for fishermen based at the Fish Lakes. Similar in character to the two Fish Lakes, Pipestone holds cutthroat trout averaging 25-35 cm in length. Casting room is available around most of the lake and tactics used for Fish Lakes apply equally well to Pipestone.

Moose Lake (PC)

cutthroat trout to 45 cm

Moose Lake is located on a bench amid mixed forest and meadow west of the Pipestone River and can be reached by a 5 km trail from the Fish Lakes. Its silty, green waters hold an abundance of cut-throat trout mostly in the 15-25 cm range. Although small, Moose's cutthroat are easy to catch and offer good sport, especially for those fishermen who haven't yet fully mastered their fly casting skills. Ample backcasting room exists around most of the lake.

Pipestone River (PC)

cutthroat trout to 35 cm
bull trout to 50 cm (1.5 kg)

From headwaters in alpine meadows below Pipestone Pass, the Pipe-stone River flows southeast to Lake Louise where it joins the Bow River. The upper reaches of the Pipestone in the Fish Lakes vicinity holds small cutthroat and the occasional bull trout.

Mosquito Lake (PC)

status: unknown

Mosquito Lake, at the headwaters of the Siffleur River, is set in alpine surroundings on the northwest side of Pipestone Pass. A 2 km hike over open ground (map and compass recommended) from the main Pipestone Pass trail leads you to the lake which usually remains frozen until mid-July. Rainbow trout were stocked in the past, but their reproductive success has never been determined since few if any anglers make it in to this isolated lake each year

Siffleur River (PC/AB)

bull trout to 60 cm (2.5 kg)
whitefish to 35 cm

Flowing northwest through a long, wide valley from the lofty heights of Pipestone Pass, the Siffleur River forms long stretches of babbling riffles interspersed with quiet pools. Although the upper Siffleur is attractive to the eye of the fisherman, its fish population is small, being made up of bull trout in the 25-35 cm range along with whitefish. The quality of fishing increases below the Banff National Park boundary which is located approximately 2 km downstream from the confluence of Dolomite Creek with the Siffleur.

Isabella Lake (PC)

rainbow trout to 65 cm (3.0 kg)
bull trout to 60 cm (2.5 kg)

Picturesque Isabella Lake, which has Dolomite Creek as both its inlet and outlet, stands out as the region's hidden treasure in terms of angling. Infrequently visited due to long approach routes, the quality of angling in Isabella should remain high. Its silted waters hold plenty of rainbow trout in the 30-40 cm range with good numbers of even larger ones present as well as the odd bull trout. Although rainbow can be taken from most spots around the lake, the area around the inlet usually proves to be the most productive. Casting room is generally available, and a wet or dry fly works with equal effectiveness.

Dolomite Creek (PC)

bull trout to 50 cm (1.5 kg)
rainbow trout to 40 cm

This fast-flowing glacial stream offers little in the way of fishing. Immediately above and below Isabella Lake the occasional rainbow can be taken while bull trout are present in the creek between Isabella Lake and the Siffleur River.

Lake Alice (PC)
status: devoid of fish

Located in a stark, rocky basin above Dolomite Creek, Lake Alice has never been stocked and contains no fish.

Dolomite Lake (PC)
rainbow trout to 40 cm

Set in the flowered alpine meadows of Dolomite Pass, the striking blue waters of tiny Dolomite Lake are visited by few fishermen. Rainbow trout were stocked in the past and now propogate themselves through natural reproduction. However, fishing is generally poor as the number of trout remaining is very limited.

Lake Katherine (PC)
cutthroat trout to 50 cm (1.5 kg)

Usually frozen until late July, the long, narrow form of Lake Katherine sits amid treeless surroundings just south of Dolomite Pass 8 km by trail from the Icefields Parkway. It's a favourite destination for fishermen since its sparkling blue waters hold plenty of cutthroat trout mostly in the 25-35 cm range. Waters in the vicinity of the several inlet creeks hold trout so long casts are not required. Around most of the lake, the bottom drops off quickly, and a wet fly fished deep here usually attracts some attention. With no tree cover, backcasting room is available from every location.

Lake Helen (PC)
brook trout to 35 cm

Set in an appealing alpine meadow, delicate Lake Helen attracts numerous hikers from the Icefields Parkway 6 km distant. Brook trout in the 20-30 cm range inhabit Helen's translucent green waters in good numbers and can generally be taken within a few metres of shore. If wind and light conditions are ideal, fish can be seen cruising about for food. Backcasting room is available around the entire lake.

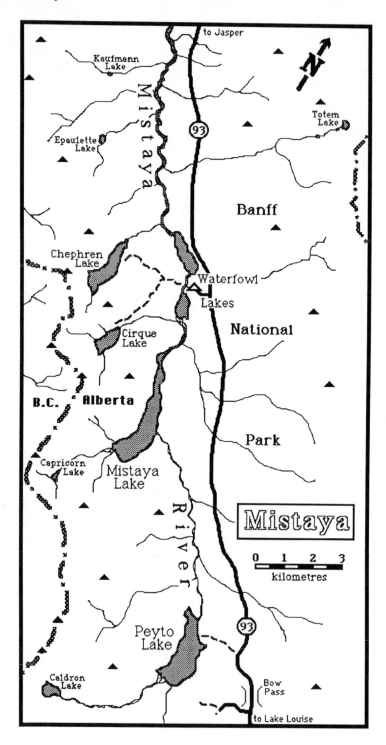

to Jasper

Kaufmann
Lake

Mistaya

93

Epaulette
Lake

Totem
Lake

Banff

Chephren
Lake

Waterfowl
Lakes

Cirque
Lake

National

B.C. **Alberta**

Capricorn
Lake

Mistaya
Lake

Park

River

Mistaya

0 1 2 3
kilometres

Peyto
Lake

93

Caldron
Lake

Bow
Pass

to Lake Louise

MISTAYA

Paralleled by Highway 93 (Icefields Parkway), the Mistaya River flows through the core of the region from Peyto Lake to the North Saskatchewan River. Well-known for the magnificent views of mountains and glaciers from the Parkway, the area also offers fine angling in several lakes notably the Waterfowl Lakes and nearby Cirque, Chephren and Mistaya Lakes which are all popular with fishermen throughout the summer. The spectacular colouration of the region's lakes is attributable to the presence of glacial silt, the much photographed blue waters of Peyto Lake being the best-known example.

Mistaya River (PC)

cutthroat trout to 50 cm (1.5 kg)
rainbow trout to 45 cm
brook trout to 45 cm
bull trout to 70 cm (4.0 kg)
whitefish to 40 cm

The Mistaya River, flowing north from Peyto Lake to the North Saskatchewan River, possesses many long stretches of fishable water most notably in the area between Mistaya and Waterfowl Lakes. Although the angling season is shortened by the long run-off which brings large amounts of silt down from the icefields to the west, early and late season fishing on the Mistaya is generally good. Depending on which section of river is being fished, a variety of species can be caught. Cutthroat are dominant in the upper reaches and bull trout in the lower, while in the stretch from Mistaya Lake through to the Waterfowl Lakes, cutthroat and brook trout make up the greastest percentage with rainbow trout present in fair numbers as well. Whitefish can also be taken from many spots along the river throughout its length. Although a short jaunt through the bush is usually required, the Mistaya is always within a kilometre or two of the Icefields Parkway.

Peyto Lake (PC)

cutthroat trout to 50 cm (1.5 kg)

Although it is admired by thousands of tourists from the viewpoint at Bow Summit each summer, Peyto Lake receives relatively few visitors to its shores. This is no doubt due to the steep 2 km trail which descends from the Icefields Parkway to lake level. Fishing in Peyto's delightful blue waters for cutthroat trout averaging 25-35 cm in length is usually slow during the height of the summer when nearby glaciers deposit large amounts of silt into the lake. As temperatures begins to cool by late summer, however, fishing in Peyto improves with the area around the lake's outlet generally being the most productive.

Caldron Lake (PC)
status: devoid of fish

Caldron Lake lies hidden in an isolated hanging valley west of the Peyto Glacier and 5 km upstream from Peyto Lake. Caldron has never been stocked and contains no fish.

Mistaya Lake (PC)
cutthroat to 55 cm (2.0 kg)
brook trout to 40 cm
rainbow trout to 40 cm

Hidden by heavy forest, Mistaya Lake goes unnoticed by most fishermen, despite the overcrowding that occurs at Waterfowl Lakes only 2 km distant. Cutthroat trout averaging 25-35 cm in length predominate in Mistaya, although the odd brook or rainbow trout occasionally makes their way in from Waterfowl Lakes. It's possible whitefish and bull trout may also be present in limited numbers. As the lake is silted much of the summer, fish tend to keep to the shallower waters in search of food, the waters around the inlet being the most productive if silting isn't too heavy. Backcasting is a problem around much of the shore, although the forest cover does break in spots.

Capricorn Lake (PC)
status: devoid of fish

Set beneath the Capricorn Glacier in a cirque high above Mistaya Lake, Capricorn Lake has never been stocked and is devoid of fish.

Waterfowl Lakes (PC)
cutthroat trout to 50 cm (1.5 kg)
brook trout to 50 cm (1.5 kg)
rainbow trout to 50 cm (1.5 kg)

With a major campground located between the lakes, Upper and Lower Waterfowl are by far the most popular fishing spots in the region. Similar in character to most other major lakes along the Mistaya River, the Waterfowl Lakes are heavily silted which accounts for their appealing blue-green colouration. Cutthroat and brook trout averaging 25-35 cm in length make up the greatest numbers with rainbow present as well. Areas around the inlets and outlets are productive at times, but are generally overfished. Casting room can be found from many locations around both lakes.

Cirque Lake (PC)

brook trout to 50 cm (1.5 kg)
rainbow trout to 45 cm

Cirque Lake lies tucked away in a side valley 5 km by trail from the Waterfowl Lakes campground. Generally silty due to run-off from glaciers at the head of the lake, Cirque fishes better in the late season for fair numbers of brook and rainbow trout averaging 20-30 cm in length. An extensive outlet strewn with deadfall usually holds trout, although many a fly will be lost to snags. The edge of the lake in the vicinity of the outlet is also protected by a wide swath of reed growth.

Chephren Lake (PC)

brook trout to 50 cm (1.5 kg)
cutthroat trout to 50 cm (1.5 kg)
rainbow trout to 50 cm (1.5 kg)

Slightly larger than Cirque Lake, Chephren Lake occupies the next side valley to the north, and offers good fishing for brook, cutthroat and rainbow trout in the 25-35 cm range despite heavy silting much of the year. Fish can usually be taken close to shore, the large amount of sunken deadfall providing excellent cover for the trout. Casting is possible from many locations even though forest cover extends down to the lake around much of the lake.

Epaulette Lake (PC)

status: devoid of fish

Located 2 km west of the Mistaya River through heavy forest, Epaulette Lake is inaccessable to all but the most determined angler. Fortunately, Epaulette has never been stocked and contains no fish.

Kaufmann Lake (PC)

status: devoid of fish

No fish are present in this tiny glacial tarn set beneath the east face of Mt. Sarbach.

Totem Lake (PC)

status: unknown

Set high in a stark, rocky basin on the flank of Mt. Murchison and accessed by an ill-defined, difficult 6 km trail from the Icefields Parkway, Totem Lake is far removed from fishing pressure. Although the lake was stocked in the past with rainbow trout, few confirmed reports about Totem ever make their way out and it is unknown whether any fish remain.

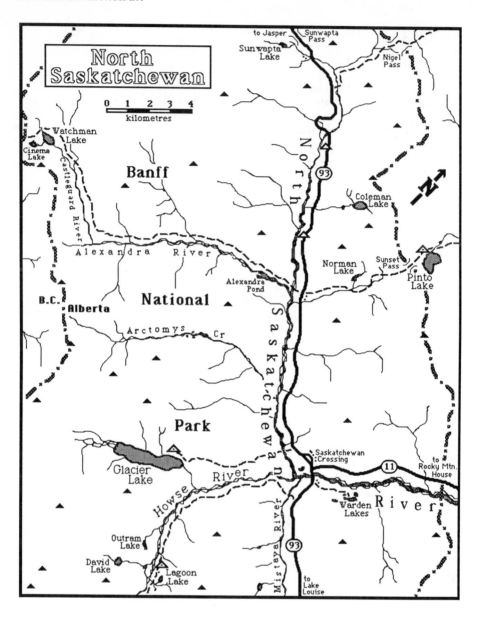

NORTH SASKATCHEWAN

Encompassing the north end of Banff National Park, the region is dominated geographically by the mighty North Saskatchewan River and its tributaries. Highway 93 (Icefields Parkway) provides the main access into the region, and is intersected by Highway 11 (David Thompson Highway) coming in from the east at Saskatchewan River Crossing where limited tourist services of gas, food and lodging are available. Hiking is required to reach the shores of most lakes in the area. The Howse River, a major tributary to the North Saskatchewan, contains David, Outram, Lagoon and Glacier Lakes within its watershed while farther north the Alexandra River and Arctomys Creek flow west to join the North Saskatchewan. Warden Lakes, a popular fishing spot, is located 2 km by trail east of the Saskatchewan Crossing Warden Station. Further north, Pinto Lake is another favourite destination. Just south of the Banff-Jasper Parks boundary at Sunwapta Pass, Sunwapta Lake lies hidden in the forest a short distance west of the highway.

North Saskatchewan River (PC)
bull trout to 70 cm (4.0 kg)
lake trout to 65 cm (3.0 kg)
whitefish to 50 cm (1.5 kg)
brook trout to 40 cm
rainbow trout to 40 cm

Flowing from its source at Saskatchewan Glacier and joined by a number of other glacial rivers, the North Saskatchewan River is heavily silted much of the year, only clearing in late summer. During run-off, fishing is very slow and usually confined to waters around clearer flowing tributary streams. When run-off is finally complete, fishing improves along the entire lenth of the river with large bull and lake trout along with whitefish making up the vast majority of fish in the river, although brook and rainbow trout are also caught on occasion. Fishing is usually productive near the mouths of the Mistaya, Howse and Alexandra Rivers.

Warden Lakes (PC)
rainbow trout to 50 cm (1.5 kg)
cutthroat trout to 45 cm

The two Warden Lakes are located on a bench south of the Saskatchewan River 2 km east of the Icefields Parkway by trail. The Lower Lake was stocked in the past with both rainbow and brook trout which failed to reproduce and the lake is now devoid of fish. Subject to winter kill, the larger Upper Lake has been stocked with rainbow, cutthroat, brook and splake, of which it is likely that only rainbow and cutthroat are now present in small numbers.

Howse River (PC)

bull trout to 65 cm (3.0 kg)
lake trout to 60 cm (2.5 kg)
whitefish to 40 cm

The Howse River flows from headwaters below historic Howse Pass to its junction with the North Saskatchewan River just west of Saskatchewan River Crossing. Flowing through a broad valley over its final 10 km, the Howse River is characterized by wide gravel flats with extensive braiding where you can fish for bull trout in the 30-40 cm range, whitefish and the occasional lake trout. Generally, fishing is very slow in the Howse, picking up somewhat in late summer and early fall when water levels recede and the river clears. A major horse trail leading to Howse Pass parallels the river for its entire length.

Lagoon Lake (PC)

bull trout to 65 cm (3.0 kg)

Almost 20 km by trail from the Icefields Parkway, Lagoon Lake lies in marshy meadows east of the Howse River near a backcountry campground and warden's cabin. Lagoon was stocked in the past with rainbow trout which apparently failed to reproduce. At present, the lake contains bull trout and possibly a few whitefish which have made their way in from the Howse River.

David Lake (PC)

rainbow trout to 35 cm

Set in a cirque directly beneath the north face of Mt. David, David Lake is well protected by a major ford of the Howse River and by steep and difficult terrain over its final 2 km of approach. Very few visitors reach the lake each year. Due to lack of information, it is has never been determined whether the rainbow trout stocked a number of years ago still exist.

Outram Lake (PC)

bull trout to 60 cm (3.5 kg)
whitefish to 35 cm
rainbow trout to 35 cm

A ford of the Howse River (passable for hikers by late summer) is required in order to reach Outram Lake's location on a bench above the west bank of the river. The lake holds bull trout and whitefish in good numbers and rainbow trout are reported to be present in fair numbers as well. Due to its lengthy and difficult access, Outram offers the promise of solitude.

Glacier Lake (PC)

lake trout to 80 cm (7.0 kg)
bull trout to 70 cm (4.5 kg)
whitefish to 50 cm (1.5 kg)

The largest lake in the region, Glacier Lake has never gained a favourable reputation for fishing due to run-off from the nearby Lyell Glacier which ensures the water is heavily silted all year long. When the waters clear in the late seson, the area around the outlet is worth a look. Bait and spin fishermen will have the best success in Glacier which holds some lake and bull trout of gigantic proportions as well as whitefish in fair numbers. Although fish can be taken from most locations along the shore, the sheer size of the lake will intimidate most fishermen.

Arctomys Creek (PC)

bull trout to 50 cm (1.5 kg)
whitefish to 35 cm

Born in the Lyell Glacier high among the peaks of the continental divide, Arctomys Creek possesses the same characteristics as other major rivers of the region. It runs very silty most of the year, only clearing up in late summer when a limited population of bull trout and whitefish can be caught in its lower reaches. Access is difficult, requiring either a near impossible ford of the North Saskatchewan River or a long ill-defined approach from the Glacier Lake trail via the west bank of the North Saskatchewan River.

Norman Lake (PC)

brook trout to 35 cm

Norman Lake, 5 km along the Sunset Pass trail from the Icefields Parkway, is bypassed by most hikers and fishermen on their way to the more renowned waters of Pinto Lake. Set in marshy and mosquito-infested meadows below Sunset Pass, the lake holds a small population of brook trout averaging 20-30 cm in length. Casting room is plentiful around the shoreline although wet feet are a definite possibility.

Pinto Lake (AB)

bull trout to 65 cm (3.5 kg)

Located on the north side of Sunset Pass just beyond the Banff National Park Boundary, Pinto Lake is very popular with outfitters and backpackers who generally pack the campground every weekend during the summer. A 14 km trail from the Icefields Parkway is the usual route of approach, although outfitters tend to favour the longer access up the Cline River from the David Thompson Highway. The lake holds plenty of good-sized bull trout which are more susceptible to bait and spin fishermen than fly fishermen.

Alexandra Pond (PC)

lake trout to 60 cm (3.0 kg.)
bull trout to 60 cm (3.0 kg.)
whitefish to 40 cm

Alexandra Pond, merely a widening of the Alexandra River, is located less than a kilometre upstream from the Alexandra's confluence with the North Saskatchewan River. Reached by a trail which bridges the North Saskatchewan, Alexandra Pond is readily accessible, but receives little fishing pressure; the early season is too silty for angling, and even after run-off is over, fishing is fairly slow for large lake, bull trout and whitefish.

Alexandra River (PC)

bull trout to 55 cm (2.0 kg)
lake trout to 55 cm (2.0 kg)
whitefish to 35 cm

A major tributary of the North Saskatchewan River, the Alexandra River offers poor to fair fishing over its entire length. The lower reaches just above and below Alexandra Pond are the most productive with whitefish, lake and bull trout present in limited numbers.

Castleguard River (PC)

bull trout to 50 cm (1.5 kg)
whitefish to 30 cm

A tributary of the upper Alexandra, the Castleguard River presents very few opportunities for anglers since only a few bull trout and whitefish are present.

Watchman Lake (PC)

cutthroat trout to 40 cm

Two days of hiking from the Icefields Parkway are required to reach Watchman Lake, an attractive body of water set in subalpine forest 2 km northwest of seldom-visited Thompson Pass. Cutthroat trout averaging 20-30 cm in length are present in the lake.

Cinema Lake (PC)

status: devoid of fish

Guarding the northwest entrance to Thompson Pass, Cinema Lake has never been stocked and contains no fish.

Coleman Lake (PC)
status: devoid of fish

Defended by a line of cliffs paralleling the Icefields Parkway, Coleman Lake is reached by only the most enterprising of individuals. It has never been stocked and no fish are present in its waters.

Sunwapta Lake (PC)
cutthroat trout to 35 cm
brook trout to 35 cm

Although it lies less than a kilometre from the busy Icefields Parkway, the pretty green waters of Sunwapta Lake receive very little attention from hikers or fishermen who are perhaps unaware of a series of intermittent game trails which lead in short order from the Sunwapta Pass parking area to the shoreline. The lake's silted waters hold small cutthroat and brook trout and may also contain the odd splake, remnant of past plantings. Backcasting room is available from most locations along the shoreline.

How long a fish grows depends on how long you listen to the fisherman.

BRAZEAU

The Brazeau River drainage constitutes the major portion of this region located in the remote southeast corner of Jasper National Park. Extended backpacking trips are required to reach most potential fishing spots in the district which include Brazeau Lake, the Brazeau River and its major tributaries, the Southesk and Cairn Rivers. To the southeast, outside the Jasper National Park boundary, Job and Obstruction Lakes, both of which can be reached via extended trails from Highway 11 (David Thompson Highway), are noted for their fine cutthroat fishing.

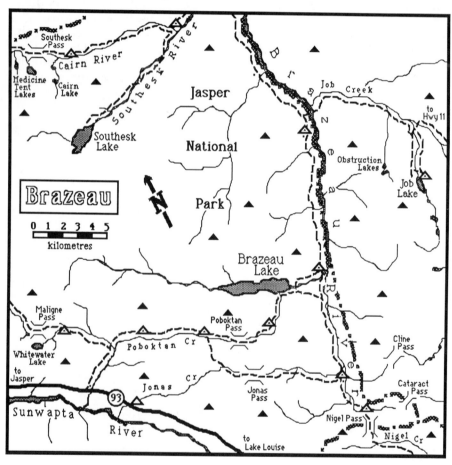

Brazeau River (PC/AB)

bull trout to 65 cm (4.0 kg)
whitefish to 45 cm

Paralleled by trails over its entire length, this major tributary of the North Saskatchewan River has never been noted for outstanding fishing in its upper reaches. Very silted much of the summer, the Brazeau fishes best in late August and early September when bull trout and whitefish and the occasional cutthroat or rainbow can be taken. Where the Brazeau River forms the boundary of Jasper National Park, national park fishing regulations are in effect.

Brazeau Lake (PC)

rainbow trout to 70 cm (4.0 kg)
bull trout to 75 cm (5.0 kg)

Set in a deep valley west of the Brazeau River, majestic Brazeau Lake is a remote 30 km by trail away from the Icefields Parkway and consequently receives little attention from fishermen. Its silted waters contain both rainbow and bull trout and although the fish are not overly plentiful, their size which averages 35-45 cm in length makes up for their numbers. A wet fly fished deep is often effective in Brazeau , the area around the outlet being particularly productive.

Job Lake [Wilson Lake, Blue Lake] (AB)

cutthroat trout to 65 cm (3.0 kg)

A lake of exceptional quality in terms of both beauty and fishing, Job Lake has long been popular with outfitters despite the long 40 km trail from the David Thompson Highway and the even longer 50+ km approach from the Icefields Parkway. Good numbers of cutthroat trout averaging 30-40 cm in length are Job's main attraction together with the lake's beautiful setting of mixed forest and meadow which affords plenty of room for backcasting.

Obstruction Lakes (AB)

cutthroat trout to 40 cm

The tiny Obstruction Lakes, located 4 km southwest of Job Creek by ill-defined trail, receive little attention from anglers each season. Set near treeline, they hold cutthroat trout in the 20-30 cm range and have an abundance of backcasting room.

Southesk River (PC)
bull trout to 55 cm (2.0 kg)
whitefish to 35 cm

Flowing east from headwaters in Southesk Lake, the Southesk River joins the Brazeau River at the Jasper National Park boundary. Seldom fished due to lengthy access routes, the river holds limited numbers of bull trout and whitefish.

Southesk Lake (PC)
bull trout to 60 cm (2.5 kg)

Poor trails and restricted access limit travel into Southesk Lake which is situated in one of the most remote corners of Jasper National Park. Bull trout are present in Southesk, although not in substantial numbers.

Cairn River (PC)
bull trout to 40 cm

A tributary to the Southesk River, Cairn River receives virtually no angling pressure. Bull trout are present in small numbers in the river which begins on the east side of Southesk Pass.

Cairn Lake (PC)
status: devoid of fish

The headwaters of the Cairn River, Cairn Lake has never been stocked and is reported to be devoid of fish.

Medicine Tent Lakes (PC)
status: devoid of fish

Set in alpine terrain on the west side of Southesk Pass, the Medicine Tent Lakes are the source of the Medicine Tent River which flows northwest to join the Rocky River. The lakes have never been stocked and contain no fish.

Whitewater Lake (PC)
status: devoid of fish

The largest of the lakes in the immediate Maligne Pass vicinity has never been stocked and is devoid of fish.

ATHABASCA

Centered on the upper Athabasca River drainage, this district encompasses much of the southwest corner of Jasper National Park. Highway 93 (Icefields Parkway) and to a lesser extent Highway 93A run through the centre of the region, paralleling the Athabasca River. Most of the region's better fishing opportunities are found within a few kilometres of these highways and include Buck, Osprey, Honeymoon, Leach, Mile 16 1/2, Horseshoe, Edwards, Colfair, Wabasso Lakes and the Valley of the Five Lakes, in addition to the Athabasca and Sunwapta Rivers. Slightly longer and more strenuous routes lead hikers to Moab, Geraldine, Fryatt, Dragon and Fortress Lakes.

Sunwapta River (PC)
bull trout to 70 cm (4.0 kg)
rainbow trout to 50 cm (1.5 kg)
brook trout to 45 cm
whitefish to 45 cm

Flowing northwest from the Banff-Jasper Boundary at Sunwapta Pass, the Sunwapta River joins the Athabasca River 3 km downstream from Sunwapta Falls. Readily accessible from the Icefields Parkway, the Sunwapta offers good fishing below the falls for bull, rainbow and brook trout, particularly near the river's confluence with the Athabasca. Bull trout predominate above the falls where angling is fair at best. With its source high among the glaciers of the continental divide, the Sunwapta runs silty for much of the year, clearing only late in the summer.

Athabasca River [upper] (PC)
bull trout to 80 cm (7.0 kg)
rainbow trout to 50 cm (1.5 kg)
brook trout to 50 cm (1.5 kg)
whitefish to 50 cm (1.5 kg)

Jasper National Park's major river flows from the Columbia Icefield north to Jasper, then swings east and exits the park, eventually turning north en route to the Arctic Ocean. South of Jasper, the Icefields Parkway follows the course of the upper Athabasca closely and provides easy access. Although it is very turbulent and muddy for much of the summer, the river does present some reasonable fishing opportunities in the late season, especially in the waters below Athabasca Falls where whitefish, bull, rainbow and brook trout can all be caught in fair numbers. Areas around the Athabasca's confluence with both major and minor tributaries generally hold trout, especially when the main river is muddy.

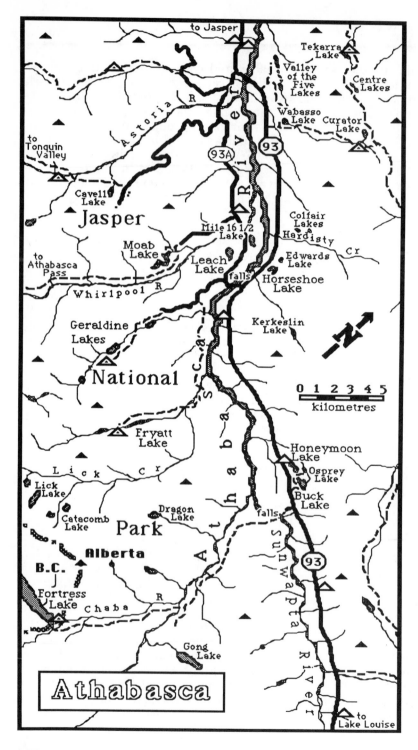

Athabasca

Gong Lake (PC)

status: devoid of trout

This large glacial lake near the headwaters of the Athabasca River has never been stocked and contains no fish.

Dragon Lake (PC)

brook trout to 40 cm

Protected by a major ford of the Athabasca River and by poorly defined access routes, Dragon Lake lies well beyond the grasp of most anglers. The lake was stocked in the past with brook trout and recent reports indicate that some trout still exist although their numbers are limited.

Fortress Lake (BC)

lake trout to 90 cm (10 kg)
bull trout to 80 cm (7.0 kg)
brook trout to 60 cm (2.5 kg)

A long 25 km access route that includes a major ford of the Chaba River leads to Fortress Lake, a 10-km long body of water situated just west of the Alberta-B.C. boundary at Fortress Pass. The lake, which holds large bull, lake and brook trout has long been popular among fly-in fishermen and outfitters' parties but has been overlooked by most hikers. Fortress' remote location ensures that the quality of fishing will remain high for many years to come.

Buck Lake (PC)

brook trout to 50 cm (1.5 kg)
rainbow trout to 50 cm (1.5 kg)

Surrrounded by heavy forest, Buck Lake sits less than a kilometre by trail from the Icefields Parkway. Buck holds both rainbow and brook trout averaging 25-35 cm in length, but since the lake's ability to hold trout has generally been dependent on regular stockings, the quality of fishing has declined somewhat in recent years. Shoreline vegetation around the entire lake will hinder fly fishermen, although adept roll casters can overcome most problems.

Osprey Lake (PC)

rainbow trout to 50 cm (1.5 kg)

This small reed-fringed lake just north of Buck and Honeymoon Lakes is only a short 15 minute walk away from the Icefields Parkway. Osprey's shallow waters hold rainbow trout averaging 25-35 cm in length and possibly the odd brook or bull trout as well. Due to the nature of the shoreline, casting is generally difficult and fly fishermen are advised to work the waters around the lake's outlet creek.

Honeymoon Lake (PC)

rainbow trout to 60 cm (2.5 kg)

Situated immediately east of the Icefields Parkway, Honeymoon Lake is a popular fishing spot for anglers who choose not to travel far beyond the safety of the highway. Rainbow trout averaging 25-35 cm in length inhabit Honeymoon's waters in fair numbers. However, reports indicate that the quality of fishing has declined somewhat in the past few years and the lake's ability to hold fish is somewhat in question.

Lick Lake, Catacomb Lake (PC)

status: devoid of fish

Two glacial lakes set high among the peaks of the continental divide at the head of Lick Creek, a minor tributary of the Athabasca River, have never been stocked and contain no fish.

Fryatt Lake (PC)

rainbow trout to 50 cm (1.5 kg)

Pinched in a narrow valley between Brussels Peak and Mt. Fryatt, Fryatt Lake is reached after a tiring 17 km hike-in from the Geraldine Lakes Fire Road. While the upper Fryatt Creek valley is a favourite haunt of climbers, fishermen are more likely to be enticed by Fryatt Lake and its population of rainbow trout. The lake is almost completely encircled by heavy timber which will cause problems for most fly fishermen.

Geraldine Lakes (PC)

rainbow trout to 55 cm (2.0 kg)
brook trout to 50 cm (1.5 kg)

Five exquisite lakes strung like pearls in a series of basins separated by short headwalls are one of the region's more popular day hikes. The first and most popular lake lies less than 2 km from the trailhead on the Geraldine Lakes Fire Road, while the upper or fifth lake lies another 6 km distant. All five lakes contain good numbers of both rainbow and brook trout ranging from 25-40 cm in length which can often be sighted well out into the clear waters. Sunken deadfall provides cover in the waters near shore, particularly in the first lake, and fishermen are advised to work these areas.

Leach Lake (PC)
rainbow trout to 65 cm (3.0 kg)

Located alongside Highway 93A, Leach Lake has gained a reputation over the years of harbouring some large fish. Rainbow trout in the 30-40 cm range are present in good numbers, their numbers maintained through regular stocking. Shallows extending far out into the lake make fishing from shore a difficult proposition. During low light conditions when many of the larger fish make their way into the shallows to feed, patient fly fishermen can be rewarded with rainbows of 60 cm or more. From a boat, which is available through rental arrangements made at sporting goods stores in Jasper, working the distinct margin separating the shallow water from the deep is usually very effective.

Mile 16 1/2 Lake J-B [Jasper-Banff]
rainbow trout to 60 cm (2.5 kg)
brook trout to 55 cm (2.0 kg)

Situated less than a kilometre north of Leach Lake on the opposite side of Highway 93A, Mile 16 1/2 Lake draws high praise from many anglers. A shallow lake similar in character to Leach, Mile 16 1/2 contains large rainbow and brook trout averaging 30-40 cm in length best fished from boats which are available for rent through arrangements made with sporting goods stores in Jasper. Consistent with other lakes of this nature, the zone between the shallow and deep waters usually holds fish. Slowly trolling a wet fly through the deeper water has also proven effective.

Moab Lake (PC)
lake trout to 75 cm (5.0 kg)
rainbow trout to 50 cm (1.5 kg)
grayling to 35 cm

A short 1 km hike at the end of a 7 km-long fire road off Highway 93A leads to the shores of pretty Moab Lake. Very popular with anglers, Moab's clear waters hold rainbow trout along with large lake trout and a limited number of grayling. Although the lake's distinctive shape allows for fishing from along much of the shoreline, a boat is strongly recommended and is available for rent on Moab through prior arrangements made with one of Jasper's sporting goods stores. Although bait and spin fishermen generally have greater success with lakers than fly fishermen, trolling a streamer deep behind a slow moving boat can be productive at times. Be sure to check fishing regulations as the outlet stream is permanently closed to angling as is the area of Moab Lake around the outlet.

Whirlpool River (PC)
bull trout to 60 cm (2.5 kg)
rainbow trout to 40 cm
whitefish to 40 cm

Paralleled for its entire distance by the historic Athabasca Pass trail, the Whirlpool River receives little pressure from fishermen above the area of its confluence with the Athabasca River. Small bull trout predominate in the upper reaches, while bull and rainbow trout along with whitefish are found in fair numbers in the lower river. Although heavily fished, the waters near the Whirlpool's confluence with the Athabasca are usually productive.

Kerkeslin Lake (PC)
status: unknown

Located high in an isolated valley north of Mt. Kerkeslin, the pristine waters of Kerkeslin Lake remain virtually untouched. Reliable reports seldom make their way out, but it is likely that Kerkeslin Lake holds a limited population of bull trout which have worked their way in over a period of time from the Athabasca River.

Horseshoe Lake (PC)
rainbow trout to 60 cm (2.5 kg)

Appropriately-shaped Horseshoe Lake sits alongside the Icefields Parkway 20 km south of Jasper. Although Horseshoe's ability to sustain trout over a period of years has long been questioned, its sparkling blue waters presently hold rainbow trout in fair numbers averaging 25-35 cm in length . The lake is ringed by loose rock which will present problems for those anglers with poor backcasts.

Edwards Lake (PC)
rainbow trout to 45 cm

Located less than a kilometre north of Horseshoe Lake, Edwards Lake is generally overlooked by the area's anglers. The lake holds rainbow trout in the 25-35 cm range which can be taken from most locations around the lake.

Colfair Lakes (PC)
rainbow trout to 50 cm (1.5 kg)

Two small lakes set in the wooded hills north of Hardisty Creek offer some really fine fly fishing to those who reach their shores. Although a number of ill-defined trails connect the Colfairs to the Icefields Parkway 2 km distant, finding a trailhead may be a problem. Best bet is to carry a map and compass. Rainbow trout in the 25-40 cm range are plentiful and tend to be particularly succeptible to the fly. Although it's doubtful, a few brook trout, remnants of previous plantings, may still exist in the lower lake.

Curator Lake, Tekarra Lake, Centre Lakes (PC)
status: devoid of fish

Companions to hikers on the Skyline Trail from Maligne Lake to Jasper, Curator, Tekarra and Centre Lakes have never been stocked and contain no fish.

Wabasso Lake (PC)
rainbow trout to 55 cm (2.0 kg)
brook trout to 45 cm

The quiet waters of Wabasso Lake lie less than 3 km by trail from the busy Icefields Parkway. A popular destination for family hikes, Wabasso also holds promise for fishermen since it contains both rainbow and brook trout in good numbers. Casting is somewhat restricted around much of the shoreline due to heavy reed growth and the proximity of the forest cover.

Valley of the Five Lakes (PC)
rainbow trout to 80 cm (7.0 kg)
brook trout to 60 cm (2.5 kg)

Set in an open valley 2 km east of the Icefields Parkway, the Valley of the Five Lakes is a favourite spot with local anglers. All five interconncted lakes hold rainbow trout, which predominate, as well as a fair number of brook trout. Some enormous rainbow trout in the 5-6 kg range having been taken from these lakes in the past. Nowadays, the First and Fifth Lakes which are the largest hold the most promise for fishermen . As all of the lakes are fairly narrow, reaching the fish holding waters is usually not a major problem, although forest cover will hamper backcasts in spots. Boats are available on the First and Fifth Lakes, and arrangements for their rental can be made in sporting goods stores in Jasper.

TONQUIN

One of Jasper National Park's most popular backcountry destinations, beautiful Tonquin Valley, ranks favourably with any area in the Rockies in terms of scenery. Two 20 km-long trails, one along the Astoria River and the other via Portal and Maccarib Creeks lead into the valley where overnight visitors are able to choose from several fine backcountry campsites as well as permanent outfitters camps and an Alpine Club of Canada hut at Outpost Lake. The centerpiece of the region, Amethyst Lake, is set beneath the spectacular castellate summits of the Ramparts and is truly one of the jewels of the Canadian Rockies; its sparkling waters home to large rainbow and brook trout. Fortunately, its location is remote enough to ensure the quality of fishing remains high. Although many of the other waters in the Tonquin area are devoid of fish, Moat Lake and the Astoria River hold the promise of fine fishing.

Amethyst Lakes (PC)

rainbow trout to 80 cm (5.0 kg)
brook trout to 60 cm (2.5 kg)

Fortunately for anglers, fishing in Amethyst Lakes rivals the area's scenic spendour and large rainbow and brook trout averaging 35-50 cm in length can be taken in good numbers all summer long. As the lakes are sizable, fishing from shore often seems a little intimidating. However, the waters are very clear, and since trout are always cruising the shallows in search of food, patient shore-bound fishermen are often rewarded. For those anglers having little success from shore, arrangements can generally be made with one of the outfitter's camps to rent a boat. Fishing from a boat generally increases fishing potential manyfold, and just trolling a wet fly while admiring the scenery will usually produce results. The stretch of the Astoria River between its outlet and a point 400 m downstream is permanently closed to angling as are areas of the lakes around the outlet and all inlet creeks. Check regulations before you go.

Moat Lake (PC)

rainbow trout to 50 cm (1.5 kg)

Moat Lake, reached by a short 2 km side trail, is situated northwest of Amethyst Lakes amid marshy meadows which contribute to the area's large insect population. It holds plenty of rainbow trout averaging 25-35 cm in length which actively feed on the surface. Backcasting room is adequate around most of the shoreline, and the lake's long, narrow shape is favourable to fly fishing since a large portion of the fishable water can be reached by shore-bound fishermen. Boats are available for rent through arrangements with outfitters on Amethyst Lakes.

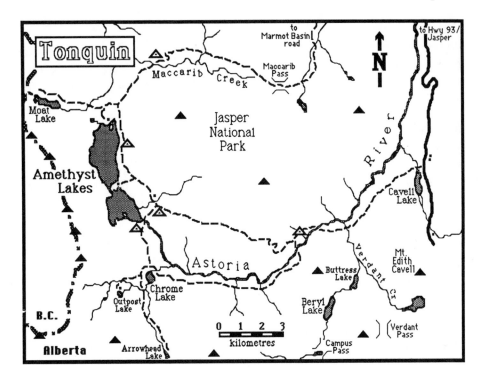

Astoria River (PC)

rainbow trout to 40 cm
bull trout to 60 cm (2.5 kg)
brook trout to 40 cm

Flowing from the Amethyst Lakes to the Athabasca River, the turbulent Astoria River possesses several fine stretches of fishable water. Most fishing activity takes place in the area of the confluence with the Athabasca and in the upper reaches within 10 km of Amethyst Lakes where rainbow trout in the 20-30 cm range predominate over bull and brook trout. Near the Athabasca where bull trout tend to predominate, the odd whitefish may also be taken.

Chrome Lake (PC)

rainbow trout to 40 cm

Located 2 km south of Amethyst Lakes by trail and surrounded by a pleasant combination of forest and meadow, Chrome holds a small population of rainbow trout averaging 25-30 cm in length but is generally overlooked by anglers intent of fishing the more renowned waters of Amethyst. Casting is possible from various spots where meadows make their way down to the shoreline. Because Chrome is often very silty due to glacial runoff, fish are generally taken in the shallower waters close to shore.

Outpost Lake (PC)
status: devoid of fish

The Alpine Club of Canada's Waites-Gibson Hut is located on the shores of tiny Outpost Lake which has never been stocked and contains no fish.

Arrowhead Lake (PC)
status: devoid of fish

Three kilometres south of Chrome Lake in Eremite Valley, appropriately-shaped Arrowhead Lake lies at the base of Eremite Glacier. Arrowhead has never been stocked and is too silted for fish to survive.

Buttress Lake/Beryl Lake (PC)
status: doubtful

Neither Buttress nor Beryl Lake has ever been stocked and their isolated location in a remote valley off Verdant Creek make it highly improbable that they contain any fish.

Cavell Lake (PC)
brook trout to 40 cm
cutthroat trout to 40 cm

Most famous as a foreground in photographs of Mt. Edith Cavell, the emerald green waters of charming Cavell Lake are seldom fished. Recent reports indicate relatively poor fishing for cutthroat and brook trout in the 25-35 cm range and in addition casting is difficult along much of the shore due to heavy forest cover, although there are a few tolerable locations near the lake's outlet.

Many fishermen catch their fish by the tale.

JASPER

Set in and around the townsite of Jasper, this popular region offers many excellent fishing opportunities where hiking ability is of no concern as roads or short trails reach virtually every lake and river. Most lakes receive regular stocking to maintain populations. Lac Beauvert, Edith, Annette and Trefoil Lakes are located on the east side of the Athabasca River in the vicinity of Jasper Park Lodge. On the wooded bench west of Jasper, Pyramid and Patricia Lakes attract plenty of attention from anglers throughout the summer. In the same area, a series of hiking trails radiating out from Jasper townsite and from the Pyramid Lake Road lead to Riley, Mina, Marjorie, Hibernia, Caledonia, Minnow, High and Saturday Night Lakes. The Miette River paralleling Highway 16 (Yellowhead Highway) as it heads west from Jasper to the B.C.-Alberta boundary offers good late summer fishing. Also from Highway 16, a short trail leads to Dorothy, Christine, Iris and Virl Lakes, while seldom-visited Cutt and Golden Lakes are located on a side trail from upper Minaga Creek.

Edith Lake (PC)
rainbow trout to 80 cm (6.0 kg)
brook trout to 60 cm (2.5 kg)

Located just east of the Maligne Lake Road some 6 km from Jasper townsite, the translucent blue waters of Edith Lake hold some very large rainbow trout indeed, although most taken are in the 25-40 cm range. Brook trout are also present in limited numbers. As Edith is a large lake which drops off sharply in most locations, fishing is better from boats which are available for rent through arrangements made with sporting goods stores in Jasper. Trolling a fly slowly behind a boat is generally productive, especially along the zone around the many deep holes in Edith. On occasion, when there is insect activity on the surface, a dry fly can be particularly effective.

Annette Lake (PC)
brook trout to 55 cm (2.0 kg)
rainbow trout to 60 cm (2.5 kg)

This very pretty lake set amid quiet woods east of the Jasper Park Lodge Road attracts plenty of picnickers as well as anglers. Extremely clear waters hold brook and rainbow trout in good numbers averaging 25-40 cm in length. Boats can be rented through arrangements made in one of Jasper's sporting goods stores, a move which greatly enhances the quality of fishing. Trolling a fly while admiring the scenery is a superb way to get the most out of Annette. For those fishermen determined to fish from shore, the eastern side of the lake where the lake bottom drops off very quickly holds the best opportunities.

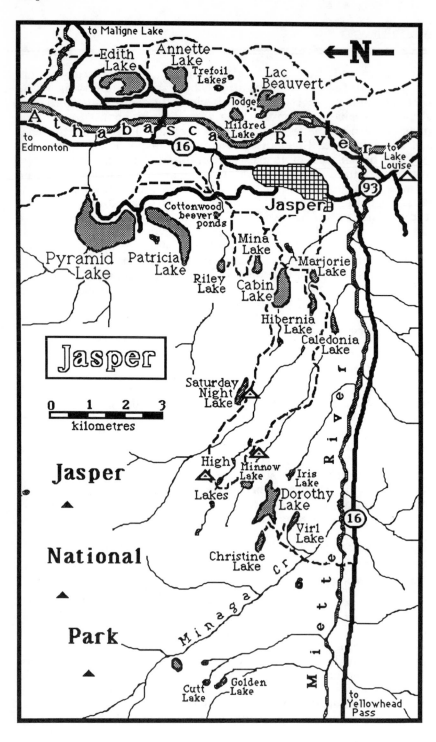

Trefoil Lakes (PC)

rainbow trout to 40 cm
brook trout to 40 cm

In the past, the fishing potential of three small lakes on the grounds of Jasper Park Lodge has been directly related to artificial stocking. The two larger lakes (Trefoil #1 and #2), still contain limited populations of rainbow trout and at last report still hold remnants of a brook trout population. The most westerly lake (Trefoil #3) is apparently devoid of fish at present. Although forest cover is sparse around the lakes, a steep shoreline will cause problems with most backcasts.

Mildred Lake (PC)

status: devoid of fish

This over-sized duck pond on the west side of the Jasper Park Lodge Road was stocked in the past, but the fish failed to reproduce.

Lac Beauvert (PC)

rainbow trout to 60 cm (2.5 kg)
brook trout to 55 cm (2.0 kg)

The sparkling green waters of Lac Beauvert, the scenic centerpiece of the Jasper Park Lodge grounds, have never been renowned for a high quality of fishing. Although a variety of fish have been stocked in the past, only rainbow and brook trout are still present in limited numbers.

Pyramid Lake (PC)

lake trout to 80 cm (6.0 kg)
rainbow trout to 55 cm (2.0 kg)
brook trout to 50 cm (1.5 kg)
splake to 60 cm (2.5 kg)
whitefish to 55 cm (1.5 kg)

Located six kilometres from Jasper by road, the region's most popular fishing spot is busy with anglers from opening to closing day. Although both rainbow and brook trout are plentiful, it's the large lake trout which attract the attention of most fishermen. In the early season, lake trout and splake can be taken in the shallower waters, but soon migrate to the colder waters as soon as the lake begins to warm. Although bait and spin fishermen are generally more successful in taking lakers than fly fishermen, trolling a streamer behind a boat can be very effective in the first weeks after the season opens. By mid-summer, rainbow and brook trout become the standard fare with lake trout caught on occasion by those anglers fishing Pyramid's very depths. Rental boats are available at the lake.

Patricia Lake (PC)
rainbow trout to 75 cm (5.0 kg)

Situated alongside the Pyramid Lake Road 5 km from Jasper, the striking blue waters of Patricia Lake are often overlooked by fishermen intent on fishing Pyramid, yet Patricia holds good numbers of rainbow trout with some very large individuals present and possibly the odd brook trout as well, remnants of past stockings. Fishing from shore is generally restricted due to tree cover, except in the area of the road where cars replace trees as the major hazard. Fortunately, boats are available for rent through Jasper sporting goods stores. Although trolling a wet fly is an effective method of fishing on Patricia, dry fly fishing often produces excellent results during calm evenings.

Cottonwood beaver ponds (PC)
rainbow trout to 35 cm
brook trout to 35 cm

A series of beaver ponds extending from the west side of the Pyramid Lake Road 3 km from Jasper hold both rainbow and brook trout in the 20-30 cm range. The marshy setting of the ponds complete with heavy vegetation growth makes access difficult and casting even more difficult.

Riley Lake (PC)
rainbow trout to 40 cm

A small reed-encircled lake 3 km by trail from the Pyramid Lake Road, Riley offers good fishing for rainbow trout averaging 25-35 cm in length. With casting from shore generally inhibited by vegetation and shallows extending out from shore around much of the lake, it's best to make arrangements with one of Jasper's sporting goods stores to rent a boat.

Mina Lake (PC)
rainbow trout to 55 cm (2.0 kg)
brook trout to 50 cm (1.5 kg)

Located on the Mina-Riley loop trail 3 km from the Pyramid Lake Road, Mina Lake is typical of many of the smaller lakes on the bench west of Jasper. Both rainbow (predominant) and brook trout are present in the lake, but backcasting is difficult from much of the shoreline because of heavy tree cover and long casts are usually required to reach fish-holding waters. Low light periods when fish tend to feed in the shallows is generally the best time to fish.

Cabin Lake

rainbow trout
status: closed

Cabin Lake, the source of Jasper's water supply, is permanently closed to angling.

Marjorie Lake (PC)

rainbow trout to 65 cm (3.0 kg)
brook trout to 50 cm (1.5 kg)

Marjorie Lake, a popular fishing destination, is an easy 15-20 minute walk from Jasper townsite along the Saturday Night loop. Its waters hold both rainbow and brook trout in good numbers with most fish taken averaging 25-35 cm in length. Boats are available through rental arrangements made with one of Jasper's sporting goods stores. If you haven't yet mastered roll casting, fishing from shore is generally a problem on account of either dense forest cover or steep banks.

Hibernia Lake (PC)

rainbow trout to 55 cm (2.0 kg)

Located on a spur trail less than a kilometre off the main Saturday Night loop, Hibernia attracts plenty of fishermen after rainbow trout in the 25-35 cm range which inhabit the lake in good numbers. Rental boats are available through arrangements made with sporting goods stores in Jasper. Although fishing from shore can also be productive, roll casting ability is important due to heavy woods all around the lake.

Caledonia Lake (PC)

rainbow trout to 55 cm (2.0 kg)
brook trout to 50 cm (1.5 kg)

Caledonia Lake is set on a forested bench 2 km by trail beyond Marjorie Lake and 5 km from Jasper. Both rainbow and brook trout are present with rainbow the dominant species. Reeds and extended shallows around much of Caledonia's shoreline make fly fishing from shore a difficult proposition, but fortunately, boats are available at the lake and can be rented through Jasper's sporting goods stores. Tactics on Caledonia range from trolling a wet fly to working a dry fly when insects are hatching.

Minnow Lake (PC)

rainbow trout to 50 cm (1.5 kg)
brook trout to 50 cm (1.5 kg)

Situated near the upper end of the Saturday Night loop, Minnow Lake receives much less attention from anglers than the more accessible waters of Marjorie, Hibernia and Caledonia. Rainbow and brook trout can both be taken from Minnow with most averaging 25-35 cm in length.

High Lakes (PC)

brook trout to 40 cm
rainbow trout to 35 cm

A series of shallow lakes located at the upper end of the Saturday Night loop, the seven High Lakes are spread out over 3 km amid mixed forest and swamp. Although all of the lakes were stocked at one time with both rainbow and brook trout, it is likely that trout are present now only in lakes #4, #5, #6 and #7 (lakes at the western end of the chain), and that brook trout predominate. Soggy feet are a certainty if a good casting spot is to be located.

Saturday Night Lake (PC)

rainbow trout to 60 cm (2.5 kg)
brook trout to 50 cm (1.5 kg)

Saturday Night Lake is the usual destination for anglers undertaking the Saturday Night loop trail. The lake's shimmering green waters hold plenty of rainbow and brook trout with rainbow averaging 25-40 cm in the majority. Fishing from shore is possible from a number of locations, although forest cover will hamper backcasting. Boats can be rented through arrangements made with sporting goods stores in Jasper.

Dorothy Lake (PC)

rainbow trout to 70 cm (4.0 kg)

Accessed by a 4 km trail from the Yellowhead Highway west of Jasper, Dorothy receives much less fishing pressure than other lakes in the immediate vicinity of the townsite. Consequently, rainbow trout are plentiful in Dorothy, most averaging 30-40 cm in length with much larger specimens taken on occasion. Although it's doubtful, the lake may also hold a few brook trout, remnants of past plantings. From a boat (available for rent through sporting goods stores in Jasper) it is generally productive to anchor in on of the numerous sheltered bays and work either a wet or dry fly.

Christine Lake (PC)

rainbow trout to 60 cm (2.5 kg)
brook trout to 55 cm (2.0 kg)

Located less than half a kilometre by trail from Dorothy Lake, Christine Lake is one of the region's few lakes offering reasonable fishing to the shore-bound angler. From a number of rocky points jutting out into the lake fish-holding waters are within easy casting distance and backcasting room generally available. Brook trout predominated in Christine for many years, but it now appears as if rainbow trout are beginning to take over. Boats are available through rental arrangements made in Jasper.

Iris Lake (PC)

rainbow lake to 40 cm

Iris Lake, located less than a kilometre below the east end of Dorothy Lake, is reached by ill-defined trails winding around Dorothy. Rainbow trout in the 25-35 cm range are the normal catch. Fly fishermen will have problems with their backcasts due to the proximity of forest cover.

Virl Lake (PC)

brook trout to 55 cm (2.0 kg)
rainbow trout to 50 cm (1.5 kg)

Set in an opening in heavy forest just east of the main Dorothy Lake trail, Virl Lake offers relative solitude for most visitors. Brook and rainbow trout averaging 25-40 cm in length are plentiful, the long, narrow character of the lake allowing anglers to reach fish-holding waters with only a minimum of roll casting ability. Fishing a wet fly deep in Virl usually produces positive results.

Miette River (PC)

rainbow trout to 45 cm
brook trout to 40 cm
bull trout to 65 cm (3.0 kg)
whitefish to 55 cm (2.0 kg)

A major tributary of the Athabasca River, the Miette River flows east from the Alberta-B.C. boundary to its junction with the Athabasca at Jasper and is closely paralleled by the Yellowhead Highway for almost its entire length. Very muddy each year during run-off, the Miette generally clears by mid-summer when rainbow, brook and bull trout can all be taken from the river's many fine pools along with good numbers of large whitefish taken in the fall when fishing is at its best.

Minaga Creek (PC)

rainbow trout to 35 cm
brook trout to 35 cm

Crossed by the Dorothy Lake trail 1 km from Highway 16, this minor tributary of the Miette River holds both rainbow and brook trout in the 20-30 cm range.

Cutt Lake (PC)

rainbow trout to 40 cm

A small lake reached from trails on upper Minaga Creek, Cutt Lake was stocked long ago with cutthroat trout and more recently with rainbow trout. Although little information is available, reports indicate that rainbow in 25-35 cm range are present in good numbers.

Golden Lake (PC)

rainbow trout to 40 cm

Located less than a kilometre from Cutt Lake, Golden Lake was stocked in the past with rainbow trout which can still be found in fair numbers.

No man has ever caught a fish as big as the one that got away.

196

MALIGNE

Spectacular Maligne Lake, set amid some of the most impressive mountain scenery the Rockies has to offer, stands out as the center-piece of the region, its world-class rainbow trout attracting anglers from far and wide.   The lake is easily accesible via a 45 km-long paved road which branches southeast off Highway 16, 5 km east of Jasper.   Lorraine, Moose, Mona and Evelyn Lakes are all located within easy hiking distance from the Maligne Lake Road terminus, while farther downstream on the Maligne River, Medicine Lake offers superb late summer fishing.   Alongside Highway 16 (Yellow-head Highway) east of Jasper, the Athabasca and Rocky Rivers, along with Jasper, Talbot, Edna and Mile 14 Lakes, present plenty of opportunities for fishermen.

Maligne Lake (PC)
rainbow trout to 90 cm (10 kg)
brook trout to 65 cm (3.0 kg)

Situated at the head of the beautiful Maligne Valley, Maligne Lake attracts crowds of visitors; the shoreline is busy all summer with photographers, while on the lake tour boats make daily sightseeing excursions.   Long regarded as an excellent fishing lake, Maligne contains large rainbow and brook trout with a few rainbow tipping the scale at 7.0 kg or better with monsters of over 10 kg not unknown. Fortunately for fishermen, boats and canoes can be rented at the lake which increases fishing potential enormously.   Trolling a fly can be very effective, particularly in the famed "Rainbow Alley" which extends from near the outlet of the Maligne River for the first few kilometres down the lake. Almost 10 km down the lake, the Sampson Narrows have also gained renown for fishing, although it is a long trip if you're rowing or paddling. For those shore bound, the area around the outlet holds some potential, as do the areas around the many inlet creeks. Maligne Lake is not usually free of ice until mid-June, well after the fishing season usually opens.

Moose Lake (PC)
brook trout to 30 cm

Lying less than a kilometre from the Maligne Pass trailhead, tiny Moose Lake draws little attention from anglers.   Brook trout were stocked in the past, but recent reports indicate they are present in very limited numbers at best.   Although forest cover is relatively heavy, casting room is availble from many locations around the lake.

197

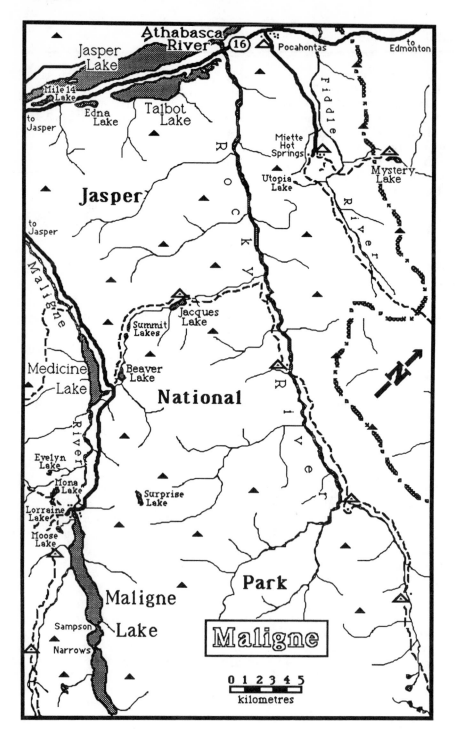

Mona Lake (PC)

brook trout to 45 cm

Situated 2 km along the Skyline Trail, Mona Lake is the largest of the lakes located to the west of Maligne Lake, its clear waters holding plenty of brook trout averaging 20-30 cm in length. Ringed by forest, Mona presents casting problems for fly fishermen. However, fish can be caught fairly close to shore from many spots provided adequate roll casting ability is applied.

Lorraine Lake (PC)

brook trout to 40 cm

Situated off to one side of the Skyline Trail opposite Mona Lake, tiny Lorraine Lake attracts many fishermen from nearby Maligne Lake on account of fair numbers of brook trout in the 20-30 cm range. Heavy reed growth and extended shallows will tend to frustrate many fly fishermen. During low light periods, however, the trout tend to work the shallows extensively for food and patient anglers are often rewarded at these times.

Evelyn Lake (PC)

brook trout to 35 cm
rainbow trout to 35 cm

This small lake located less than a kilometre northwest of Mona Lake is generally overlooked by the crowds at Maligne Lake 4 km distant. Evelyn holds both brook and rainbow trout in small sizes.

Surprise Lake (PC)

status: doubtful

Only experienced route finders armed with map and compass find their way into secluded Surprise Lake located some 4 km east of the Maligne Lake Road. Surprise was stocked in the past with brook trout which apparently failed to take hold. If any fish were found today in Surprise Lake, it would definitely be a surprise.

Maligne River [upper] (PC)

rainbow trout to 60 cm (2.5 kg)
brook trout to 55 cm (2.0 kg)

The Maligne River between Maligne Lake and Medicine Lake offers several stretches of outstanding fly fishing for plentiful numbers of rainbow and brook trout in the 25-40 cm range. The best areas are found just below the outlet on Maligne Lake and just above the inlet on Medicine Lake. Check regulations as the season on the upper Maligne River is reduced to protect spawning fish.

Medicine Lake (PC)

rainbow trout to 70 cm (4.0 kg)
brook trout to 60 cm (2.5 kg)

Located alongside the Maligne Lake Road some 10 km downstream from Maligne Lake, Medicine Lake ranks favourably with some of the best fishing lakes in the Rockies with its good numbers of large rainbow and brook trout. Water levels on Medicine fluctuate dramatically during the year, the lake nearly doubling in size at the height of the run-off in early July. As the lake level recedes beginning in August, fishing picks up, and continues to improve into September when the upper portion of the lake is little more than a mud flat, crisscrossed by various channels of the Maligne River. During this time of the year, there is excellent fly fishing for large rainbows in Medicine, whether from a boat in the main part of the lake, or from the river bank in the mud flats. Boats are available for rent through prior arrangement with sporting goods stores in Jasper.

Beaver Lake (PC)

brook trout to 55 cm (2.0 kg)
rainbow trout to 40 cm

Set in a pleasant valley less than 2 km from the Maligne Lake Road, shallow Beaver Lake is a popular spot for family picnics as well as for fishing. At one time, extremely large brook trout in the 5-6 kg range inhabited the lake, but trout in that size have never returned, although brook trout are still dominant in Beaver and a few rainbow are present as well. The entire shoreline is made up of heavy reed growth, a strong deterrent to fly fishing. Fortunately, boats are available for rent and can be reserved through sporting goods stores in Jasper. When conditions are right, Beaver Lake offers some excellent dry fly fishing.

Summit Lakes (PC)

status: devoid of fish

Two small lakes situated at the height of land on the Jacques Lake trail have been stocked in the past with brook trout which failed to reproduce. At present, no fish exist in the lakes.

Jacques Lake (PC)

bull trout to 70 cm (4.0 kg)

A popular backpacking destination 12 km by trail from the Maligne Lake Road, pretty Jacques Lake contains bull trout averaging 30-40 cm in length in good numbers. Casting room is restricted by forest cover around much of the lake, and fly fishermen are generally more successful in the outlet creek which holds plenty of pan-sized bull trout.

Jasper Lake (PC)

bull trout to 70 cm (4.0 kg)
rainbow trout to 50 cm (1.5 kg)
brook trout to 50 cm (1.5 kg)
whitefish to 50 cm (1.5 kg)

Merely a widening of the mighty Athabasca River, the shallow waters of Jasper Lake attract little attention from anglers despite its impressive variety of fish which includes whitefish, bull, rainbow and brook trout, as well as pike, ling, chub and suckers. Fishing is generally restricted to the channels through which the main river flows, but unfortunately these areas are usually near-impossible to reach due to extensive shallows making up the vast majority of the lake. Anglers are advised to work the waters in and around the lake's inlet and outlet where the Athabasca is reduced to a more reasonable width.

Mile 14 Lake J-E [Jasper-Edmonton] (PC)

rainbow trout to 40 cm
brook trout to 40 cm

Located appropriately enough 14 miles or 23 km from Jasper on the north side of the Yellowhead Highway, Mile 14 Lake receives moderate angling pressure each summer for fair numbers of brook and rainbow trout in the 20-30 cm range. Heavy reed growth around much of the shore restricts casting.

Edna Lake (PC)

rainbow trout to 40 cm
brook trout to 40 cm

Edna Lake, situated less than a kilometre west of Talbot Lake, is similar in character to other lakes along the Athabasca River. It holds both brook and rainbow trout ranging from 20-30 cm in length and while casting is difficult around much of the lake due to extended shallows, fish can be taken fairly close to shore during low light conditions.

Talbot Lake (PC)

rainbow trout to 50 cm (1.5 kg)
whitefish to 40 cm
northern pike to 90 cm (10.0 kg)

Separated only by the Yellowhead Highway, the clear waters of Talbot Lake stand in stark contrast to the silted waters of Jasper Lake opposite. Its shoreline is generally active with fishermen, most in search of the lake's large pike many of which exceed the 5.0 kg mark in weight. Whitefish are plentiful with rainbow trout, ling and chub is also present in limited numbers. Spin and bait fishermen are normally more successful than fly fishermen at Talbot due to the extensive shallows and reed growth around the lake.

Rocky River (PC)

bull trout to 60 cm (2.5 kg)
rainbow trout to 40 cm
brook trout to 40 cm
whitefish to 45 cm

The Rocky River joins the Athabasca as a major tributary just east of Talbot Lake. The Rocky generally clears sooner than the Athabasca, offering fine river fishing from mid-summer on for bull, rainbow and brook trout along with whitefish which can be taken in good numbers from the lower reaches of the river within easy walking distance of the Yellowhead Highway. Of particular interest to fishermen are the waters around the Rocky's confluence with the Athabasca which is a short hike downstream from Highway 16. Bull trout predominate in remoter upper sections accessed by trail from Jacques Lake.

Fiddle River (PC)

bull trout to 55 cm (2.0 kg)
rainbow trout to 40 cm
whitefish to 40 cm

The Fiddle River begins high in the Miette Range and joins the Athabasca River as a minor tributary just inside the eastern boundary of Jasper National Park. The lower reaches are accessible from both the Yellowhead Highway and from the Miette Hot Springs Road. The upper Fiddle, accessed from trails beginning at Miette Hot Springs, holds whitefish, bull and rainbow trout in good numbers with bull trout becoming the dominant species the further upstream you fish.

Utopia Lake (PC)

status: unknown

Hidden high on the flank of Utopia Mountain, Utopia Lake receives few, if any, visitors each year. The lake was stocked in the past with cutthroat trout but it has never been determined whether any fish still exist. Recommended for only the most hardy of souls outfitted with a map and compass.

Mystery Lake (AB)

rainbow trout to 45 cm
brook trout to 45 cm

Mystery Lake, protected by a troublesome ford of the Fiddle River, is located just outside the Jasper National Park boundary. Although it is becoming more popular as a backpacking destination, Mystery is still far removed from the crowds and presently holds plenty of brook and rainbow trout, averaging 20-30 cm in length. It's designated as a High Mountain Lake in the fishing regulations.

NORTH BOUNDARY

Set in the remote, rugged north end of Jasper National Park, this isolated area is bounded on the west by Mt. Robson Provincial Park and on the north by Willmore Wilderness Provincial Park. Jasper's famed North Boundary Trail cuts through the centre of the region and provides access for horse parties and backpackers. The Snake Indian River parallels the North Boundary Trail from the eastern trailhead at Celestine Lake to the alpine environs of Snake Indian Pass. To the south of this drainage, the Snaring River makes its way east from the heights of the continental divide and like much of the rest of the territory, remains virtually untravelled. North of Jasper National Park the Willmore Wilderness offers some fine fishing along the Berland and Wildhay Rivers and at Rock and Moosehorn Lakes. In the southwest corner of the region, Highway 16 (Yellowhead Highway) serves as a major thoroughfare, passing alongside Yellowhead and Lucerne Lakes. From the highway, trails extend into the seldom visited upper Miette River and cross the continental divide into Mount Robson Provincial Park.

Yellowhead Lake (BC)

lake trout to 75 cm (5.0 kg)
rainbow trout to 50 cm (1.5 kg)
whitefish to 40 cm

Situated alongside Highway 16 (Yellowhead Highway) just west of the continental divide at Yellowhead Pass, Yellowhead Lake is one of the region's few readily accessible lakes. The lake holds large lake trout averaging 40-50 cm in length as well of plenty of smaller rainbow trout and whitefish. In the early season the odd laker can be taken by fly fishermen, but as the season progresses, rainbows and whitefish become the normal catch. Due to the size of the lake, the best tactic is trolling a fly from a boat which is available through rental arrangements made with sporting goods stores in Jasper.

Lucerne Lake (BC)

lake trout to 70 cm (4.5 kg)
rainbow trout to 50 cm (1.5 kg)
whitefish to 40 cm

Little more than a downstream extension of Yellowhead Lake, Lucerne Lake offers the same variety of fish and the same general fishing strategies that work on its larger neighbour to the west are applicable on Lucerne. If shore-bound, the areas around the inlet and outlet usually hold a fair amount of fish.

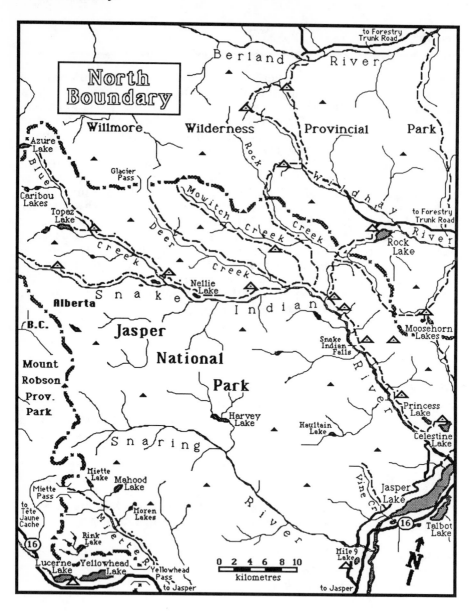

Rink Lake (PC)
status: devoid of fish

Rink Lake, located in a side valley to the west of the Miette River beneath the peaks that form the B.C.-Alberta boundary, has never been stocked and contains no fish.

Moren Lakes (PC)
status: devoid of fish

Set in a isolated valley to the east of the upper Miette Valley, the two small Moren Lakes have never been stocked and reportedly contain no fish.

Mahood Lake (PC)
status: unknown

This large lake set in a side valley west of the Miette River headwaters has never been stocked. Due to its isolated position, few fishermen ever make their way into Mahood, so although unconfirmed, it is possible that bull trout have made their way into the lake from the Miette River.

Miette Lake (PC)
bull trout to 50 cm (1.5 kg)

The headwaters of the Miette River is an arduous 25 km hike from the Yellowhead Highway. Reached by only a few hikers and outfitters each summer, Miette Lake holds a limited number of bull trout averaging 30-40 cm in length.

Snaring River (PC)
bull trout to 60 cm (2.5 kg)
rainbow trout to 40 cm
whitefish to 45 cm

This major tributary to the Athabasca River joins the Athabasca 17 km east of Jasper and offers fine river fishing in its lower reaches for bull and rainbow trout as well as plenty of whitefish in the early fall. While its upper sections are located far beyond the reach of the average fisherman, it is easily accessed from the Celestine Lake Road which provides access to the lower Snaring.

Mile 9 Lake (PC)

rainbow trout to 40 cm
brook trout to 40 cm

Situated alongside the Celestine Lake Road, Mile 9 Lake attracts many fishermen from the nearby Snaring River campground. Its shallow waters hold rainbow and brook trout in good numbers, most averaging 20-30 cm in length. Casting room is generally restricted around most of the shoreline.

Harvey Lake (PC)

status: unknown

Hidden deep within the Snaring River drainage, Harvey Lake remains a mystery to most fishermen. Stocked in the past with rainbow trout, it has never been determined whether fish are still present and due to difficult access, Harvey will likely keep its secrets for many years to come.

Vine Creek (PC)

rainbow trout to 30 cm
brook trout to 30 cm

The lower reaches of Vine Creek which are within easy walking distance of the Celestine Lake Road contain a series of beaver dams. These dams have been stocked in the past with both rainbow and brook trout. However, reproductive success among the trout planted has been limited at best and fish are present in small numbers.
Note: To reach the Celestine and Princess Lakes and North Boundary Trail trailheads, the upper portion of Celestine Lake Road must be driven. Due to narrow and dangerous corners, travel is limited to one direction for specific hours during the day. Check with the Parks Canada Information Centre in Jasper.

Celestine Lake (PC)

rainbow trout to 65 cm (3.0 kg)

Celestine Lake, a short 2 km hike from the end of the rough and sometimes hair-raising 33 km-long Celestine Lake Road, attracts numerous fishermen and sightseers alike each summer. The lake's appealing green waters hold rainbow trout averaging 25-40 cm in length, but due to extended shallows around much of the lake and heavy forest cover, fly fishermen will encounter problems. Fortunately, boats are available for rent through prior arrangement with one of Jasper's sporting goods stores.

Princess Lake (PC)
brook trout to 50 cm (1.5 kg)

Located alongside the Celestine Lake trail, the long, narrow form of Princess Lake is generally overlooked by fishermen en route to Celestine despite the fact that Princess holds fair numbers of brook trout ranging from 20-35 cm in length. Ringed by reeds, Princess will cause troubles for most fly fishermen. Early morning and late evening when the fish tend to enter the shallows to feed will the most successful time of day for fly fishing.

Snake Indian River (PC)
bull trout to 55 cm (2.0 kg)
rainbow trout to 40 cm
whitefish to 45 cm

Constant companion to the eastern half of the North Boundary Trail, the Snake Indian River and its tributaries form the main artery of the entire region. Running muddy much of the summer, the Snake Indian offers little in the way of fishing until early August when rainbows, bull trout and whitefish can be taken along the entire length of the river, the areas around the confluence with tributaries usually offering the best fishing. Many of the river's overflow lakes hold trout, although marsh generally accompanies these areas. Only a small number of foot or horse parties regularly make their way beyond thunderous Snake Indian Falls located 21 km from the eastern trailhead at Celestine Lake. The distance from Celestine Lake to the Berg Lake trailhead via the North Boundary Trail is a staggering 175 km.

Haultain Lake (PC)
status: unknown

Set in a valley to the southwest of the Snake Indian River, secluded Haultain Lake remains virtually untouched by civilization. Although the lake was stocked in the past with both cutthroat and rainbow trout, unconfirmed reports indicate that only a few rainbow are still present.

Nellie Lake (PC)
bull trout to 50 cm (1.5 kg)
rainbow trout to 35 cm

This large, shallow lake located 50 km from the Celestine Lake trailhead offers only limited opportunities for fishermen. The marshy shoreline, complete with reeds, makes casting difficult. Bull and rainbow trout along with the odd whitefish tend to make their way to and from the nearby Snake Indian River, but never seem to be present in large numbers in the lake.

Topaz Lake (PC)

rainbow trout to 55 cm (2.0 kg)
bull trout to 70 cm (4.0 kg)

Set in the Blue Creek drainage, the most scenically impressive corner of the entire North Boundary region, Topaz Lake attracts only a limited number of visitors due to the extremely long access of over 60 km from the Celestine Lake trailhead. Topaz holds rainbow and bull trout in the 30-45 cm range in good numbers, ample reward for the few fishermen who do make it in each year.

Caribou Lakes (PC)

rainbow trout to 50 cm (1.5 kg)
bull trout to 70 cm (4.0 kg)

Another in the chain of sparkling lakes to the west of Blue Creek, the Caribou Lakes contain plenty of good-sized rainbow and bull trout. Angling quality should remain high in these lakes for many years to come as fishing pressure will undoubtedly be light.

Azure Lake [Indigo Lake] (PC)

rainbow trout to 50 cm (1.5 kg)
bull trout to 70 cm (4.0 kg)

Much like Topaz and Caribou Lakes to the south, beautifully-coloured Azure Lake offers much to those who put forth the extra effort to reach its shore. Outstanding scenery and excellent fishing for rainbow and bull trout averaging 30-40 cm are all wrapped up in this package. Fortunately, distances are great enough to ensure that Azure will remain unspoiled for many years to come.

Rock Lake (AB)

lake trout to 90 cm (10.0 kg)
bull trout to 65 cm (3.0 kg)
whitefish to 50 cm (1.5 kg)
rainbow trout to 40 cm

Situated in a heavily wooded valley just west of the Wildhay River and accessed from the Forestry Trunk Road via the Willmore Wilderness Park Road, Rock Lake attracts many fishermen each season. The lake's deep waters hold some lake trout of immense proportions as well as whitefish, bull trout, rainbow trout and the odd pike. Although it is possible to fish from shore from a number of locations, a boat is strongly recommended since trolling a streamer deep can be very effective at times. The campground at Rock Lake is very popular and is usually filled to capacity each weekend during the summer.

Moosehorn Lakes (AB)

cutthroat trout to 40 cm

Seldom visited, the Moosehorn Lakes are located just outside the north boundary of Jasper National Park and accessed by two main trails, one from the Celestine Lake Road and the other from Rock Lake - both over 30 km in length. Although few accounts make their way out, the lakes are reported to contain cutthroat trout averaging 20-30 cm in length. Both are listed in the fishing regulations as High Mountain Lakes.

Berland River (AB)

bull trout to 85 cm (7.5 kg)
rainbow trout to 50 cm (1.5 kg)
whitefish to 50 cm (1.5 kg)
grayling to 40 cm

The Berland River, which eventually joins the Athabasca River near Edson, is situated in the heart of the Willmore Wilderness Provincial Park and provides excellent river fishing most notably for large bull trout. In addition to bull trout, rainbows, whitefish and grayling are also present in good numbers. Less heavily fished, the upper reaches of the Berland and its tributaries are accessible only by trail.

Wildhay River (AB)

bull trout to 60 cm (2.5 kg)
rainbow trout to 40 cm
whitefish to 45 cm
grayling to 35 cm

A tributary to the Berland River, the Wildhay River offers fine stream fishing particularly in the vicinity of Rock Lake. Bull and rainbow trout, along with whitefish and a few grayling are all present. Accessible by the Willmore Wilderness Park Road for all but the extreme upper reaches, the Wildhay is understandably popular among river fishing enthusiasts.

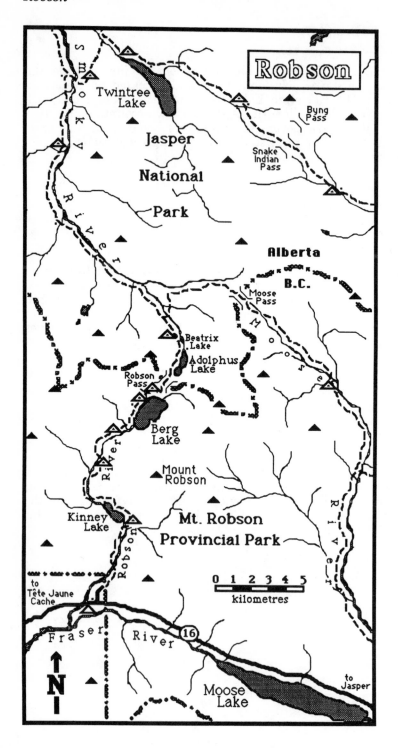

ROBSON

Dominated by the presence of awe-inspiring Mt. Robson, the highest point in the Canadian Rockies, this region represents the pinnacle in mountain scenery. Glacier-mantled peaks towering over pristine lakes attract visitors from all corners of the world. Although the area's angling potential has never gained the stature of the surrounding physical beauty, perservering fishermen are generally rewarded for their efforts. Berg Lake, set at the base of Mt. Robson is a prime backpacking destination, and along the same access trail you'll also find Kinney Lake. Beyond Berg Lake, Jasper National Park's noted North Boundary Trail leads adventuresome hikers past Adolphus, Beatrix and Twintree Lakes and the Smoky River before crossing Snake Indian Pass into the Snake Indian River drainage. Moose Lake and the Fraser River situated alongside Highway 16 (Yellowhead Highway) receive plenty of fishing pressure during the summer months.

Moose River (BC)

bull trout to 60 cm (2.5 kg)
rainbow trout to 45 cm
whitefish to 40 cm

With its source high among the peaks that straddle the continental divide, Moose River flows south from humble beginnings to join the upper Fraser River as a major tributary just east of Moose Lake. Much of the upper Moose River lies far beyond the reach of most hikers and remains the domain of grizzly bears interrupted only by the occasional horse party. Bull and rainbow trout in the 25-35 cm range as well as a few whitefish can be taken along the entire length of the river. Fishing pressure is light in the lower reaches and virtually nonexistent in the remote upper Moose.

Robson River (BC)

bull trout to 60 cm (2.5 kg)
rainbow trout to 40 cm
whitefish to 35 cm

From its source at Berg Lake, the Robson River roars through the Valley of a Thousand Falls into Kinney Lake before finally emptying into the Fraser River. With the upper section far too torrential to hold fish, all angling on the Robson should be confined to the final 6 km before the confluence where whitefish, bull and rainbow trout can all be taken in limited numbers. Due to its glacial source, the Robson River runs silted much longer than most rivers, generally clearing only for a few short weeks in the fall.

Moose Lake (BC)

lake trout to 90 cm (10.0 kg)
bull trout to 75 cm (6.0 kg)
rainbow trout to 65 cm (3.0 kg)
kokanee to 60 cm (2.5 kg)
whitefish to 50 cm (1.5 kg)

Almost 10 km in length, Moose Lake is a highly visible companion to people driving Highway 16 (Yellowhead Highway). Moose's waters, which remain silted much of the summer, hold a variety of fish with lake and bull trout predominating. Although large lake and bull trout in excess of 5 kg are taken regularly, fly fishermen will likely have the most success with the lake's rainbow population, particularly if you try trolling a fly around the mouth of one of Moose's many inlet streams. Although fishing a streamer in the deep water may attract the odd laker or bull trout, bait and gang troll fishermen generally have more success here. Be aware of strong winds that occasionally sweep through Yellowhead Pass.

Fraser River [upper] (BC)

bull trout to 70 cm (4.0 kg)
rainbow trout to 50 cm (1.5 kg)
whitefish to 40 cm

The upper Fraser River between Yellowhead Lake and Tete Jaune Cache possesses long stretches of fishable water along with several major waterfalls below which the fishing is generally very good. Bull and rainbow trout predominate with whitefish present in fair numbers as well. This entire section of the Fraser is paralleled by the Yellowhead Highway which affords easy access to all of the river's fishing spots. Run-off is usually complete by mid-summer when fishing begins to pick up appreciably.

Kinney Lake (BC)

rainbow trout to 50 cm (1.5 kg)

Perpetually silted due to the in and outflow of the Robson River, Kinney Lake situated 5 km along the Berg Lake trail has never been able to sustain a large fish population and only moderate numbers of rainbow trout inhabit the lake. The outlet area is generally the most productive area, particularly later in the season when the lake's silt levels are at their lowest.

Berg Lake (BC)
rainbow trout to 40 cm

Blessed with one of the most exquisite settings anywhere in the mountain world, Berg Lake is busy with photographers and sight-seers throughout the summer months. The stunning glacier-clad north face of Mt. Robson towering above the lake dotted with ice floes is a sight that few people forget. Despite being a strenuous17 km hike-in from the Yellowhead Highway, the lake remains one of the most popular backpacking destinations in the Rockies, but unfortunately for anglers, fishing in ever-silty Berg can be regarded as poor at best with rainbow trout present in small and ever-dwindling numbers.

Smoky River (PC)
bull trout to 70 cm (4.0 kg)
rainbow trout to 35 cm
whitefish to 40 cm

The upper Smoky River offers several kilometres of fine stream fishing as it flows north from Adolphus Lake. Meandering quietly back and forth across the broad valley north of Robson Pass, it possesses plenty of fine holes where bull and rainbow trout are present in fair numbers. Progressing downstream, the Smoky begins to accumulate tributaries and increase appreciably in size, with the result that rainbows decrease in number and bull trout and whitefish become predominant. Access is via the North Boundary Trail which follows the course of the Smoky River to a point approximately 10 km from the northern boundary of Jasper National Park, whereupon the main trail swings east towards Twintree Lake.

Twintree Lake (PC)
rainbow trout to 70 cm (4.0 kg)

Located in the most remote corner of Jasper National Park along the North Boundary Trail, Twintree Lake is a distant 65 km hike from the Berg Lake trailhead, and an even more distant105 km hike from the Celestine Lake Road trailhead. Suffice to say that Twintree Lake receives very little fishing pressure each year. A large lake, Twin-tree is generally silted for much of the summer, the fishing picking up only as the lake begins to clear in August. Large rainbow, many in the 40-50 cm range, are present in Twintree, although their num-bers are not overwhelming. Due to the size of the lake, fishermen are advised to work the waters around any inlet creeks where the water is liable to be clearer.

Adolphus Lake (PC)

rainbow trout to 45 cm
brook trout to 45 cm

Set in open subalpine forest less than 1 km north of Robson Pass in Jasper National Park, Adolphus Lake offers some respite from the crowds at nearby Berg Lake. The headwaters of the Smoky River hold rainbow and brook trout averaging 23-35 cm in their clear waters and while casting is no problem around most of the shoreline, extended shallows in some spots will require long casts.

Beatrix Lake (PC)

rainbow trout to 35 cm

Located less than 1 km downstream from Adolphus Lake, tiny Beatrix Lake is little more than a widening of the Smoky River. Rainbow trout in the 20-30 cm range are present as well as the odd brook trout which makes its way into Beatrix from Adolphus from time to time. Heavy brush around the lake will cause problems for most fly fishermen.

Truth: *when one fisherman calls another fisherman a liar.*

INDEX

Index

No honest man is a successful fisherman.